ONE HUNDRED
INDOOR GAMES
YOU CAN PLAY

ONE HUNDRED
INDOOR GAMES
YOU CAN PLAY

GUILD PUBLISHING

Dedicated to the memory of George Hervey

First published in 1982 by
The Hamlyn Publishing Group
This edition published in 1988
by Guild Publishing
by arrangement with
The Hamlyn Publishing Group Limited
a division of The Octopus Publishing Group,
Michelin House, 81 Fulham Road,
London SW3 6RB

Printed and bound in Great Britain by Purnell Book Production Ltd.

CN 8269

Acknowledgment
The Publishers wish to acknowledge the kindness of Waddingtons
Playing Card Company Limited, who supplied the cards for the
card game illustrations.

First published in 1981
under the title *The Complete Book of Indoor Games*
by The Hamlyn Publishing Group Limited

Contents

Board and Tile Games

Dice Games

Roulette 274

Introduction

The first requirement of this introduction is to define the scope of this book in relation to its title. By 'indoor games' is meant those sedentary games which require no more physical energy than the laying of a card or the throwing of dice.

Bridge and poker players might claim that a long session requires stamina, but it does not need physical dexterity, athleticism or agility. Therefore such pursuits as table tennis, badminton and snooker, although played indoors, are not included. They are sometimes called indoor games, but might be more properly thought of as indoor sports.

Secondly the word 'complete' is not meant to imply that every game ever invented which uses cards, tiles, dice, counters and such like is included. No book has ever achieved such a feat, and none ever will. Nor would the reader wish to buy a book which used some of its space to describe how to toss a coin in a game of heads and tails, or how to play Noughts and Crosses or even Snakes and Ladders. Nor has it been thought feasible to include the proprietary games which proliferate annually, and many of which are in any case based on the old games.

The object has been to include those standard games which have stood the test of time and have so caught popular fancy as to have earned a right to be included, and those games which while they might not have become so widespread, yet have their followers and will repay those who make the effort to learn them. Anybody who masters all or most of the games in this book can claim with as much justification as the next man to be a complete games player.

The book has been based upon the great success of two earlier books, *The Hamlyn Illustrated Book of Card Games* and *The Illustrated Book of Table Games*. The best of each have been amalgamated, and some new games added. Thus there are a number of writers to be acknowledged. The late George F. Hervey wrote all the articles concerning card games. Paul Langfield wrote the articles on Chess and Checkers. Jeremy Flint wrote the article on Backgammon. Francis Roads wrote the article on Go. Rodney Headington wrote the article on Hex. David Pritchard wrote the articles on Reversi, Wari, Mah Jong and Dominoes. The present editor wrote the articles on Roulette and Dice games.

The largest part of the book concerns card games, and a description of the arrangement of them is best left to an extract from George Hervey's introduction to the book in which they originally appeared:

'Card games do not admit of a precise arrangement. In this book they have been arranged according to the number of players who may take part at one table; as, however, most card games can be played, in one form or another, by a varying number of players, it is more correct to say that the games have been arranged according to the number of players for which they are best suited; but party games and banking games are grouped separately, and among the party games some will be found suitable for members of the younger generation who may find that playing a game of cards is a less noisy pastime than playing an electric guitar. It is not an ideal arrangement, but it has the merit of convenience, and is less arbitrary than arranging the games in alphabetical order, and more practical than arranging them by their family resemblances. Most card games have a number of variations. Only the more popular ones have been given a place in this book, and, with some rare and inevitable exceptions, descriptions of them follow the description of the parent game.

The aim of the present writer is nothing higher than to explain how the various games are played; and when no authoritative organisation has laid down the scoring, rules of play and appropriate penalties for breaking them, the practice that he recommends is that of the majority of experienced players. If here and there he has broken form and given a few hints on skilful play, it is not to compete with the text books, but because without them the bare bones would be unreadable. When the play of a deal is summarized, the standard practice of underlining the card that wins the trick (the player leading to the next trick) is followed.'

George Hervey was one of the best of all writers on card games, and while he points out that his aim was 'nothing higher than to explain how the various games are played', his descriptions of sample games nevertheless convey the elements of good play.

This principle was also followed in the other parts of the book, and learners of new games will find that pointers on strategy will start them thinking along the right lines.

It is hoped that readers will find the articles on the games they already know entertaining and perhaps instructional, and that they will derive a lifetime's pleasure from learning some new games.

P.D.A.

8

Card Games

Bisley

SINGLE-PACK

Remove the four Aces from the pack and place them face upwards in a row on the table. Deal nine cards in a row to the right of them, and the rest of the pack in three rows of thirteen cards each, below them (see illustration). When the four Kings become available they are placed above their respective Aces.

The Aces are built on upwards and the Kings downwards in suit-sequences. It does not matter where the two sequences meet.

Only the bottom card of a column is available for play. It may be built either on its Ace- or King-foundation, packed on the bottom card of another column, or itself be packed on. Packing

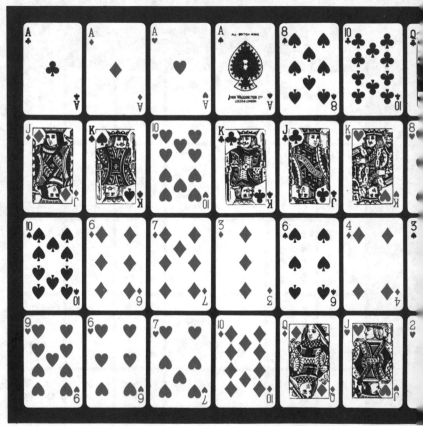

may be either upwards or downwards in suit-sequence, and the player may change this at his convenience. A space left vacant in the layout, by the removal of a card, is not filled.

In the layout below, the **K** ♦ is played above the **A** ♦, the **2** ♠ is built on the **A** ♠, and the **2** ♥ on the **A** ♥. This exposes the **3** ♠ which is built on the **2** ♠. The **Q** ♦ is built on the **K** ♦. The **9** ♦ is packed on the **10** ♦, and the **8** ♦ on the **9** ♦. Now the **8** ♣ is packed on the **9** ♣, exposing the **2** ♣ which is built on the **A** ♣. And so on.

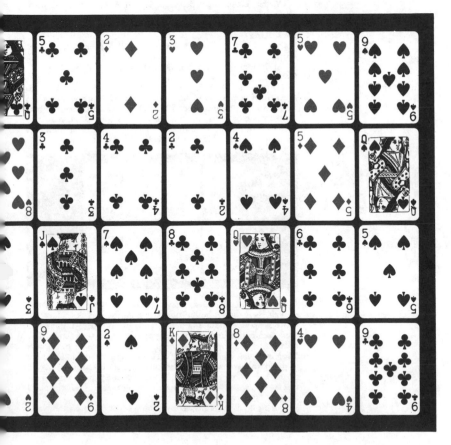

Calculation

SINGLE-PACK

Calculation, or Broken Intervals, is a one-pack patience that is well-named, because it is necessary to calculate at the turn of every card, and it offers more scope for skilful play than any other patience.

Any **Ace**, any **2**, any **3** and any **4** are placed in a row on the table to form four foundations. The object of the game is to build, regardless of suits, the remaining forty-eight cards on them, as follows:

On the **Ace** in the order Ace, 2, 3, 4, 5, 6, 7, 8, 9, 10, Jack, **Queen, King**.

On the **2** in the order **2, 4, 6, 8, 10, Queen, Ace**, 3, 5, 7, 9, **Jack, King**.

On the **3** in the order **3, 6, 9, Queen, 2**, 5, 8, **Jack, Ace**, 4, 7, 10, **King**.

On the **4** in the order **4, 8, Queen, 3, 7, Jack, 2, 6, 10, Ace**, 5, **9, King**.

The cards are dealt from the pack one at a time, and every card must either be built on a foundation or played to any one of a waste heap below each foundation. The pack is dealt only once, but play from a waste heap may continue after it has been exhausted. Only the top card of a waste heap may be played; it may be built on a foundation and may not be played to another waste heap.

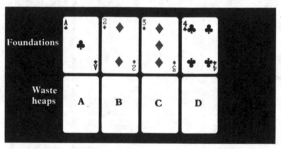

The cards in the pack are now dealt one at a time. Suppose a **10** is dealt, as it cannot be built on a foundation it is best played to waste heap **B**. Next a **6** is dealt; it is built on the 3-foundation. Next comes an **8**, and, of course, is built on the 4-foundation. The next card is a **King**. It must be played to a waste heap, but as a **King** is the last card to be built on a foundation it would be wrong to play it to waste heap **B** and so cover the **10**. It should be played to another waste heap, and many experienced players would now reserve this waste heap for Kings. Play continues in this way until all forty-eight cards have been dealt.

If the play is carefully thought out, by building on the waste heaps descending sequences of two to four or more cards, towards the end of a game excellent progress will be made.

Demon

SINGLE-PACK

Demon is probably the best known of all the many one-pack patiences. It is sometimes known as Fascination, sometimes as Thirteen, and, in America, as Canfield, because it was reputedly invented by Richard A. Canfield, a well-known gambler of the late 19th century, whose practice it was to sell the pack for $52.00 and pay $5.00 for every card in the foundation row when the game came to an end. It was not altogether as profitable as it may seem, because for every player he had to employ a croupier to keep an eye on him during the play.

Thirteen cards are dealt face downwards in a pile and the top card is faced. The pile is known as the heel, and four cards are dealt face upwards in a row to the right of it. The next card of the pack is dealt face upwards and placed above the first card of the row. It indicates the foundations.

The **10 ♦** is the first of the four foundations, and the **3 ♦** is the top card of the heel. As they become available, the other three 10s are played to the right of the **10 ♦**, and the object of the game is to build on them round-the-corner suit-sequences up to the 9s. The four cards to the right of the heel are packed in descending sequences of alternate colours. As a start, therefore, the **J ♦** is built on its foundation-card; the **4 ♣** is packed on the **5 ♥** and the **3 ♦** on the **4 ♣**. The card in the heel below the **3 ♦** is turned and, if it cannot be built on a foundation or packed on a card in the layout, is played to the space left vacant by the **J ♦**. The next card in the heel is then exposed.

The bottom card of the four columns may be built on a foundation, but a sequence may be moved from one column to another only as a whole, and then only if the sequence can be packed on the next higher card of a different colour.

The stock is dealt to a waste pile in batches of three cards at a time, but if there is less than three cards at the end of the stock they are dealt singly. The stock is dealt and redealt until the game is won, or lost because no further move can be made.

When all the cards in a column have been played, the space that is left must be filled at once with the top card of the heel and the next card of the heel exposed. A space must not be filled from the cards in hand, and when the heel is exhausted, spaces are filled from the waste heap, and the player need no longer fill a space at once, but leave it vacant until a suitable card is available.

Klondike

SINGLE-PACK

The demon (see page 13) and the Klondike are probably the two best-known and most popular of the one-pack patience games. In England the name of Canfield is sometimes attached to the Klondike. This name, however, is a misnomer, and to be corrected, because Canfield is the name that in America is given to the patience that we in England call the demon.

Twenty-eight cards are dealt face downwards in slightly over-lapping rows of seven cards, six cards, five cards, four cards, three cards, two cards and one card. The bottom card of each row is turned face upwards (see below).

As they become available, Aces are played as foundations to a row above the layout; the object of the game is to build on the Aces ascending suit-sequences to the Kings.

An exposed card at the bottom of a column is available to be built on a foundation, or it may be packed in a descending sequence of alternate colour. A sequence may be moved from one column to another, but only as a whole and when the highest card of the sequence may be placed on the next higher card of another colour. When an exposed card is played, the face-downwards card immediately above it is turned face upwards; when a whole column is moved, the space must be filled by a King which may or may not have a sequence attached to it.

The stock is dealt one card at a time to a waste heap, of which the top card is available for building on a foundation or packing on a column in the layout. Only one deal is allowed.

An Ace must be played to the foundation row as soon as it becomes available, but all other cards may be left in position if the player prefers to wait on the prospect of finding a better move later in the game.

In the layout shown below the **5♦** is packed on the **6♣**, and the card under the **5♦** is turned face upwards. The **J♣** is packed on the **Q♥**, and the **K♦** moved to fill the space vacated by the **J♣**. The card under the **K♦** is now turned face upwards. And so on.

Klondike has been the subject of several variations. One of the best is **JOKER KLONDIKE**. It is played in the same way as the parent game, but with the Joker added to the pack. Whenever the Joker becomes available for play it must be built on a foundation as the next card in sequence. Other cards, if in correct sequence, are built on it, but when the natural card that it replaces becomes available it is substituted for the Joker which is built on another foundation.

A player may choose on which foundation he will build the Joker. If it becomes available for play before a foundation has been started it must remain in its position until an Ace turns up and a foundation started.

La Belle Lucie
SINGLE-PACK

La Belle Lucie, or the Fan, is one of the classical one-pack patiences; it has a very pleasing layout. The entire pack is spread on the table in seventeen fans of three cards each and one of a single card, as illustrated.

As the Aces become available they are placed above the layout as foundations, to be built on in ascending suit-sequences to the Kings. Only the end card of each fan and the single card are available for play. They may be built on a foundation, packed on the end card of another fan in descending suit-sequence, or themselves be packed on in descending suit-sequences. A space made by playing off a complete fan is not filled.

When all possible moves have been made, all the cards except those played to the foundations, are picked up, shuffled, and redealt in fans of three. If one or two cards are left over they make separate fans. Two redeals are allowed.

In the layout illustrated the A ♥ and A ♣ are played to the foundation row. The 2 ♥ is built on the A ♥, and the 7 ♣ is packed on the 8 ♣. This releases the 2 ♣ that is built on the A ♣. The J ♦ is packed on the Q ♦, the J ♥ on the Q ♥, and the A ♠ followed by the 2 ♠ go to the foundation row. And so on.

Little Spider

SINGLE-PACK

The two red Aces and the two black Kings (or the two black Aces and the two red Kings) are placed in a row on the table to serve as foundations. The remaining forty-eight cards are dealt, face upwards, in two rows of four cards each, one above the foundation cards, the other below them.

The object of the game is to build ascending suit-sequences on the Aces to Kings, and descending suit-sequences on the Kings to Aces.

During the deal a card may be built from the upper row on any of the four foundation cards, but from the lower row only on the foundation card directly above it.

After every batch of eight cards has been dealt, the top cards of all eight piles are playable and may be built on any foundation cards or packed on any other pile in the layout. The piles are packed in ascending or descending, continuous sequences (an Ace ranks below a 2 and above a King) regardless of suit. A space made by removing an entire pile is not filled.

In the layout illustrated, the Q ♣ may be built on the K ♣ and the 2 ♥ on the A ♥. The 10 ♣ may be packed on the J ♠, and the 5 ♣ on the 6 ♠. And so on.

Maze

SINGLE-PACK

Maze is an excellent patience because some skill is necessary if it is to be successful.

The fifty-two cards of the pack are dealt face upwards in two rows of eight cards each, and four of nine cards each. The four Kings are then discarded. This leaves four spaces, or six in all, because as well as the spaces left by the discard of the Kings, the spaces at the end of the first and second rows are taken into the layout for the play (see illustration).

The object of the game is to arrange the forty-eight cards in four ascending suit-sequences, from Aces to Queens, beginning with an Ace at the extreme left of the top row and ending with a Queen at the extreme right of the bottom row. The sequences follow on, from the end of one row to the beginning of the next, as in reading and writing. Only one card may be moved at a time.

The rules for moving a card into a space are:

1. The card must be in suit-sequence one higher than the card on the left of the space or one lower than the card on the right of the space, and it is to be assumed that not only are the rows continuous but that the bottom row is continuous with the top row.

2. When a space occurs on the right of a Queen it may be filled with any Ace, as an alternative to the card one lower in suit-sequence than the card on the right of the space.

Suppose the layout is as in the illustration. After the four Kings have been discarded, the space left vacant by the **K ♥** may be filled by any Ace, or with the **9 ♠** (by reason of the **10 ♠** on the right of the space) or the **8 ♠** (by reason of the **7 ♠** at the end of the bottom row). The space at the extreme right of the top row may be. filled either with the **2 ♥** or **4 ♥**, that at the extreme right of the second row either with the **10 ♥** or **10 ♠**. The space left vacant by the **K ♦** may be filled either with the **Q ♣** or **5 ♠**.

To begin the game. Play the **A ♠** to the top left corner of the layout, and the **10 ♥** to its vacant place. Play the **5 ♦** to the left of the **6 ♦** in the top row, and the **J ♦** to the left of the **Q ♦** in the bottom row. Play the **10 ♠** to the extreme right of the second row, and the **2 ♠** followed by the **3 ♠** to the right of the **A ♠** in the top row. Play the **5 ♠** to the left of the **6 ♠**, the **J ♣** to the left of the **Q ♣** and the **4 ♠** to the left of the **5 ♠**. The **5 ♥** is played to the left of the **6 ♥**, the **9 ♥** to the left of the **10 ♥** and the **9 ♠** to the left of the **10 ♠**. Now the **5 ♦** in the top row may be played to the right of the **4 ♦** and the **4 ♠** to the right of the **3 ♠** in the top row. With the **A ♠**, **2 ♠**, **3 ♠** and **4 ♠** in position, the game progresses well.

Paganini

DOUBLE-PACK

Paganini is a double-pack patience game, similar in principle to but more interesting than, the single-pack game known as spaces. It was composed by Mr Charles Jewell.

The entire pack is dealt face upwards on the table in eight rows of thirteen cards each, as shown in the accompanying illustration.

The object of the game is so to arrange the cards that each row consists of one suit beginning with an Ace (on the left) and ending with a King (on the right). No row is singled out for any particular suit; the player makes his own decision but, having made it, must not alter it.

Play begins by moving one of the Aces to the extreme left of a row. It will be appreciated, therefore, that as the game proceeds the whole of the layout is moved one space to the left so to speak. When a card is moved it leaves a space in the layout which is filled with the next higher card of the same suit as the card on the left of the space. Filling a space leaves another space in the layout. In turn this is filled in the same way, and so on, until a run is brought to an end by removing a card from the right-hand side of a King, because no card is available to be played to the space on the right of a King.

The game calls for a show of skill. To begin, a player has to decide which of the eight Aces he will move first and to the extreme left of which of the eight rows he will move it to. Then, whenever a card is moved in the layout, there is, at all events early in the play, a choice of two cards to fill the available space. It will be seen, therefore, that when all eight Aces have been moved to the extreme left of the layout, each move will offer the choice of filling one of eight spaces with either of two cards.

The layout in the illustration is not as difficult as it may appear. Indeed, with a little care the game should be won.

After a general survey of the possibilities in the game, the A ♥ in the bottom row should be moved to the extreme left of the row; the Q ♥ in the fifth row is moved to the space left vacant by the A ♥; and the 9 ♣ in the bottom row is moved into the space left vacant by the Q ♥. The space left vacant by the 9 ♣ may be filled either with the 2 ♥ in the second row or the one in the seventh row. Consideration shows that it should be filled with the one in the second row, because the 6 ♣ in the top row can be moved into the vacant space, the A ♣ in the fifth row can be moved to the extreme left of the top row, the 6 ♣ in the top row can be moved to the space in the second row left vacant by the 2 ♥, and either the 2 ♣ in the second row or that in the fourth row can be moved into the space (alongside the A ♣) left vacant by the 6 ♣. And so on.

Royal Parade

DOUBLE-PACK

Royal Parade is a popular two-pack patience with the alternative names of Financier, Hussars and Three Up.

Twenty-four cards are dealt in three rows of eight cards each (see illustration). Aces take no part in the game and are discarded. The cards in the layout must be arranged so that the top row consists of eight 2s, the middle row of eight 3s, and the bottom row of eight 4s, and these cards must be built on in suit-sequences at intervals of three cards, namely:

2	3	4
5	6	7
8	9	10
J	Q	K

In the layout illustrated the A ♦, in the top row, and the A ♣, in the bottom row, are discarded: the 4 ♠, in the middle row, is moved to the space in the bottom row left vacant by the discard of the A ♣, and the 7 ♠, in the top row, built on it. Either the 3 ♥ or 3 ♣, both in the top row, may be moved to fill the space in the middle row left vacant by the 4 ♠, and clearly the 3 ♥ should be chosen because the 6 ♥, in the bottom row may be built on it. And so on.

When all moves have been made, eight cards are dealt to waste heaps below the layout. Aces, as they are dealt, are discarded; other cards are used to build on the foundations or to fill spaces in the layout. Play continues in this way, making moves after each deal of eight cards to the waste-heaps, until the pack is exhausted. Only the top cards of the waste heaps may be moved to the layout.

Saint Helena

DOUBLE-PACK

Saint Helena, or Napoleon's Favourite, is a two-pack patience in which the packs are not shuffled together but used one after the other. Although the game gives a player some scope for ingenuity and the exercise of his memory, it is such a simple game that one rather doubts that it received its name because it was Napoleon's chief amusement during his last years.

An Ace and a King of each suit are arranged in two rows, the Kings above the Aces. Twelve cards are then dealt, clockwise, beginning above the left-hand King, as shown in the diagram:

The Kings are built on in descending suit-sequence to the Aces, and the Aces in ascending suit-sequences to the Kings; with the restriction that cards dealt to spaces 1, 2, 3, 4 may be built only on the Kings, cards dealt to spaces 7, 8, 9, 10 only to the Aces, and cards dealt to spaces 5, 6, 11, 12 to either.

When all moves have been made the spaces are filled from the pack, and when no further moves are to be made, another twelve cards are dealt to cover the cards in position.

When the pack has been exhausted, the restriction of play is lifted, and cards may be built on any one of the twelve surrounding waste heaps. Also, the top card of each waste heap may now be packed on either in ascending or descending suit-sequence.

Three deals in all are allowed. The waste heaps are picked up in reverse order 12 . . . . 1, and turned face downwards, so that the bottom card of the twelfth waste heap becomes the top card of the re-made stock. No shuffling is allowed.

Spider

DOUBLE-PACK

There are several variations of Spider. The one described in this article is deservedly considered the best, and, indeed, among the best of all patiences, because it frequently calls for deep analysis. According to *Redbook Magazine* it was the favourite patience of the late President Franklin D. Roosevelt.

Forty cards are dealt to the table in four overlapping rows of ten cards each: the first, second and third rows face downwards, the fourth row face upwards, as in the illustration.

Foundation cards are not played to the centre. The game is to build within the layout, descending suit-sequences on the eight

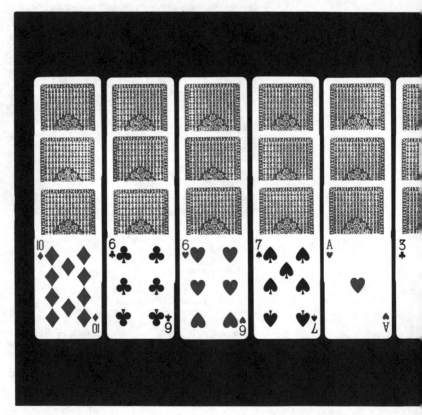

Kings to the Aces. A completed sequence is discarded, so that the game is won when the table is cleared of all cards.

The cards at the bottom of the columns may be packed in descending sequences irrespective of suit and colour, and when a card is moved from one column to another the face-downwards card immediately above it is turned face upwards and becomes available for play.

In the diagram any of the three sixes may be packed on the **7 ♠** and the **9 ♦** may be packed on either of the tens. Two cards will thus be exposed.

When all the cards have been moved from a column, the space may be filled by any exposed card or sequence of cards.

After all possible moves have been made, and spaces filled, ten cards are dealt from the stock, face upwards, one to the bottom of each column, overlapping the cards in position.

Play is continued in this way until the stock is exhausted. The last deal from the stock will, of course, be of only four cards.

Sultan
DOUBLE-PACK

Sultan, sometimes, but rarely, known as Emperor of Germany, is a two-pack patience that calls for some skill if it is to be successful.

The eight Kings and one Ace of Hearts are removed from the pack and arranged on the table as shown in the illustration. With the exception of the central King of Hearts they serve as foundations to be built up in suit-sequences to the Queens, the Aces ranking between the Kings and the 2s.

On each side of the foundations, deal a column of four cards, as shown in the illustration. It is known as the divan, and the cards dealt to it are available to be built on the foundations. When one is played, the space is filled either from the stock or from the waste heap, but need not be filled immediately.

The pack is turned one card at a time to a waste heap, and may be dealt three times.

Management of the divan is of great importance. The general rule is not to fill a space with a card that is unlikely to be wanted during the immediate deal. If, for example, a foundation is built up to a 7, and both 8s are already buried, the 9s and higher cards should be played to the waste heap, because if used to fill a space in the divan they would be wasted.

Windmill

DOUBLE-PACK

The game known as Windmill or Propeller gets its name from the layout. Any King is placed face upwards on the table, and two cards are dealt above it, two below it, and two on each side of it, to form a cross (see illustration). The first four Aces that are dealt, whether to the layout or as the stock is turned, are played to the angles of the cross.

The object of the game is to build on the central King a descending, round-the-corner, sequence of fifty-two cards, regardless of suit and colour, and ascending suit-sequences, regardless of suit and colour, on the four Aces to the Kings.

In the layout shown, the A ♦ is played to an angle of the cross, the Q ♦ is built on the K ♠, and the J ♥ on the Q ♦. At any time a card may be taken from an Ace-foundation and played to the King-foundation, but only one card may be taken from each Ace-foundation during the building of any one sequence on the King-foundation.

The stock is turned to a waste heap, and a space in the layout must be filled from the waste heap, or from the stock if there is no waste heap.

There is no second deal, but when the stock is exhausted, the waste heap may be taken up and the first card dealt. If it can be played to a foundation, the next card is dealt, and so on. The game, however, comes to an end when a card can no longer be played to a foundation.

All Fours

All Fours is known in America as Old Sledge. It is a game for two players played with the full pack of fifty-two cards, which rank from Ace (high) to 2 (low). The game is won by he who first scores 7 points. The points are scored as follows:

High. The player who is dealt the highest trump in play scores 1 point.

Low. The player who is dealt the lowest trump in play scores 1 point.

Jack. The player who wins the Jack of trumps (if it is in play) scores 1 point.

Game. Each player counts the honours among the tricks he has won, and, counting the Ace as 4, the King as 3, the Queen as 2, the Jack as 1 and the Ten as 10, the player with the highest total scores 1 point. If there is equality the non-dealer scores the point.

The points are not counted until the end of the deal, but they should be understood from the start because they illustrate the object of the game.

Six cards are dealt in bundles of three to both players, and the thirteenth card is turned up to determine the trump suit.

The non-dealer now declares whether he will stand or beg. If he says 'I stand' he accepts the turned-up card as the trump suit and play begins. If he says 'I beg' he rejects the turned-up card as the trump suit, and the dealer must either accept or refuse the proposal to make another suit trumps. To refuse he says 'Take one'. The non-dealer then scores 1 point for gift and play begins. To accept he says 'I run the cards'. He deals three more cards to his opponent and three to himself, and turns up the next card to determine the trump suit. If this is the same suit as the original trump suit, he runs the cards again, and continues to run them until a different trump suit is turned up. In the rare, but not impossible, event of the pack being exhausted without a different trump suit being turned up, there is a redeal by the same player. If the turned-up card is a Jack, the dealer scores 1 point, and if, when the cards are run, the turned-up card is again a Jack, the dealer again scores 1 point.

Play begins when the trump suit has been determined, and if the cards have been run, the players first discard from their hands enough cards to reduce the number held to six. The non-dealer leads to the first trick. His opponent must follow suit or trump. Unlike at most games, however, a player may trump even though he is able to follow suit, but he must not discard if he holds either a card of the suit led or a trump. If he does he has revoked and his opponent scores 1 point.

The winner of a trick leads to the next, and so on until all six tricks have been played. The players then turn up their tricks and score for High, Low, Jack and Game.

These four scoring features are fundamental to the game and are counted whenever it is possible to do so. If, for example, there is only one trump in play it counts 2 points, because it is both High and Low.

The deal passes in rotation.

ALL FOURS FOR FOUR PLAYERS is played with two players playing in partnership against the other two in partnership.

The method of play is the same as in the parent game, except that only the dealer and the opponent on his left (eldest hand) look at their cards to determine the trump suit. When they have done this, but not before, the other two players look at their cards and come into the game for play.

If a player exposes a card it is liable to be called by an opponent.

SEVEN UP is a variation of the parent game that receives its name from the method of scoring.

Both players (or both sides if four are playing) begin with seven counters each. Every time that a point is scored the player (or side) that wins it puts a counter aside, and the player (or side) who first gets rid of his counters wins the game. If both go out in the same deal, the winner is the one who first counts out when the points are scored for High, Low, Jack and Game.

ALL FIVES is a variation of the parent game that is played for 61 points up. For convenience the score is best kept on a cribbage board (see Plate 11).

The mechanics of the game are the same as those of the parent game, and points are pegged when the following trumps are won in a trick: Ace 4 points, King 3 points, Queen 2 points, Jack 1 point, Ten 10 points and Five 5 points. After the hand has been played, the honours are counted as in the parent game, to determine the point for Game, with the addition that the player who has won the 5 of trumps scores 5 points for it.

Bezique

The standard game of Bezique is played by two players, with two packs of cards from which the 6s, 5s, 4s, 3s and 2s have been removed. The cards rank in the order: **A 10 K Q J 9 8 7**.

Eight cards are dealt to each player in packets of three, two, three. The remaining forty-eight cards (the stock) are placed face downwards on the table, and the dealer exposes the top card to denote the trump suit. It is placed alongside the stock, and if it is a **7** he scores 10 points.

The non-dealer leads to the first trick. As at most games the winner of a trick leads to the next, but it is a feature of bezique that a player is under no obligation to follow suit to the card led. The object of the game is to score points for declaring certain cards and combinations of cards. The declarations, and the points that may be scored for them, are as follows:

Double Bezique = 500 points. Two **Q ♠** (or **Q ♣** if Spades or Diamonds are trumps) and two **J ♦** (or **J ♥** if Spades or Diamonds are trumps).

Sequence in Trumps = 250 points. **A 10 K Q J** of the trump suit.

Any Four Aces = 100 points.

Any Four Kings = 80 points.

Any Four Queens = 60 points.

Any Four Jacks = 40 points.

Bezique = 40 points. **Q ♠** (or **Q ♣** if Spades or Diamonds are trumps) and **J ♦** (or **J ♥** if Spades or Diamonds are trumps).

Royal Marriage = 40 points. **King** and **Queen** of the trump suit.

Common Marriage = 20 points. **King** and **Queen** of the same plain suit.

A player scores 10 points if he holds a **7** of the trump suit and exchanges it for the turn-up card; and 10 points are scored for playing a **7** of the trump suit.

When a player has won a trick he may declare by placing the appropriate cards face upwards on the table. He may make as many declarations as he chooses, always provided that the declarations do not involve the same cards. If the exposed cards show more than one declaration the player must announce which declaration he intends to score, and leave the other to be scored when he wins another trick. A card that has once scored cannot again be used to form part of a similar declaration. As an example, a player may expose **K ♠ Q♠ J ♦** score 40 for bezique and announce 'Twenty to come' meaning that the next time he wins a trick he will score 20 points for the common marriage of the King and Queen of Spades. He may not expose a second Jack of Diamonds and score bezique with the Queen of Spades. The cards that have been declared, and so exposed on the table, remain a part of the player's hand and he may play them to later tricks.

Tricks should be gathered and kept by the player who wins them, because at the end of a deal a player scores 10 points for every Ace and every 10 that he has won. They are known as brisques.

When both players have played to a trick they replenish their hands from the stock: winner takes the top card, loser the next.

When the stock is exhausted the last eight tricks are played, and the game takes on a rather different character. Now, if a player has a card of the suit that has been led he must play it, and he must win a trick if he is able to. No further declarations may be made, and the aim of the player is to win brisques and the last trick for which 10 points are scored.

The deal passes to the other player, and so alternately, until one of them has reached an agreed number of points, usually 2,000.

The score cannot be kept satisfactorily with pencil on paper. It is best to use the special bezique markers that take the form of indicators marked as clocks on thin cardboard.

The following deal, played by two experienced players, illustrates many of the finer points of good play.

South dealt, and the hands were:

Clubs were trumps, the 10 of Clubs having been turned up.

The turn-up card is important because it is a sequence card, and a high one at that since it ranks immediately below the Ace.

The main features of North's hand are that he holds two sequence cards (the Queen and Jack of Clubs), a 7 of trumps to exchange for the valuable 10, and three Queens, which put him well on the way to a declaration of four Queens.

The main features of South's hand are a bezique Queen (the Queen of Spades) and three low trumps, including the 7; but, of course, as yet South does not know that North holds both the Queens of trumps, so that a sequence for him is impossible. It is South's lead, and it is necessary for him to win a trick to exchange the 7 of Clubs for the 10. An inexperienced player might be tempted to lead an indifferent card, such as the 7 of Hearts, hoping that North will have nothing to declare and will refuse to win the trick. This, however, is very artless play, and the better play is for South to lead his highest trump because it compels North to use a sequence card if he wants to take the trick and make a declaration. So . . .

Trick 1 South led the 9 of Clubs. North, who appreciated the importance of the turn-up card, won with the Queen of Clubs. This was North's best play, although it suffers from the defect that it reduces North's chance of declaring four Queens, and it informs South that virtually he has no hope of a sequence because North would hardly play a sequence card if he lacked a duplicate. North exchanged the 7 of Clubs for the turn-up card, and scored 10 points. He drew the King of Clubs (giving him no less than four of the five sequence cards), and South the 9 of Hearts.

Trick 2 North led the 9 of Diamonds, and South played the 7 of Hearts. North declared the royal marriage and scored 40 points, making his total 50 points. North drew the King of Hearts, and South the Ace of Hearts.

Trick 3 North led the 7 of Hearts, and South played the 9 of Diamonds. North declared the common marriage in Hearts and scored 20 points, making his total 70 points. North drew the Ace of Clubs, and South the Jack of Hearts.

Trick 4 North now held a sequence, but, in order to declare it, he had first to win a trick. A Heart must be led, and he chose the Queen. Undoubtedly it was the best lead. The Ace of Hearts is not a good lead, because, if trumped, it will cost North a brisque; and it is better for North to save for four Kings, instead of for four Queens, because not only does it gain 20 more points, but North had already played a Queen so the chance of drawing a Queen was slightly less than that of drawing a King. South played the 9 of Hearts. North declared his Ace, 10 and Jack of Clubs, and scored 250 points for the sequence, giving him a total of 320 points. South had not yet scored. North drew the 10 of Spades, and South the Jack of Diamonds.

At this point the hands were:

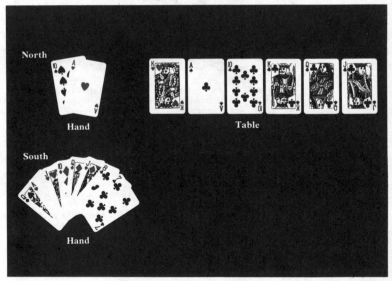

North

Hand

Table

South

Hand

Trick 5 North's trumps were no longer of vital importance to him, and could be played if desired. The two Kings were important because North had made up his mind to save for Kings, and it is an error of tactics to change one's mind during the game. The Aces and 10s were important, because they furnish brisques. So North led the Jack of Clubs. South had a bezique in his hand, but unfortunately he could not win the trick and declare it. The best he could do was to play the Jack of Hearts. North drew the 8 of Diamonds, and South the Queen of Diamonds.

Trick 6 North led the 8 of Diamonds. South won with the 10 of Diamonds, putting away a brisque for himself, and declared bezique. South's 40 points for bezique was his first score, and he was a long way behind North's 320 points. South drew the 10 of Hearts, and North the Ace of Clubs.

Trick 7 South now had the lead. He chose the 7 of Clubs and scored 10 points, making his total 50. It was the best lead, because the lead of either Heart would probably be trumped and a brisque lost. He had to save for four Queens, and the Jack of Diamonds was out of the question since there was always the possibility of declaring double bezique. North was more or less compelled to win with the Queen of Clubs. North drew the 8 of Diamonds, and South the Queen of Spades.

Trick 8 North led the 8 of Diamonds, and South won with the 8 of Clubs and declared four Queens (60 points) giving him a total of 110. North, with a total of 320 points, was still well ahead, but he noted with some concern that South would be able to declare double bezique if he was lucky enough to draw the other Jack of Diamonds. South drew the 9 of Spades, and North the 8 of Spades.

Trick 9 South led the 9 of Spades, and North won with the 10 of Spades. North drew the Jack of Spades, and South the 8 of Spades.

Trick 10 North led the 8 of Spades, and South played the other 8 of Spades. North drew the 8 of Hearts, and South the Jack of Hearts.

Trick 11 North led the 8 of Hearts, and South won with the 10 of Hearts. South drew the King of Diamonds, and North the 8 of Hearts.

At this point the hands were:

The score was North 320 points, South 110 points.

Trick 12 South led the Jack of Hearts, and North played the 8. It would not have been good play for North to win with the Ace of Hearts because, though this would have given him a brisque, it is better for North to save for four Aces now that he held three. South laid down his King of Diamonds and scored a common marriage (20 points), giving him a total of 130 points. South drew the 7 of Spades, and North the Ace of Spades.

Trick 13 South led the 7 of Spades. North won with the Jack of Spades, and declared four Aces (100 points). This raised his total to 420, and he had a good lead on South, whose score was only 130 points. North drew the Jack of Clubs, and South the 9 of Spades.

The hands were now:

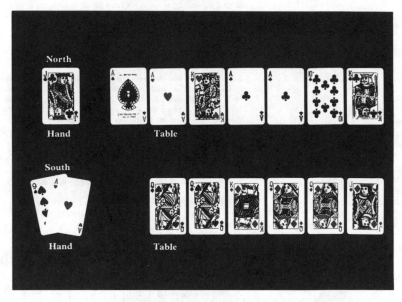

North
Hand   Table

South
Hand   Table

and South's hand with its three bezique cards was not without possibilities.

Trick 14 North led the Jack of Clubs, and South played the 9 of Spades. North drew the Jack of Spades, and South the 9 of Hearts.

Trick 15 North led the Jack of Spades, and South played the 9 of Hearts. North drew the King of Clubs, and South the Jack of Diamonds.

Trick 16 Now, of course, the whole game changed, because South held a double bezique, though he had to win a trick before he could declare it. If the stock is nearly exhausted it is proper for North to lead trumps in an attempt to prevent South from winning a trick. It was, however, too early in the game for these tactics, so North led the Ace of Spades, hoping that it would not be trumped, and South, who had no trump in his hand, discarded the married Queen of Diamonds. North drew the 10 of Diamonds, and South the 10 of Clubs, a vital card.

Trick 17 North, who by this time suspected that South held double bezique, led the Ace of Hearts, hoping that South would still not be able to trump. This time, however, he was doomed to disappointment, because, of course, South was able to win with the 10 of Clubs and declare double bezique. The score of 500

34

points for double bezique raised South's total to 630 and gave him a lead of 210 points because North's score was only 420 points. South drew the Ace of Spades, and North the King.

Trick 18 South, who had no further use for his bezique Jacks, led a Jack of Diamonds. North won with the 10 of Diamonds and declared four Kings (80 points), raising his score to 500 points. North drew the 9 of Clubs, and South the Ace of Diamonds.

Trick 19 North led the 9 of Clubs, and South played the Jack of Diamonds. North drew the 8 of Clubs, and South the Ace of Diamonds.

The hands were now:

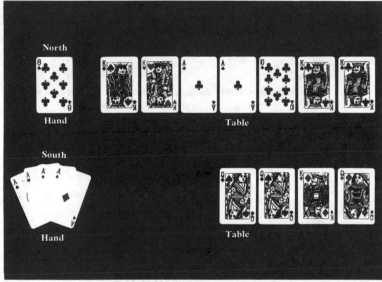

Trick 20 North now suspected that South was on the point of declaring four Aces. His tactics, therefore, had to be aggressive, and, since the other 10 of Clubs had been played, his trumps were all winners, and he played them to prevent South from declaring. North led the Ace of Clubs, and South played the Queen of Spades. North drew one 7 of Diamonds and South the other.

Trick 21 North led the Ace of Clubs, and South played the 7 of Diamonds. North drew the Queen of Hearts, and South the 10 of Spades.

Trick 22 North led the 10 of Clubs, and South played the Queen of Spades. North declared the common marriage in Hearts (20 points) raising his total to 520 points. North drew the King of Spades, and South the 7.

Trick 23 North led the King of Clubs, and South played the 7 of Spades. North drew the King of Diamonds, and South the 10 of Hearts.

Trick 24 (last trick) North led the King of Clubs, and South played the Queen of Diamonds. North scored 10 points for the last trick bringing his total to 530 points. South's score was 630 points, and from the time that he declared double bezique North had little chance to overtake him. He did well, however, to prevent South from declaring four Aces and so adding another 100 points to his score. North drew the King of Hearts, and South picked up the 7 of Clubs exposed on the table.

After picking up their cards from the table, the hands of the two players were:

North   South

The play to the last eight tricks was:

North	South
K ♥	A ♥
7 ♦	A ♦
K ♦	A ♣
K ♠	A ♠
Q ♥	10 ♥
K ♠	10 ♠
8 ♣	K ♦
K ♥	7 ♣

South was lucky to win all his brisques, giving him a score of 100 points: North won six brisques for a total of 60 points. The final score, therefore, was: South 730 points; North 590 points.

Altogether a fine deal, and one worth studying, because it illustrates the importance of playing for double bezique. For the first half of the deal North was well ahead, but after South had won the highest prize that the game has to offer, it was practically impossible for North to win the deal, and all his efforts had to be directed towards preventing South from gaining an even bigger lead. North played well to reduce South's lead of 210 points (gained at the seventeenth trick) to 140.

RUBICON BEZIQUE has the advantage over the parent game that, as long ago as 1887, a committee of the Portland Club drew up a code of laws under which it should be played.

It is very similar to the parent game, and, like it, is a game for two players, but four packs of cards, not two, are used, and there are some differences in the preliminaries, the scoring and the routine of the game.

In the preliminaries, nine cards (not eight) are dealt to each player, either singly or in packets of three, and there is no turn up of the top card of the stock, so that the peculiar value of the 7 of trumps is lost.

The scoring is the same as in the parent game, with the following additions:

36

Carte Blanche = 50 points. If either player is dealt a hand without a court card he is entitled to score for carte blanche. Both players are entitled to score it. Before a player can score, however, he must show his hand to his opponent. Thereafter, each time that he draws a card from the stock he may show it to his opponent and score 50 points if it is not a court card.

Ordinary Sequence = 150 points. **A 10 K Q J** of any suit other than the trump suit.

Triple Bezique = 1,500 points. Three **Q ♠** and three **J ♦** (or **Q ♣** and **J ♥** if either Spades or Diamonds are trumps).

Quadruple Bezique = 4,500 points. Four **Q ♠** and four **J ♦** (or **Q ♣** and **J ♥** if either Spades or Diamonds are trumps).

Last Trick = 50 points.

The routine differs from that of the parent game in the following essentials:

1. A game is complete in one deal.
2. Trumps are determined by the first marriage or sequence declared by either player.
3. The tricks are left exposed on the table until such time as a brisque is played. After this the tricks are gathered and turned in the usual way.
4. If a card is played from a declared combination, subsequently the combination may be filled by adding an appropriate card and the declaration scored again.
5. If a player has declared two marriages in the same suit, he may rearrange the Kings and Queens on the table and declare two more marriages.
6. Brisques are disregarded for scoring except to break a tie or to save a player from being rubiconed.
7. If a player fails to score 1,000 points he is rubiconed. His score is added to (not subtracted from) that of his opponent, who adds a further 1,300 points (not 500) for the game. Further, if a player fails to score 100 points, the winner adds an extra 100 points to his score.

BEZIQUE FOR THREE PLAYERS is played with three packs of cards, and the players compete all against all. The play is the same as in the parent game with the addition of a score of 1,500 points for triple bezique.

BEZIQUE FOR FOUR PLAYERS is played with six packs of cards, or 192 cards in all. Two play in partnership against the other two.

The dealer places twenty-four cards face downwards in a pile on the table, and on this he places a marker so that the players will be warned when the stock is nearing exhaustion. He deals nine cards to each of the four players and places the remainder of the pack (132 cards in all) face downwards on top of the marker.

In general, the play follows that described under rubicon bezique (above) but there are some differences in the scoring and in declaring.

Carte Blanche = 100 points.

Double Carte Blanche = 500. Both partners being dealt hands without a court card.

Quintuple Bezique = 13,500 points. Five **Q♠** and **J♦** (or **Q♣** and **J♥** if either Spades or Diamonds are trumps).

Sextuple Bezique is so unlikely that no score has been alloted to it. Should it occur, the correct score is 40,500 points.

Any Four Aces = 1,000 points.
Any Four Tens = 900 points.
Any Four Kings = 800 points.
Any Four Queens = 600 points.
Any Four Jacks = 400 points.

The game bonus is 1,000 points, the rubicon 2,500 points and brisques are disregarded.

In all other essentials the scoring is the same as in rubicon bezique. The partnership principle, however, introduces two new features in the methods of declaring combinations. First, after winning a trick, a player may either declare or leave it to his partner to do so. Secondly, a player may declare a combination either with his own cards (including those on the table already declared by him) or with one or more of his own cards and one or more of his partner's declared cards. Indeed, since a player holds only nine cards, quintuple bezique (and sextuple bezique if it occurs) can only be declared with the help of partner.

The player on the left of the dealer leads to the first trick.

Beyond these additions, the play follows that of rubicon bezique.

SIX-PACK BEZIQUE, sometimes, but rarely, known as Chinese Bezique, is a game for two players, and generally considered the most popular variation of the family. Sir Winston Churchill was a keen player and an able exponent of the game.

Six packs are shuffled together and both players lift a part of the pack and show the bottom cards to determine choice of seat and deal. The one who shows the higher card has the choice, and would be advised to pass the deal to his opponent because there is a slight disadvantage in dealing. If equal cards are shown the players cut again.

The dealer takes a number of cards at random off the top of the pack, and the non-dealer estimates how many have been taken. If his estimate proves correct he scores 150 points. The dealer deals twelve cards, one by one, to his opponent and himself, and scores 250 points if he has taken exactly twenty-four cards from the top of the pack.

There is no turn-up to determine the trump suit. It is determined, as in rubicon bezique (above), by the first declared marriage or sequence by either player.

The declarations are scored for as follows:

Sequence in Trumps = 250 points.
Sequence in a Plain Suit = 150 points.
Royal Marriage = 40 points.
Common Marriage = 20 points.

Bezique = 40 points	If Spades are trumps bezique is **Q♠** and
Double Bezique = 500 points	**J♦**; if Diamonds are trumps **Q♦** and **J♠**; if Hearts are trumps **Q♥** and **J♣**;
Triple Bezique = 1,500 points	and if Clubs are trumps **Q♣** and **J♥**.
Quadruple Bezique = 4,500 points	

Four Aces in Trumps = 1,000 points.
Four Tens in Trumps = 900 points.
Four Kings in Trumps = 800 points.
Four Queens in Trumps = 600 points.
Four Jacks in Trumps = 400 points.
Any Four Aces = 100 points.
Any Four Kings = 80 points.
Any Four Queens = 60 points.
Any Four Jacks = 40 points.
Carte Blanche = 250 points.

The non-dealer leads to the first trick. It is not compulsory to follow suit, and the card that is led holds the trick unless a higher card of the same suit is played or a trump is played to the lead of a plain suit. As points are not scored for brisques, nor for winning tricks, the tricks are not gathered and turned but left face upwards on the table in a pile. The winner of a trick may score for a declaration. He takes the top card of the stock (the loser takes the next card of the stock) and leads to the next trick.

A declaration is made by placing the appropriate cards face upwards on the table. They are left there and are available for play as though in the hand of the player. Declarations are scored when made, and the same card may be counted in a declaration more than once.

No declaration may be made after the last two cards of the stock have been drawn. The players then pick up any cards they have on the table and play off the last twelve tricks. As in the parent game, a player must now follow suit to the card led, and must win a trick if he is able to.

Every deal constitutes a game, and the player with the higher score wins. He adds 1,000 points to his score, and rubicons his opponent if he has failed to score 3,000 points.

EIGHT-PACK BEZIQUE is identical with six-pack bezique (above) except for the increased number of cards and the following differences in the routine and scoring:

1. Each player is dealt fifteen cards.
2. The scores for beziques are:
   Bezique = 50 points.
   Double Bezique = 500 points.
   Triple Bezique = 1,500 points.
   Quadruple Bezique = 4,500 points.
   Quintuple Bezique = = 9,000 points.
3. In the trump suit the scores are for:
   Five Aces = 2,000 points.
   Five Tens = 1,800 points.
   Five Kings = 1,600 points.
   Five Queens = 1,200 points.
   Five Jacks = 800 points.
4. A player who fails to score 5,000 points is rubiconed.

California Jack

California Jack is played with the full pack of fifty-two cards, the Ace ranking high the 2 low. It is a game for two players that derives from all fours (see page 28) but is generally considered an improvement on it.

The non-dealer cuts the pack and exposes the bottom card to decide the trump suit. The dealer deals six cards, one at a time, to each player, and places the remainder of the pack face upwards on the table, taking the precaution to square it up so that only the top card can be seen.

The non-dealer leads to the first trick. The winner of a trick takes the top card of the stock, the loser the next card. A player must follow suit if he can, and he loses 1 point if he revokes.

When the stock is exhausted and the last six cards have been played, the tricks won by each player are examined, and 1 point is scored for winning High (Ace of trumps), Low (2 of trumps), Jack (Jack of trumps) and Game (majority of points, counting each Ace won as 4 points, each King as 3 points, each Queen as 2 points, each Jack as 1 point, and each Ten as 10 points).

The game is won by the player who first scores 10 points.

The player should aim to keep both winning and losing cards in his hand because if the exposed card of the stock is valuable he will wish to win it, but if it is not, he will wish to lose the trick on the chance of the next card of the stock being a more valuable one. The Tens, of course, are the cards to go for.

A good California Jack hand. There are two good cards for trick-winning and three for losing

SHASTA SAM is a variation of the game in which the stock is placed face downwards on the table instead of face upwards. It is a less skilful game as, of course, the winner of a trick does not know what card he will draw.

Casino

Although Casino (sometimes erroneously spelt cassino) is essentially a game for two, played with the full pack of fifty-two cards, it may be played by three or four. The only difference is that if three players take part they play all against all, and if four take part two play in partnership against the other two.

The dealer deals two cards face downwards to his opponent, then two face upwards to the table, and then two face downwards to himself. This is repeated, so that both players end with four cards each, and there are four exposed cards (the layout) on the table. The remaining forty cards (the stock) are placed face downwards on the table.

The numeral cards count at their pip values. The Ace counts as 1, and the court cards are used only for pairing: they have no pip value.

The object of the game is to take in cards which score as follows:

The 10 ♦ (Great Casino) = 2 points.
The 2 ♠ (Little Casino) = 1 point.
The majority of cards (27 or more) = 3 points.
The majority of Spades (7 or more) = 1 point.
Each Ace = 1 point.
All cards in the layout (the Sweep) = 1 point.

Each player in turn, beginning with the non-dealer, plays a card until both players have exhausted their four cards. When this occurs, the same dealer deals four more cards to his opponent and four to himself, but none to the layout. Play continues in this way until the stock has been exhausted. In all, therefore, there are six deals to complete the game, and before making the final deal the dealer must announce it. If he does not, his opponent has a right to cancel the deal.

When a player plays a card from his hand he has the choice of several plays.

He may *Pair*. If, for example, there are one or more 5s in the layout, he may play a 5 from his hand and take it up as a trick with all the other 5s in the layout. A court card, however, may be paired with only one card of the same rank at a time.

He may *Combine*. It is an extension of pairing that allows a player to pick up cards from the layout of the total pip value of a card in his hand. Thus a player playing a 9 may take up a 7 and a 2, or a 6 and a 3 from the layout, or all four cards if they are in the layout.

He may *Build*. He may play a card to a card in the layout to make up a total that he is in a position to take with another card in his hand. If, for example, a player holds a 9 and a 2, and there is a 7 in the layout, he may build the 2 on the 7, so that the next time he plays (provided his opponent has not forestalled him) he may play the 9 and take all three cards as a trick. The build may be continued by either player up to a maximum of five cards, but a build can be taken only as a unit. The player who has built must take up the combination when next it is his turn to play, unless he prefers to win something else, or he decides to make another build.

He may *Call*. It is an extension of building that allows a player to earmark one or more combinations for subsequent capture. Suppose, for example, a player holds in his hand two 8s and that there is a 5 and a 3 in the layout (see illustration). He could, of

Layout

Hand

course, combine one of his 8s with the 5 and 3 in the layout, but this would only give him three cards in the trick. The better play, therefore, is for him to play one of his 8s to the layout and announce 'Eight'. Then, when next it is his turn to play, provided his opponent has not forestalled him, he may play his other 8 and pick up all four cards in the trick.

When a player cannot pair, combine, build or call, he must play one of his cards to the layout. It is known as trailing. It is advisable to play a low card, but not an Ace, little casino or a Spade.

When the last eight cards have been played any left in the layout are the property of the winner of the final trick, but it does not count as a sweep.

This ends the game, except for the formality of the players examining their tricks and counting their scores.

There is no penalty for making a build incorrectly, or for capturing cards to which a player is not entitled, because his opponent has the opportunity to see the error and demand that it is corrected. If, however, a player makes a build when he has no card in his hand to capture it or trails when he has a build in the layout, he automatically forfeits the game. If a card is faced in the pack, or if the dealer when dealing exposes a card, other than when dealing cards to the layout, the exposed card is played to the layout and the dealer plays the hand with fewer than four cards.

Casino is sometimes considered a game for children. It is, however, very far from being so. Among card players it is widely spoken of as one of the best of all two-handed games and it is often played for high stakes. To be successful a player needs an elephantine memory, and the capacity to deduce from the card played by an opponent what cards he is most likely to be holding in his hand.

ROYAL CASINO is an improvement on the parent game because the court cards play a more important part. The Aces count 1 or 14 (at the option of the player), the Kings 13, the Queens 12 and the Jacks 11, and they may be used for combining and building. Thus an 8 and a 4 may be taken with a Queen, a 6, a 4 and a 3 with a King, and so on.

Twenty-one points constitute the game.

In **DRAW CASINO**, after the first round of a deal, the forty undealt cards are placed face downwards on the table to form a stock. Then each player, after playing, draws a card from the stock to bring the number of cards in his hand up to four. When the stock is exhausted the hands are played out and the count made as in the parent game.

SPADE CASINO may be played either as royal casino (above) or as the parent game, with the addition that the Ace, Jack and 2 of Spades count 2 points each, and all the other Spades 1 point each.

Game is 61 points, and it is convenient and customary to keep the score on a cribbage board.

Comet

Two 52-card packs, with the same design on their backs, are used alternately. The packs must be prepared by rejecting all the Aces, putting all the red cards into one pack and all the black cards into another, and interchanging a red and a black 9.

Eighteen cards are dealt to each player, one at a time, and the remaining twelve cards are put aside; they play no part in the game. The non-dealer begins the game by playing one of his cards, face upwards, to the centre of the table. The players then, alternately, build up on it by rank only. Suits are disregarded. Any number of cards, provided they are of the proper rank, may be played in one turn. The four 8s, for example, may be built on a 7, the four Jacks on a 10, and so on. When a player is unable to build it is a stop, and his opponent begins a new sequence by playing any card he chooses. Obviously a King is always a stop.

The 9 of the opposite colour is called the comet. It may represent any card that the holder chooses, but may be played only in turn. It is a stop, and the player who plays it begins a new sequence.

The player who is first to get rid of all the cards in his hand is the winner. He scores the total of pips left in his opponent's hand, the court cards counting as 10 each. If both players are stopped and both are left with cards in their hands, both hands are counted. The lower hand wins and scores the value of his opponent's hand less the value of his own. If a player wins the hand while the comet is in the hand of his opponent he scores double. If a player wins by playing the comet, he doubles his score, and if he wins the hand by playing the comet as a 9 he quadruples his score.

COMMIT is a variation of the parent game that is suitable for more than two players. It is played with the standard pack of fifty-two cards from which the 8 of Diamonds has been removed, and as many other 8s and 7s as may be necessary for the players to be dealt an equal number of cards.

The players place an equal number of units into a pool.

The player on the left of the dealer begins by playing any card to the centre of the table. The others play cards on it as able, and not necessarily in rotation. The cards played must follow in sequence. Only the 6 of Spades may be played on the 5 of Spades, the 8 of Clubs on the 7 of Clubs, and so on.

The 9 of Diamonds is the comet and may be played either when all the players are stopped or when the holder of it has played regularly and is unable to continue the sequence. After it has been played, any player in rotation may either continue by playing the 10 of Diamonds on it, or the card next above that for which the comet has been substituted.

The player who plays the comet receives 2 units from each of the other players, and any player who plays a King receives 1 unit from each of the other players. The player who is first to get rid of his cards wins the pool, and receives 2 units from a player who has been left with the comet in his hand, and 1 unit for each King.

Cribbage

Cribbage is believed to have been developed out of the older card game of Noddy, by Sir John Suckling in the reign of Charles I. Originally it was a two-handed game, but variations for three and four players are now known.

The two-handed game is the most popular, and of it there are three variations: 5-card, 6-card and 7-card. Points won are marked with a peg on what is known as a noddy board. It is oblong in shape, has a double row of holes, thirty in each row, and is divided, for convenience in scoring, into groups of five holes. The board is placed between the two players; both start from the same end of the board and peg their scores first along the outer row of holes and then along the inner row—once round the board at the 5-card game, twice round at the 6-card game and three times round at the 7-card game. In each case the game ends when one player reaches the game hole from which he started. Thus, at 5-card cribbage the game is 61 holes, at 6-card 121 holes, and at 7-card 181 holes.

FIVE-CARD CRIBBAGE FOR TWO PLAYERS, which is the original game, is generally considered the most scientific of the variations. In the manner of scoring it is unique, and the play is different to that of most card games, because it calls for no effort of memory. Good judgement and concentration are the chief qualities that lead to success.

The full pack of fifty-two cards is used. The players cut for deal; the lower deals first. When cutting for deal, and for scoring sequences, the cards rank in order from Ace (low) to King (high), but, for counting, the King, Queen and Jack count 10 each and the other cards at their pip values. Five cards are dealt to each player, and the non-dealer pegs 3 holes (Three for Last) as compensation against the advantage of the first deal of a game.

The players look at their cards, and then place two of them face downwards on the right of the dealer. These four cards are known as the *Crib*. The non-dealer then cuts the pack, and the dealer turns up the top card of the cut and places it on top of the pack. The card is known as the *Start*, and if it is a Jack the dealer pegs 2 holes (Two for his Heels).

Scores are made partly in play and partly by the scoring values of the cards in hand. The latter, however, are not pegged until the play ends.

During the play of the hand, scores are made as follows:

If a player plays a card of the same rank as the previous one played, he pegs 2 for a *Pair*, but court cards pair only rank with rank—that is to say King with King, Queen with Queen and Jack with Jack.

If a player plays a third card of the same rank as a pair he pegs 6 for *Pair-Royal*.

If a player plays a fourth card of the same rank as a pair-royal he pegs 12 for a *Double Pair-Royal*.

A *Sequence* (or *Run*) is pegged at 1 for each card with a minimum of three cards and a maximum of seven. The cards need not be of the same suit, nor need they be played in sequential order, but, as the Ace is low, **A K Q** is not a sequence, and a sequence is destroyed by a pair or an intervening card. If the dealer plays a 7 and the non-dealer a 5, the dealer may now play a 6 and peg 3, and the non-dealer may continue either with a 4 or an 8 and peg 4.

If a player plays a card which, with those already played, adds up to *Fifteen* he pegs 2, and, again, if they total *Thirty-one* he pegs 2.

Out of this an important point arises. If, when the player whose turn it is to play cannot do so without exceeding thirty-one, he says 'Go'. His opponent then plays a card or cards up to the limit. If the cards that he plays bring the total up to exactly thirty-one he pegs 2; if not he pegs 1 (One for Last).

This ends the play, and the players, beginning with the non-dealer, count their scores by combining their own cards with the start. The dealer then exposes the crib (it is his exclusive property) and any values that he finds in it (making full use of the start) he pegs to his score. Should either player hold the Jack of the same suit as the start he pegs 1 (One for his Nob). If a player holds in his hand three cards all of the same suit he pegs 3 for a *Flush*, and 4 if the start is of the same suit. In the crib, however, nothing is scored for a flush unless, with the start, it is a flush of five; if it is the dealer pegs 5.

Two other features of the scoring call for special mention. First, a player must count his hand aloud, and if he overlooks any score, either in play or otherwise, his opponent may call 'Muggins', point out the omission, and peg the score for himself. Secondly, if a player reaches the game hole before his opponent has gone half-way round the board a *Lurch* is scored, that is to say the winner scores two games instead of only one.

Points are scored during the play by a player adding the value of the card played by the opponent to a card played from his own hand. Thus if a 10 or court card is led, and a player plays a 5, he scores fifteen and pegs 2 holes (Fifteen-Two as it is called for short). If a 6 is led, and he plays another 6, he scores for a pair and pegs 2. Again, a 4 is led, he plays a 6, and the opponent plays a 5: he pegs 3 for a sequence and 2 for fifteen. And so on.

The general principles of play may be illustrated in an elementary deal.

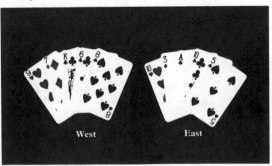

West   East

East is the dealer.

West holds a sequence of four. As a result the King of Clubs will go to the crib, and for his other card he must choose between the 6 of Clubs and the 9 of Hearts. There is not much in it, but as the 6 of Clubs is of the same suit as the King, there is a slight advantage in discarding the 9 of Hearts, because the 6 of Clubs (along with the King) might help to give East a flush in his crib.

East has an easy choice of discards. Indeed, it is obvious that he will discard the Ace of Clubs and 3 of Diamonds.

West cuts the cards, and East turns up the King of Spades.

The position is now:

Start   Crib

West   East

West leads the **7** ♦ and says 'Seven'. It is his best lead because if East plays an 8 and pegs 2 for fifteen, West can play the **6** ♣ and peg 3 for sequence. He will not, of course, play the 8 ♠, because if East holds another 8 he will play it and not only peg for a pair-royal but for thirty-one as well.

In the event, East cannot play an 8 and score for fifteen. His best play, therefore, is the **10** ♣ announcing 'Seventeen'. This makes it impossible for a fifteen to be scored against him.

West has no better play than the **8** ♠ announcing 'Twenty-five', because the closer the total to 31 the better is the chance that East will be unable to play.

East plays the **5** ♠ announcing 'Thirty'.

West says 'Go' and as East has not got an Ace he pegs One for Last.

The hands are now counted.

West is not helped by the start. All he can score is 2 for fifteen and 3 for sequence. This with his Three for Last gives him a score of 8.

East pegs 6 for fifteen (two 10s and the **K** ♠ in the start, each combined with the **5** ♠) and 2 for the pair of 10s. In the crib he finds an Ace, a King a 9 and a 3. With the start this gives him 2 for the pair of Kings. He, therefore pegs 10 holes, making 11 in all as he has already pegged One for Last.

SIX-CARD and SEVEN-CARD CRIBBAGE FOR TWO PLAYERS. The 6-card and 7-card variations of cribbage differ very little from the 5-card game. There is, in fact, no difference in the play nor in the crib, and very little in the mechanics of the game. The only differences of importance, apart from the number of cards, are that the non-dealer does not receive Three· for Last, that the cards are played out to the end (the player failing to score for go leading again, thus giving his opponent the chance of making a pair or fifteen) and that in the 6-card variation the play is twice round the board (121 holes) and in the 7-card three times round (181 holes).

The general principles explained for the parent game hold good at the 6-card variation. It is to be noted, however, that in the 6-card variation the number of cards in hand and in the crib are the same, from which it follows that it is not so important for the non-dealer to make an effort of trying to baulk the crib by his discard. The two objectives – preserving any values in hand and baulking opponent's crib – are in this case on the same level, and either objective may be preferred, as the nature of the hand dictates.

THREE-HANDED CRIBBAGE. Five cards are dealt to each player, and an extra one to the crib, to which each player contributes one card only. There is no Three for Last. The start is cut for in the usual way. The player on the left of the dealer plays first, and has first Show. He deals the succeeding hand. The score may be pegged on a triangular board open in the centre, or on the regular board furnished with a pivotted arm that permits a third player to peg. The game is once round the board.

FOUR-HANDED CRIBBAGE. Two play as partners against the other two, the partners sitting facing each other. Each player is dealt five cards and discards one to the crib, which is the property of the dealer. The player on the left of the dealer plays first. The others follow in clockwise rotation. Consultation between partners is not allowed, nor may they prompt each other, but a player may help his partner in the count of the hand or crib. The cards are played out to the end, as in the 6-card and 7-card variations. Game is usually twice round the board (121 holes).

Ecarté

Écarté is played with a 32-card pack; that is to say with a pack from which the 2s, 3s, 4s, 5s, and 6s have been removed. The cards rank in the order: King (high), Queen, Jack, Ace, 10, 9, 8, 7 (low).

The two players are deal five cards each, either in packets of three and two, or two and three, and the rest of the pack is placed face downwards on the table, between them. To determine the trump suit the top card of the pack is turned face upwards. After looking at his cards, the non-dealer either plays or proposes. If he proposes, the dealer has the choice of either accepting or playing, and if he accepts both players may exchange any or all of their cards for others from the pack. By agreement the exchange of cards may continue until the pack is exhausted.

The non-dealer has first lead. The object of the game is to win three tricks, called the Trick. The winner scores 1 point for this, and if he wins all five tricks (the Vole) he scores 2 points. The game is won by the player who first wins 5 points, and it is customary to count a treble if a player wins the game and his opponent has failed to score; a double if his opponent has scored only 1 or 2 points, and a single if his opponent has scored 3 or 4 points.

So far, then, *écarté* appears to be childishly simple. The game, however, lends itself to a number of refinements that raise it to the level of an adult game. If the non-dealer does not propose, but plays, and fails to make the Trick, the dealer scores 2 points instead of only 1. In the same way, if the dealer refuses a proposal, and plays, and fails to make the Trick, the non-dealer scores 2 points. The value of the Vole (2 points) is not affected by playing without proposing.

Another important feature of the game is that if the dealer turns up a King as trumps, or if a player is dealt the King of the trump suit, he scores 1 point. The point can be scored by the non-dealer only if he declares the King before he makes the opening lead, and by the dealer only if he declares it before he plays to the first trick. A player is under no compulsion to declare the King, and, indeed, sometimes it is better to sacrifice the point for declaring the King than to declare it and so disclose to the opponent that this important card is held against him.

With the score West 3 points, East 4 points, East deals and the 8 ♠ is turned up.

West   East

East decides to play and must win the game if he handles his cards correctly. In the event he loses the game by incautious play. He leads **K ♣** on which West plays **7 ♣**. West does not declare the **K ♠** because East has played without proposing and, therefore, will lose 2 points if he fails to win the Trick. On the other hand, if he wins the Trick, declaring the King will be of no help to West.

East is lulled into a false sense of security, and unaware that the **K ♠** is against him he assumes that it is safe to lead **Q ♠**. West wins with **K ♠**, leads **Q ♦** to force East to win with **J ♠**, and comes to the last two tricks, and with them wins the game, with **A ♠** and **A ♥**

There are a number of stock hands, holding which a player should play and not propose, and equally refuse the opponent's proposal. The more important of them are set out below. In all cases Spades are trumps:

1. Any three trumps supported by two inferior cards in outside suits— **♠ J 10 7 ♥ 8 ♦ 10**
2. Any two trumps supported by three cards in one outside suit— **♠ 10 8 ♥ J 8 7**
3. Any two trumps supported by the King and a low card in an outside suit, and one indifferent card in another suit— **♠ A 8 ♥ K 7 ♦ 9**
4. Any one trump supported by four cards headed by the King (or Queen) in an outside suit— **♠ J ♥ K 9 8 7** (or **Q J 8 7**)
5. Any one trump supported by three cards headed by a court card in an outside suit, and any high court card in another suit— **♠ 10 ♥ J 10 7 ♦ Q**
6. Any hand that contains three queens (or better) and even though it may lack a trump card— **♥ Q 7 ♦ Q 7 ♣ K**
7. Any hand that contains four high cards (King, Queen, Jack) and even though it may lack a trump card— **♥ K ♦ Q J ♣ Q 7**

These stock hands are based on the Law of Probability, supported by the experience of the best players, who set great store on them. So far as the dealer is concerned, they are the minimum types of hands for him to play on. In a number of cases he may do better if he follows his luck, or decides to play on what is called a hunch, but the non-dealer should never propose when holding a hand similar to one of the above types. The reason is that he has the opening lead, and, at écarté, the opening lead is of vital importance.

East deals and the **10 ♠** is turned up.

West plays and if he leads **Q ♥** he wins the Trick no matter how East plays.

If, however, West had dealt, East would be on lead and if he led the **K ♦** he would win the Trick no matter how West played. In fact, West would be hard put to save the Vole, and, indeed, would do so only if he retained the **J ♣** and not the **Q ♥**. An experienced player would, of course, retain the **J ♣** (although the **Q ♥** is a higher card) because he holds three Hearts and only one Club, and since there are only eight cards in a suit it is about seven to five on that East's last card is a Club and not a Heart.

The deal is of some interest because it illustrates the danger of leading the Queen of trumps, unless the King has been turned up as trumps. It will be seen that if West decides to lead the **Q ♠**, East wins with the **K ♠**, runs his Diamonds (scoring the Trick) and West will save the Vole only if he retains the **J ♣**. On the other hand, it is to be noted that the lead of the singleton King of trumps is nearly always a good lead, and rarely damages the leader's hand.

As a general rule it is best for a player to play when he cannot see his way to discarding more than two cards; but if a player's hand guarantees him the Trick, or virtually so, he should propose or accept, because if the proposal is refused he is on easy street (since the Trick is more or less in his pocket) and if the proposal is accepted he has the opportunity to convert his hand into one on which he may win the Vole.

Stock   West

German Whist

German Whist is a very simple game. Each player is dealt thirteen cards. The remaining twenty-six cards are placed face downwards between the players and the top card is turned face upwards to denote the trump suit.

The non-dealer leads to the first trick. Thereafter the player who wins a trick leads to the next, and so on. A player must follow suit if he can. If he cannot he may either trump or discard. The winner of a trick takes into his hand the exposed card from the top of the stock: the loser takes the next card from the stock (he does not show it to his opponent) and turns up the next card of the stock.

When the stock is exhausted, the players play out the remaining thirteen cards, and at this stage of the game the player with a good memory will know exactly which cards his opponent holds.

The game is complete in one deal, and the player who wins the majority of tricks receives an agreed number of points per trick for all in excess of those won by his opponent. If both players win thirteen tricks, there is, of course, no score.

Although german whist is a simple game it offers good memory training for those who aspire to succeed at more advanced games, and, at the same time, gives exercise in the technique of card play.

If a player holds a strong trump suit he should lead his trumps early in the game so as to command the game in the later stages of the play, and if the exposed card is a trump it is always good play to make an effort to win it.

On the other hand, it is not always good play to win a trick. Much depends on the value of the exposed card. The 9 ♦ is exposed. West leads the 7 ♦ and East holds ♦ Q 6 3. East should play 3 ♦, and allow West to win the trick. It is not worth while wasting the Q ♦ which should be kept in hand for better things later in the game. By contrary, if the J ♦ is the exposed card, East should win the trick with the Q ♦, because now he is exchanging the Q ♦ for an equivalent card and adding a trick to his total.

It is advisable to hold command of as many suits as possible, because it enables one to take a trick whenever the exposed card is worth winning, without losing control of the suit.

West holds the hand opposite.

Spades are trumps, and the exposed card is K ♣.

The K ♣ is worth winning, but leading the A ♣ is not the best play. West will win the trick, but the value of his hand will remain unchanged. West should prefer to lead the K ♦, because if it wins the trick his hand will be that much better, and if East is able to win the trick with the A ♦, West's Q ♦ has been promoted to top Diamond.

Gin Rummy

Many variations of rummy (see page 139) are known, but for two players the one generally preferred is Gin Rummy with the Hollywood scoring, so called because during the war it was taken up with much publicity by the cinema stars.

The game is played with a full pack of fifty-two cards that rank from King (high) to Ace (low). The players cut to determine who deals first, but, thereafter, the player who wins a hand deals for the next one.

Ten cards are dealt to each player and the next card is turned face upwards and placed on the table between the players; it is known as the up-card. The rest of the pack is placed faced downwards alongside it.

The object of the game is to meld one's cards into sets of three or four of the same suit, and into sequences of three or more of the same suit. Sets and sequences must be independent of each other: a player is not allowed to meld the same card into a sequence and a set.

The non-dealer has first choice of taking the up-card into his hand. If he does not, he must offer it to the dealer. If either player takes the up-card, he discards a card from his hand face upwards on the table. If neither player takes the up-card, the non-dealer takes the top card of the stock and discards a card from his hand to cover the up-card. The dealer then has the option of taking into his hand either the card that the non-dealer has discarded or the top card of the stock. When he has taken one of them into his hand, he, too, discards a card from his hand. The discards are placed one on top of the other, so that only the card immediately discarded can be seen, and the discard pile must not be examined by the players while the deal is in play.

Play continues in this way—each player in turn either taking the top card of the discard pile or the top card of the stock—until one of them elects to go down (called knocking) or there are only two cards left in the stock. Neither may be drawn, and if the player who draws the fiftieth card discards without knocking, the deal is declared a draw; neither player scores and the same dealer deals again.

The player who knocks must do so after drawing a card and discarding, and his unmelded cards must not exceed a total of 10 points—court cards count 10 points each and the others their pip values.

Unless a player has declared gin (*i.e.* knocked with all his cards melded) his opponent can reduce his loss by adding cards from his hand to the melds exposed by his opponent.

North, who has not declared gin, knocks with the melds on the left.

South holds in his hand:

      ♠ J 6 3 2 ♥ Q A ♦ Q J ♣ K 6

and reduces his loss by adding the 6♠ and A♥ to North's sequences, and the K♣ to his set of Kings.

Play now ceases, and the score is made up as follows:

1. The unmelded cards of the players are totalled to determine their respective point-counts.

2. A player who has declared gin scores 25 points plus his opponent's point-count.

3. If gin has not been declared: if the knocker's point-count is less than that of his opponent's, the knocker wins the hand and scores the difference between the two point-counts; if the opponent's point-count is less than that of the knocker or if the two point-counts are equal, the opponent wins the deal and scores 20 points for undercutting plus the difference (if any) between the two point-counts.

The scores are recorded on a sheet of paper ruled as follows:

	Jack	Sam	Jack	Sam	Jack	Sam
Box 1						
Box 2						
Box 3						
Box 4						
Box 5						

Every deal won and score entered is known as a box. The first time that a player scores he enters the points in the first column only. The second time that he scores he enters them in the second column and adds them to his score in the first column. The third time that he scores he enters them in the third column and adds them to the scores last entered in the first and second columns. Thereafter, every time that a player scores he adds his score to the scores last entered in all three columns.

When the score of a player in a column reaches a total of 100 points or more, the column is closed. The winner of a column scores 100 points for winning it, and a further 20 points for each box that he has won in excess of those won by his opponent. If, however, the opponent has won more boxes than the winner of the column, the opponent scores 20 points for each box that he has won in excess of those won by the winner of the column, and this score is deducted from that of the winner of the column.

If a player fails to score in any column he is blitzed, and the total score of the winner of the column is doubled. The player who has been blitzed in any column makes his first, or second, score in the next column which has not been won.

The game ends when all three columns have been won.

If a player wins all three columns, his final score is determined by adding together the total scores of all three columns. If a player wins two columns (his opponent one column) the final score is determined by adding together the total scores of the winner of the two columns, and subtracting the lower score from the higher.

Honeymoon Bridge

Thirteen cards are dealt to each player and the remaining twenty-six cards are placed face downwards between them.

The non-dealer leads to the first trick. Thereafter the player who wins a trick leads to the next. A player must follow suit if he can. The winner of a trick takes the top card of the stock, the loser takes the next card. The first thirteen tricks are played without a trump suit, and the tricks do not count in the final score.

When the stock is exhausted, the two players bid as in bridge (see page 83) the dealer first; bidding continues until one player passes a bid, double or redouble. The player who does not make the final bid leads to the first trick, and the play continues as in the regular game except that only two, instead of four, players are competing. The players score as in bridge.

If a player revokes during the play of the first thirteen tricks, or if he draws a card out of turn, or sees more than one card when drawing from the stock, his opponent, when it is his turn to draw from the stock, may look at the two top cards and take either. Other irregularities are governed by the laws of bridge.

In HONEYMOON BRIDGE WITH A WIDOW the players sit in adjacent seats and the cards are dealt into four hands (as in the regular game) of twelve cards each. The remaining four cards (the widow) are placed face downwards in the centre of the table.

The players bid as in the regular game (the dealer bids first) and when a bid has been passed, doubled or redoubled, the player who has won the declaration takes up the widow hand and, without showing it to his opponent, takes one card into his own hand, one into his dummy, and gives the other two cards to his opponent to take one into his hand and the other into his dummy.

The player who has won the declaration may demand the opening lead to be made either by his opponent or by his opponent's dummy.

Thereafter the play and scoring proceed as in the regular game.

In SEMI-EXPOSED HONEYMOON BRIDGE the players sit in adjacent seats and the cards are dealt as in the regular game, except that the first six cards to the dummies are dealt face downwards in a row, the remaining cards, six face upwards on top of them and one face upwards by itself.

The dealer bids first, and the bidding ends when a bid has been passed, doubled or redoubled. The hand on the left of the player who has won the declaration leads to the first trick. The play and scoring are as in the regular game, except that a player may play from his dummy only a face-upwards card. When a face-upwards card has been played, the card under it is turned face upwards, and becomes available for play.

Jo-jotte

Although Jo-jotte was invented by Ely Culbertson in 1937, it is not altogether a modern game, but a variation of the old French game of belotte in itself very similar to klaberjass (see page 61) and its several variations.

It is a game for two players, and played with the short pack, namely a pack from which all cards below the rank of 7 have been removed.

The rank of the cards varies. If there is a trump suit, the cards of the suit rank in the order: **J 9 A 10 K Q 8 7**. In plain suits, or if the hand is played in No-Trumps, the order is: **A 10 K Q J 9 8 7**.

Each player is dealt six cards (either singly, or in bundles of two or three) and the thirteenth card of the pack is placed face upwards on the table. It is known as the turned card.

There are two rounds of bidding. The non-dealer bids first. He may either accept the suit of the turned card as trumps, or pass. If he passes, the dealer has the same option. If both players pass, the non-dealer may name any suit, other than that of the turned card, as trumps, or he may declare No-Trumps or he may pass. If he passes for the second time, the dealer has the same option. If both players pass twice the hand is abandoned and the deal passes, but if either player names a suit as trumps, his opponent may overbid it by declaring No-Trumps, but not by naming another suit as trumps. Either player may double his opponent's declaration, and any double may be redoubled.

When the declaration has been determined (doubled, redoubled or passed) the dealer deals three more cards to his opponent and to himself, and he places the bottom card of the pack face upwards on top of the undealt cards of the pack. It has no significance in play but is solely informatory and, therefore, is known as the information card.

The player who has made the final declaration is known as the declarer: his opponent as the defender.

At this stage of the game the defender may announce that instead of defending against the declarer's contract he will himself become declarer at a Nullo contract; a contract, that is, to lose every trick. The declarer may now declare a Slam. It is a contract to win every trick either in the suit originally named by him (he cannot change the suit) or in No-Trumps.

The defender then announces his melds, if he holds any. A meld is four of a kind (except 9s, 8s and 7s at No-Trumps, and 8s and 7s in a suit declaration). A meld carries a score of 100 points and is scored (as at bridge (see page 126)) above the line. Only the player with the highest-ranking meld may score for it, and he may score for a second meld if he holds one.

Next, beginning with the defender, the players score for sequences, and for this purpose the cards take their normal rank of Ace (high), King, Queen, Jack, 10, 9, 8, 7. For a sequence of five cards the holder scores 50 points above the line, for a sequence of four 40 points, and for a sequence of three 20 points. If two sequences are of equal length, that headed by the highest card takes precedence. If both sequences are equal, a sequence in the trump suit wins over one in a plain suit; if both sequences are in plain suits neither is scored for. Only the player with the higher-ranking sequence may score for it, and he may score for any other sequences that he may hold.

Defender   Declarer

Clubs are trumps. Defender scores 200 points above the line for his melds of 10s and Queens, and the declarer cannot score for his meld of Kings because in the trump suit the 10 is higher than the King.

Defender   Declarer

Hearts are trumps. Neither player has a meld. Defender declares his 4-card sequence in Spades but he cannot score for it because the declarer has an equal sequence in the trump suit (Hearts). The declarer, therefore, scores 40 points above the line for his 4-card sequence in Hearts and a further 20 points for his 3-card sequence in Diamonds.

Finally, it is to be noted that if the declarer elects to play the hand in the same suit as the turned card, either player if he holds the 7 of the suit may exchange it for the turned card.

The player who leads to a trick may lead any card that he chooses. The second player is limited in his play; for he must obey the three rules that follow:

1. He must follow suit if he can.
2. If a trump has been led he must not only follow suit if he can, but win the trick by playing a higher trump if he holds one.
3. If a plain suit has been led and he is unable to follow suit, he must win the trick by trumping if he can.

Second player may discard a worthless card only when he is unable to obey one or other of these three rules.

Winning a trick has no value in itself. What counts is winning tricks with certain cards in them: these are scored as follows:

For winning the Jack of trumps   20 points
For winning the 9 of trumps   15 points
For winning any Ace or 10   10 points
For winning any King or Queen   5 points
For winning the last trick (except at Nullo)   10 points

The example that follows is a simple one to illustrate the mechanics of the game.

Hearts are trumps. The turned card is **K ♠**: the information card **Q ♦**.

Defender leads **A ♣**, and the play is:

Defender	Declarer
A ♣	**Q ♣**
10 ♣	**10 ♥**
8 ♦	**A ♦**
J ♦	**7 ♦**
8 ♣	**8 ♥**
9 ♥	**9 ♦**
10 ♠	**9 ♠**
Q ♠	**A ♥**
7 ♥	**J ♥**

Declarer scores for taking:

Jack of trumps (♥)	20 points
A ♥	10 points
A ♦	10 points
10 ♥	10 points
10 ♣	10 points
Q ♠	5 points
Last trick	10 points
	75 points

Defender scores for taking:

9 of trumps (♥)	15 points
A ♣	10 points
10 ♠	10 points
Q ♣	5 points
	40 points

In addition to the above, if a player holds the King and Queen of the trump suit (if there is one) he may score 20 points provided he announces 'Jo' when he plays the King and later 'Jotte' when he plays the Queen. He cannot score for the combination if he plays the Queen before the King.

Game is won by the player who first scores 80 points below the line, which may be made in one hand or in a series of part-scores, and the player who wins the rubber (best out of three games) scores a bonus of 300 points.

The declarer of a Nullo contract scores a bonus of 200 points if he loses every trick; if he takes a trick, however, his opponent scores 200 points for the first and 100 for every subsequent trick.

The declarer of a Slam scores a bonus of 500 points if he wins every trick; and if a player wins every trick but has not bid Slam he scores a bonus of 100 points.

Scoring below the line, towards game, is calculated as follows:

1. If the declarer's total score, including melds, sequences, trick scores and bonuses (if any) is greater than the defender's total score, he scores his trick score below the line, and the defender scores his trick score above the line.

2. If the defender's total score is greater than the declarer's, the two trick scores are added together and scored by the defender below the line.

3. If the contract is doubled or redoubled, the player with the higher total scores both his and his opponent's trick score, doubled or quadrupled, below the line.

4. If there is a tie in total points, the trick scores of both players are put in prison and awarded to the player who obtains the higher total in the following deal.

Klaberjass

Klaberjass is probably better known in America than in England, because under the names of Clabber, Clobber, Clubby, Klab and Klob, it occurs in Damon Runyon's amusing stories, and in 1937 a variation of the game, under the name of jo-jotte (see page 57) was publicized by Ely Culbertson. Despite the similarity of names it is not identical with the Hungarian game of kalabriás, which is a game for three or four players. There may have been a common ancestor, or possibly the game was taken to the New World by Central European immigrants and there adapted as a two-handed game with klaberjass as a bowdlerized version of kalabriás.

The game is played with a pack from which the 6s, 5s, 4s, 3s and 2s have been removed. In the trump suit the cards rank in the order J 9 A 10 K Q 8 7; and in the other three suits A 10 K Q J 9 8 7.

Six cards are dealt to both players, in two bundles of three cards each. The next card of the pack is turned face upwards on the table (it is known as the turn-up card) and the rest of the pack is placed face downwards so as partly to cover it.

The non-dealer bids first. He may *take-it* (*i.e.* accept the turn-up card as the trump suit); *pass* (*i.e.* refuse to accept the turn-up card as the trump suit); or *schmeiss* (*i.e.* offer to play with the turn-up card as the trump suit or throw in the hand, as his opponent prefers). If the opponent says 'Yes' to a schmeiss there is a fresh deal; if he says 'No' the hand is played with the turn-up card as the trump suit.

If the non-dealer has passed, the dealer may either take-it, pass or schmeiss.

If both players pass there is a second round of bidding. Now the non-dealer may name any one of the other three suits as trumps, or he may schmeiss (*i.e.* offer to name one of the other three suits as trumps or throw in the hand, as his opponent prefers), or he may pass. If he passes, the dealer may name one of the other three suits as trumps, or throw in the hand.

When a player accepts or names a trump suit, the bidding ends, and the player who has accepted or named a suit as trumps is called the maker.

There is never more than two rounds of bidding, and when the trump suit has been settled, the dealer deals three more cards, one at a time, to the two players. He then turns up the bottom card of the pack and places it on top of the pack. It takes no part in the play, and is put where it is only to be seen.

If either player has been dealt the 7 of the trump suit, he may exchange it for the turn-up card.

Only sequences are melded, and for melding the cards rank in the order from Ace (high) to 7 (low). A 3-card sequence counts 20 points, a 4-card or longer one 50 points.

The non-dealer begins by announcing the value of his best sequence. If his best sequence is of three cards he says 'Twenty'; if of four or more cards he says 'Fifty'. If dealer has a better sequence he says 'No good'; if he lacks a better sequence he says 'Good'; if he has an equal sequence he askes 'How high?'. The non-dealer then announces the top card of his sequence. The dealer then says whether it is good, no good, or if he has a sequence headed by an equal card. In this last event neither player scores unless one of the sequences is in the trump suit, which wins over a sequence in a plain suit.

The non-dealer leads to the first trick; thereafter the winner of a trick leads to the next. A player must follow suit if he can, and if he cannot he must play a trump if he holds one. If a trump is led, the second player must win the trick if he can.

After the first trick has been played, the player with the highest meld shows it and scores for all sequences in his hand. His opponent cannot score for any sequences that he may hold.

A player who holds the King and Queen of the trump suit may score 20 points so long as he announces 'Bella' immediately after he has played the second of them to a trick. If a player holds the Jack of the trump suit, as well as the King and Queen, he may score for the sequence as well as for bella.

When all the cards have been played, each player examines his tricks and scores points for winning in his tricks:

Jasz (the Jack of the trump suit)	20 points
Menel (the 9 of the trump suit)	14 points
Any Ace	11 points
Any 10	10 points
Any King	4 points
Any Queen	3 points
Any Jack (except Jasz)	2 points
Last Trick	10 points

If the maker's total, including melds and cards won, is higher than the opponent's, each scores all the points he has won. If the totals of the two players are equal, the opponent scores the points he has won, the maker nothing. If the opponent's total is higher than that of the maker's, the two totals are added together and the opponent scores them.

The player who first reaches 500 points wins the game.

KLABERJASS FOR FOUR PLAYERS is played in partnership, two playing against two. Eight cards are dealt to each player, and the dealer turns up his last card for trumps.

Each player in turn, beginning with the player on the left of the dealer, may either take-it or pass. There is no schmeiss. If all four players pass, there is a second round of bidding during which each player in turn has a right to name the trump suit. If all four players pass the second round of bidding there is a fresh deal.

The player who names the trump suit becomes the maker, and his side must score more than the opposing side.

The player on the left of the dealer leads to the first trick.

Pinocle [*]

Pinocle in its original form is a game for two players similar to bezique (see page 30). It is played with a pack of forty-eight cards, namely a pack that consists of **A 10 K Q J 9** (in this order) in each of the four suits, duplicated.

Twelve cards are dealt to both players, either three or four cards at a time, and the next card is turned face upwards to indicate the trump suit. The rest of the pack is placed face downwards on the table to half cover the exposed card.

The object of the game is to win tricks that include those cards which carry a scoring value when won in a trick, and to meld certain combinations of cards that carry a scoring value.

When taken in a trick each Ace scores 11 points, each 10 scores 10 points, each King 4 points, each Queen 3 points, and each Jack 2 points. The player who wins the last trick scores 10 points.

The values of the melds are:

Class A

A 10 K Q J of the trump suit	150 points
K Q of the trump suit (royal marriage)	40 points
K Q of a plain suit (common marriage)	20 points

Class B

Pinocle (**Q ♠** and **J ♦**)	40 points
Dis (**9** of the trump suit)	10 points

Class C

Four Aces – one of each suit	100 points
Four Kings – one of each suit	80 points
Four Queens – one of each suit	60 points
Four Jacks – one of each suit	40 points

The non-dealer leads to the first trick. Thereafter the winner of a trick leads to the next. It is not necessary for a player to follow suit to a led card. The winner of a trick replenishes his hand by taking the top card of the stock; the loser of the trick takes the next.

After a player has won a trick and before drawing from the stock, he may meld any of the above combinations. To meld he places the cards face upwards on the table in front of him, where they remain until he decides to play them to a trick, or until the stock is exhausted. Melding is subject to the three rules that follow:

1. Only one meld may be made at a turn.
2. For each meld, at least one card must be taken from the hand and placed on the table.
3. A card already melded may be melded again so long as it is in a different class, or in a higher-scoring meld of the same class.

---

*Pinocle is frequently spelt pinochle, but the Oxford Dictionary does not sanction the H.

That is to say, if Hearts are trumps a player may meld ♥ K Q and score for the royal marriage, and later he may add ♥ A 10 J and score for the sequence. He cannot first declare ♥ A 10 K Q J and score for sequence and later declare the royal marriage.

If the dealer turns up a dis as the trump card he scores 10 points. Thereafter a player holding a dis may count it merely by showing it when winning a trick. He may count the dis and make another meld at the same time. After winning a trick, the holder of a dis may exchange it for the trump card.

The player who wins the twelfth trick may meld if he is able to. He then draws the last face-downwards card of the stock and must show it to his opponent. The loser of the trick takes into his hand the card exposed on the table.

The last twelve tricks are now played off. During this period of play a player must follow suit if he can to the card led; if he cannot he must trump the trick if he holds a trump. If a trump is led the second player must win the trick if he can.

Melds are scored when they are declared. The score for cards won in tricks are added after the hand has been played out, a total of 7, 8, or 9 points is counted as 10.

Every deal may constitute a game, or the players may prefer that the winner will be he who first reaches an agreed figure.

At pinocle skill and experience count for much. An ability to remember which cards have been played contributes much towards success. When it comes to playing off the last twelve cards, the experienced player will never be in any doubt about which cards his opponent holds. Thus, when playing to the last trick before the stock is exhausted, a player should be able to weigh up the merits of winning the trick and melding, preventing his opponent from melding, or losing the trick and so obtaining the exposed trump card to add to his trump length in the final play off.

Piquet

Piquet is probably the best known of all card games for two players; there is no doubt that it is more skilful and interesting than any other. It is played with a 32-card pack, namely a pack from which the 6s, 5s, 4s, 3s and 2s have been removed, sometimes called the short or piquet pack. The cards rank from Ace (high) to 7 (low) and he who cuts the higher card has the right of first deal; he would be advised to take it because there is some advantage to be gained from it.

Twelve cards are dealt to both players in packets of either twos or threes, and the remaining eight cards (*talon*) are placed face downwards on the table between the players. The non-dealer may now exchange any five of his cards with the five top cards of the talon. He need not exchange as many as five cards, but he must exchange at least one, and, if he has not exchanged five cards, he may look at those that he was entitled to draw. The dealer may exchange cards up to the number that remain in the talon. He, too, must exchange at least one card. If he does not exchange all the cards, he may look at those that he was entitled to, but he must show them to his opponent if he does. The players place their discards face downwards on the table in front of them. The discards of the players should not be mixed together as, during the play of the hand, the players are entitled to look at their own discards.

The score is made up in three ways: the count of the hand; the count during the play of the cards; the extraordinary scores.

The hand is counted in the following way:

1. The *Point*, which is the number of cards held in the longest suit. The player who holds the longest suit wins the point, and scores 1 point for each card that he holds in it. If the number of cards in the suits held by the players is the same, the player with the highest count (Aces 11, Kings, Queens and Jacks 10 each, and other cards at their pip values) wins the point. If the count is equal neither player scores.

2. *Sequences*, which must not be of less than three cards of the same suit, are won by the player who holds the most cards in one sequence. As between sequences of equal length, the highest wins. For a sequence of three (tierce) 3 points are scored; for a sequence of four (quart) 4 points are scored. For a sequence of five (quint) 15 points are scored; for a sequence of six (sixième) 16 points; for a sequence of seven (septième) and for a sequence of eight (huitième) 18 points.

3. *Quatorzes* and *Trios* are any four or three cards of the same rank higher than the 9. The player who holds the superior quatorze or trio wins. Thus, a player who holds a trio of Aces will win even though his opponent may hold trios of Kings *and* Queens. In the same way, a player who holds trios of Aces, Kings, Queens and Jacks, will score nothing if his opponent holds a quatorze of 10s. Quatorzes are scored at 14 points each; trios at 3 points each.

The count of the hand must be declared in the order: point,

sequence, quatorze and trio, and, on demand, a player must show any combinations of cards for which he has scored. In practice, however, this is rarely necessary, because the opponent is usually able to infer from his own cards what cards are held against him by his opponent.

When counting the hand a player is not compelled to declare all that he holds. It is in order, and sometimes the very best play, to mislead one's opponent by declaring less than one holds in order to conceal one's strength. The practice is known as sinking. The player who holds a quatorze of Aces may declare only a trio. The opponent may inquire which Ace is not being reckoned, and the player may name any Ace he chooses, because the explicit reply: 'I do not count the Ace of Clubs' is not a guarantee that the player does not hold this card.

After the non-dealer has counted his hand he leads a card. The dealer then counts his hand and plays a card to the non-dealer's lead. Two cards constitute a trick, and it is compulsory for the second player to follow suit to the led card if he can do so. If not he may play any card he chooses, because there is no trump suit. The player who leads to a trick scores 1 point, and if his opponent wins it he scores one point for doing so (except in the case of the last trick, when he scores 2 points) and leads to the next trick, scoring 1 point for the lead. After all twelve tricks have been played, the player who has won most tricks scores 10 points for having done so (Ten for the Cards, as it is called). There is no score to either player if they win six tricks each.

There are four extraordinary scores:

1. *Carte Blanche.* If a player is dealt a hand that contains no court card he may claim carte blanche and score 10 points. It takes precedence over any other scoring combination, but the player must announce his carte blanche as soon as he picks up the cards dealt to him, and he must show his hand, though he need not do so until after his opponent has discarded.

2. *Pique.* If a player scores in hand and play 30 points, before his opponent scores anything, he wins a pique and scores 30 points for it. Only the non-dealer can win a pique, because he scores 1 point for the first lead before the dealer counts his hand; this, of course, automatically rules out the dealer from scoring for a pique.

3. *Repique.* If a player scores in hand alone a total of 30 points, before his opponent scores anything, he wins a repique and scores 60 points for it. Either player may score for a repique, because points in hand are counted in priority to those won in play.

4. *Capot.* If a player wins all twelve tricks he wins a capot and scores 40 points, not 10, for the cards. The capot, however, is not counted towards a pique because the points are not scored until the hand has been played.

The players deal alternately, and a *partie* (game) consists of six deals (three deals each). At the end of the *partie* the player with the higher score deducts from his score that of his opponent, and adds 100 points to the result. If, however, one player fails to score 100 points, he is rubiconed, and the player with the higher score adds the two scores together, and a further 100 points. If the score after six deals is equal, each player has one more deal, and if the score still remains equal the *partie* is a draw.

Most card games are played in silence. Piquet is a continuous dialogue. When a player counts his hand he declares his point, sequences, quartorzes and trios, and his opponent confirms whether they are 'Good', 'Not good' or 'Equal' and, if equal, the player announces the pip total which his opponent declares 'Good', 'Not good' or 'Equal'. Then, during the play of the hand, the two players announce their scores as each trick is played.

At piquet it is customary to call the non-dealer the elder (hand) and the dealer the younger (hand). The deal below (after both players have discarded) illustrates the method of scoring and is not to be accepted as an example of good play.

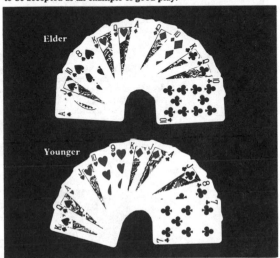

Elder : 'Point of four'.
Younger : 'Making?'
Elder : 'Thirty-nine.'
Younger : 'Not good.'
Elder : 'Queens and Tens – six'. (He counts his score for his trios without waiting for younger to confirm that the count is good. He knows that his trio of Queens is good because, from his own cards, he can see that younger cannot hold a quatorze or a better trio than one of Jacks. His announcement 'Queens and Tens' means that he holds three Queens and three 10s. If he held four Queens and three 10s he would announce 'Fourteen Queens and three Tens'.)

Elder, who has no more to count, leads the Ace of Spades – 'Seven'.

Younger now counts his hand.

Younger : 'Point of four – forty,' (Elder has a right to ask in which suit the point is. In this case, however, he has no need because he knows from his own cards that it can only be in Hearts.) 'and tierce to the Jack – seven.' (Here, again, elder has no need to ask because, from his own cards, he knows that the tierce must be in Hearts.)

Younger plays the Queen of Spades on elder's Ace of Spades, and repeats his score – 'Seven'.

The rest of the play is:

Elder		Younger	
J ♠	'Eight'	K ♠	'Eight'
Q ♥	'Eight'	A̲ ♥	'Nine'
K ♥	'Nine'	J̲ ♥	'Ten'
10̲ ♠	'Ten'	7 ♣	'Ten'
8̲ ♠	'Eleven'	8 ♣	'Ten'
K̲ ♣	'Twelve'	A ♣	'Eleven'
10 ♦	'Twelve'	10̲ ♥	'Twelve'
Q ♦	'Twelve'	9̲ ♥	'Thirteen'
Q ♣	'Thirteen'	J̲ ♣	'Fourteen'
A̲ ♦	'Fourteen'	J ♦	'Fourteen'
10̲ ♣	'Fifteen'	K ♦	'Fourteen'

Elder, winning the trick–'Sixteen, and the cards twenty-six.' This ends the deal with the score at Elder 26, Younger 14.

A player's first consideration must be the point. The importance of scoring for the point cannot be over-estimated, because not only does it add to a player's score, but it protects him against a pique or repique, and, of course, scoring for point diminishes the opponent's score to the same extent. Normally, therefore, a player should retain his longest suit intact and discard from shorter suits. This, however, does not always hold good, particularly if the longest suit consists mainly of low cards, and the shorter suits of high ones. The inexperienced player who is dealt:

will be tempted to retain the Spades, and discard from the other suits, with a view to scoring for point and sequence. The experienced player will know that the better course is to discard all five Spades, because the only card that will raise the suit from a quart to a sixième is the Jack of Spades, and the odds are about three to one against drawing it. It is likely that retaining the Spades will win the point, but almost certainly it will result in the loss of the cards. This will make a big difference to the score, and always the cards must be considered together with the point. If the non-dealer holds a long suit headed by top cards, usually it guarantees the point and the cards. The suit, therefore, must be preserved at all costs, but this is of much less importance for the dealer because he may never obtain the lead.

A good general rule emerges. The discards of the non-dealer should be made towards obtaining an attacking hand; that of the dealer towards obtaining a defensive hand; that is to say a hand in which there is some strength in as many suits as possible.

Subject to these considerations, it is best to discard from as few suits as possible, and, once a player has made up his mind to discard from a suit, he should discard the whole of it, unless it is necessary to retain the suit guarded. Sequence cards should be retained in preference to non-sequence cards, and, of course, cards that help to make up trios and quatorzes should never be discarded if it is to be avoided.

Playing to the score is very important, particularly in the last deal of a *partie*. As an example: If a player is well ahead, and sees the opportunity to gain a rubicon, he should discard cautiously and play so as to prevent his opponent from saving the rubicon by scoring 100 points. By contrary, if a player is in danger of being rubiconed, he should be prepared to take some risks, since only a big score will save him. It must be remembered, however, that if a player is rubiconed his score is added to that of his opponent, so if there is no chance of saving the rubicon he should play to keep his score down. To this end he should declare only equities or those scores that will save pique and repique, and he should aim to divide the cards.

AUCTION PIQUET originated in Oxford, and was developed by some British prisoners of war during the war of 1914.

The bidding takes place before the discard. It is opened by the non-dealer. He may pass, and if he does and the dealer does also, there is a redeal by the same player. The lowest bid that may be made is one of Seven. It is an undertaking to win, or lose, seven of the twelve possible tricks. There is no penalty for a bid out of turn nor for an underbid, because these irregularities merely give information to the opponent.

The most interesting feature of the game is the minus bid. It is an undertaking to lose the stated number of tricks. It ranks neither above nor below a normal (plus) bid. In a minus deal the player scores everything good in his opponent's hand. A player may double a bid made by his opponent, and the player who has been doubled may redouble or shift to a higher bid.

After bidding, the players discard. The routine is the same as at the parent game except that there is no compulsion for the players to discard at least one card.

The declarations follow, and the players may declare the point, sequences, trios and quatorzes in any order they choose. Sinking is allowed in plus deals but not in minus ones.

The scoring is as follows:

The value of point, sequences, trios, quatorzes, cards and capot, are the same as in the parent game.

In plus deals pique (30 points) is obtained on the score of 29 and repique (60 points) on the score of 30. In minus deals both pique and repique are obtained on the score of 21.

The *partie* (six deals) is worth 150 points, and rubicon is under 150 points. In the event of a tie a seventh deal is played and the *partie* ends if it is tied.

A player scores 10 points for every trick won in a plus deal (or lost in a minus deal above (or below) the declared contract.

If a player fails to make his contract the opponent scores 10 points for every trick by which he is short.

Overtricks and undertricks are effected by doubling and redoubling, but scores in hand and play are not.

Although a player scores 1 point for winning a trick he does not score for leading a losing card, nor an additional 1 point for winning the last trick:

Tablanette

Tablanette is a game for two players that is easy to learn and worth learning because it is remarkably fascinating to play.

From a full pack of fifty-two cards, six cards are dealt face downwards to the two players, and four cards face upwards to the table between them. The rest of the pack is temporarily set aside. If any Jacks are dealt to the table they are removed, placed at the bottom of the pack, and the spaces filled with cards from the top of the pack.

The non-dealer plays first. If he plays a card of the same rank as any of the four cards on the table, he takes the card; or, if there are any two or three cards on the table whose values if added together equal that of the card played, he takes these cards. For this purpose a King counts 14, a Queen 13, and an Ace either 11 or 1. The Jack plays a special part in the game and its function will be explained later. The other cards count at their pip values.

If the cards on the table and the player's hand are:

he will play the **K ♥** and take the **K ♠** from the table. If he holds:

he will play the **A ♥** and take the **2 ♥** and **9 ♣** from the table, because together they total 11, a value of an Ace.

The card played and those taken from the table are kept in a pile, face downwards, on the table by the player who took them.

If at any time a player is able to take all the cards on the table (there may be only one, or there may be more than four) he announces 'Tablanette' and scores the total value of all the cards taken plus the value of the card he has played. If, for example, the cards on the table are:

and a player holds any of the other three Kings, he will be able to announce 'Tablanette', because his King will take the **K ♠** and the other three cards whose values total 14. The score for this will be 42 points (*i.e.* 14 × 3).

The special function of the Jack is that playing it allows the player to take all the cards on the table, but it does not allow him to score for a tablanette. Obviously, therefore, a Jack is an excellent card to hold, because playing it compels the opponent to play a lone card to the table and when there is only one card on the table the player whose turn it is to play is in a good position to score a tablanette.

The players play in rotation until they have exhausted their six cards. The dealer then deals another six cards to each, and so on until the pack is exhausted.

When the last batch of six cards has been played, any cards left on the table are taken by the player who last took a card from the table.

The players examine the cards they have taken, and score 1 point for the 2 ♣ and for every Ace, King, Queen, Jack and 10 (except the 10 ♦ which scores 2 points). Finally, if a player has taken 27 or more cards he scores 3 points.

The deal passes in rotation, and the game is won by the player who first scores a total of 251 points.

There is more skill in the game than may be apparent at first sight. If, for example, there is only an 8 on the table and the player holds:

his best play is the 4 ♥, because no one card has a value of 12 and the opponent, therefore, cannot score a tablanette.

As at all card games it is very important to keep in mind the cards that have been played. The opponent has scored a tablanette and the player holds:

He has to play a card to the table, and the natural tendency is to play the 3 ♥, because this will give the opponent a minimum score if he can again announce 'Tablanette'. But if no 3s have been played, but a 10 has, then it is better to play one of the 10s, because the chances are against the opponent holding the remaining 10, and there is a possibility that he holds one of the remaining three 3s.

TABLANETTE FOR THREE PLAYERS is played in the same way as the parent game, except that the players are dealt four cards (instead of six) at a time.

Black Maria

Black Maria, sometimes known as Black Lady and sometimes as Slippery Anne, is very similar to hearts and its several variations. (see page 111). It is considered best played as a game for three, but may be played by more.

The 2 of Clubs is removed from the pack, and seventeen cards are dealt to each player. The cards rank in the normal order from Ace (high) to 2 (low) and, after a player has looked at his cards, he passes three of them to his right-hand opponent and receives three from his left-hand opponent, which he must not look at until he has passed three on.

When the exchanges of cards have been made, the player on the left of the dealer leads to the first trick. Thereafter, the player who wins a trick leads to the next. A player must follow suit to the led card provided he can do so. Otherwise he may discard any card he chooses. There is no trump suit.

The object of the game is to avoid winning a trick which contains a penalty card. These cards, and the penalties that go with them, are:

Every card in the Heart suit—1 point each.
The Ace of Spades—7 points.
The King of Spades—10 points.
The Queen of Spades (Black Maria)—13 points.
The deal passes in rotation clockwise.

The game introduces two features: the discard and the play of the cards.

The inexperienced player, if he is dealt a high Spade, will assume that he cannot do better than pass it on to his right-hand opponent. It is, however, not always the best play. Provided a number of low Spades are held in support of the high ones, it is very often better to retain the high cards with a view to controlling the suit during the play of the hand. Indeed, a player who has been dealt any Spades or Hearts lower than the Queen would be well advised to keep them in order to protect himself against any top cards in the suits that may be passed on to him. The main principle of discarding should be to try and set up either a void suit—in order to get rid of penalty cards by discarding them during the play—or at obtaining long suits, provided low cards in them are held. A player who has been dealt:

cannot do better than pass on the three Diamonds. The Spades must be kept to protect against receiving a high card in the suit, the Hearts are adequately protected, and there is nothing to fear in Clubs.

An ability to count the cards is the first essential to success. Towards the end of a deal an experienced player will know pretty well which cards are still left to be played, and he will be able to make a shrewd guess who holds them. It is in the end-play, therefore, that opportunity comes for skilful play.

After fourteen tricks have been played the players should know who holds the remaining cards.

West is on lead and leads the **6 ♠**, North plays the **2 ♠** and East, perforce, wins with the **K ♠**. Now, if East returns the **5 ♦** West must win with the **7 ♦** and North saddles him with the **Q ♠** (Black Maria). If, however, East returns the **3 ♣**, North will have to win with the **6 ♣** on which West will have played the **A ♠**.

East's play will be directed by the score, and whether it is more advantageous to him to saddle West or North with all 20 points. The strategy is quite ethical so long as East puts his own interest first and is not moved by malice aforethought.

FOUR-HANDED BLACK MARIA is played in the same way as the parent game, except that no card is removed from the pack, and every player, therefore, receives thirteen cards. The players may play all against all, or two in partnership against the other two.

FIVE-HANDED BLACK MARIA is played in the same way as the parent game, but the 2 of Diamonds as well as the 2 of Clubs is removed from the pack. Each player, therefore, is dealt ten cards.

Cut-throat Bridge

Many suggestions have been made to make bridge (see page 83) suitable for three players. The most satisfactory is towie (see page 80) but what has become known as Cut-throat Bridge is the original and the simplest of the three-handed variations.

The players take seats at random and after drawing for deal, shuffling and cutting in the regular way, the dealer deals thirteen cards each to the three players and to a fourth hand that is temporarily set aside.

The auction, beginning with the dealer, is conducted as in the parent game, and when a player's bid, double or redouble has been passed by the other two players, the player on his left leads to the first trick. The player who has obtained the final contract then sorts the fourth hand, spreads it in front of him on the table, and plays it as his dummy, against the other two players in partnership with each other,

The play and scoring are the same as in the parent game, except that if a player loses his contract both his opponents score the penalty points. The winner of a rubber receives a bonus of 700 points if neither opponent has won a game, but 500 points if either has.

Very clearly the game is a gamble, because the players must bid in the hope of finding the cards they need in the dummy hand.

A variation designed to make the game less speculative is for every player to be dealt seventeen cards and the fifty-second card face downwards to the dummy. After looking at their cards, and before bidding them, every player contributes four of them, face downwards, to the dummy. This way, every player knows four out of the thirteen cards that he is bidding for.

In another variation, instead of bidding for the dummy, an agreed number of deals (that must be divisible by three) are played, and, in turn, every player plays the dummy against the other two playing in partnership.

In this variation rubbers are not played, but the player who bids and makes game scores a bonus of 300 points. There is no vulnerability.

Knaves

Knaves, a game for three players, is so called because the four Knaves are penalty cards and the object of the players is to avoid winning tricks that contain them.

Seventeen cards are dealt to each player and the last card is turned face upwards on the table to denote the trump suit. It takes no other part in the game.

The player on the left of the dealer leads to the first trick; thereafter the player who wins a trick leads to the next. A player must follow suit, if he can, to the card led. If he cannot he may either trump or discard a card of a plain suit.

The player who wins a trick scores 1 point for it, but 4 points are deducted from a player's score if he wins the Knave of Hearts, 3 points if he wins the Knave of Diamonds, 2 points if he wins the Knave of Clubs, and 1 point if he wins the Knave of Spades. The aggregate score for each deal, therefore, is 7 points (*i.e.* 17 points for tricks minus 10 points for Knaves) unless one of the Knaves is the card turned up to denote the trump suit. Game is won by the first player to score 20 points.

The players play all against all, but skilful play introduces temporary partnerships that add much to the interest of the game. If, for example, one player is in the lead and the other two are trailing behind, they will combine with the aim of preventing the leading player from winning still more, even if they cannot reduce his score by forcing him to win tricks that contain Knaves. In the same way, if two players have an advanced score, and the third is down the course, the two who are ahead will so play that such points as they cannot themselves win will go to the player with the low score rather than to the one with the high score.

The game, therefore, gives ample scope for clever play. Until the last Knave has been played, a player has to strike a balance between the incentive to take a trick, and so score a point, and the fear of being saddled with a Knave, resulting in a loss.

There is much more in the game than appears on the surface. Consider the hands on the left.

No score to anyone.

East deals and the 7 ♣ is turned up.

With his preponderance of trumps North appears to be in a position to score well. In reality his hand is far from being a good one, because, though the trumps give him the advantage of winning tricks, this advantage is more than offset by the fact that he is in the dangerous position of being forced to take Knaves. Indeed, North is very likely to come out with a poor score; against good play by West he will be hard put to avoid taking the Knaves of Hearts and Diamonds—for a loss of 7 points—and, in any case, he can hardly avoid taking one of them.

Ombre

Ombre is a Spanish game of considerable antiquity. It was introduced into England by Katherine of Braganza, who married Charles II in 1662, and it immediately became very popular. Nowadays it is rarely played in Great Britain, but it is popular in Denmark (which saw the publication of a book about it in 1965) and it is played in Spain under the name of trefillo and in Latin America as rocamber. It deserves to be more popular.

The game is played with a pack of forty cards *i.e.* the regular pack from which the 10s, 9s and 8s have been removed. It is not a difficult game to play, but it is first necessary to master the rather involved and unusual order of the cards.

In plain suits the cards in the *red* suits rank in the order: **K Q J A 2 3 4 5 6 7**; those in the *black* suits rank in the normal order: **A K Q J 7 6 5 4 3 2**.

In trump suits if a *red* suit is trumps the order of the cards is: **A ♠** (Spadille), **7** (Manille), **A ♣** (Basto), **A** (Punto), **K Q J 2 3 4 5 6**; if a *black* suit is trumps the order of the cards is: **A ♠** (Spadille), **2** (Manille), **A ♣** (Basto), **K Q J 7 6 5 4 3**.

The three top trumps, Spadille, Manille and Basto, are collectively known as Matadores. The holder of one need not follow suit with it to a trump lead, but he must play one if a higher matadore is led and his hand contains no other trump card.

To determine the dealer, a card is dealt face upwards to each player in turn, and he who is first to receive a black Ace is dealer. It is here to be noted that, as in all games of Spanish origin, in dealing and play the game progresses anti-clockwise.

Nine cards are dealt to each player in bundles of three. The remaining thirteen cards are placed face downwards in the centre of the table.

Each deal is complete in itself. One player (ombre) plays against the other two playing in partnership. The player on the right of the dealer has first option of being ombre. It carries two privileges: he names the trump suit, he may discard from his hand as many cards as he chooses and draw fresh cards from the stock. If the player on the right of the dealer wishes to become ombre he says 'I play'. His right-hand neighbour may then announce that he wishes to become ombre, and, by so doing, he tacitly agrees that he will play without exchanging any of his cards. The first player may then reconsider the position, and is entitled to remain ombre if he is willing to play without exchanging any of his cards. If the second player passes, the third player (the dealer) may announce that he wishes to play without discarding. Again, the first player has a right to reconsider and may remain ombre without discarding.

If all three players pass, that is to say, if none wishes to play ombre the deal is abandoned.

If the first player is allowed to play ombre unopposed, he discards as many cards as he chooses from his hand, and draws cards from the stock to replace them. The second player does the same, and then the dealer. If any cards are left in the stock after the three players have made their exchanges, the dealer is entitled to look at them. If he does he must show them to the other two players: if he does not, the other two may not.

Ombre now names the trump suit and leads a card. The game proceeds, anti-clockwise, every player following suit, if he can, to the led card, or trumping or discarding if he cannot. The winner of a trick leads to the next, until all nine tricks have been played.

At the beginning of a deal each player puts an agreed sum in a pool. Now . . .

Sacardo. If ombre wins more tricks than either of his opponents individually, he takes all that is in the pool.

Codille. If one of the opponents wins more tricks than ombre, ombre pays him a sum equal to the amount in the pool, and the amount in the pool is carried forward to the next deal.

Puesta. If ombre and one, or both, of his opponents win the same number of tricks, ombre doubles the amount in the pool and it is carried forward to the next deal.

The deal does not pass in rotation. After every deal the dealer for the next is determined by dealing the cards, face upwards, until one player receives a black Ace.

The deal that follows is a simple one to illustrate the mechanics of the game:

West	North	East
♥ K 7	♥ none	♥ 4 5 6
♦ 6	♦ 7	♦ 2 3 4 5
♠ 7 5	♠ J 6 4 3 2	♠ Q
♣ Ma Ba K 5	♣ Q J 6	♣ 7

North deals.

West says: 'I play'. East and North pass.

West discards 7♥ 6♦ 7♠ 5♠. He draws 3♥ Q♦ A♦ 4♣.

East discards 4♥ 5♥ 6♥. His hand is of no value and he hopes to end with a void suit. He draws Q♥ A♥ Spa.

North discards 7♦ J♠ 6♠ 4♠ 3♠ 2♠. He draws J♥ 2♥ K♦ J♦ K♠ 3♣.

The hands are now:

West	North	East
♥ K 3	♥ J 2	♥ Q A
♦ Q A	♦ K J	♦ 2 3 4 5
♠ none	♠ K	♠ Q
♣ Ma Ba K 5 4	♣ Q J 6 3	♣ Spa 7

West names Clubs as the trump suit.

His hand is none too good, but the lead of a trump is called for. He, therefore, leads K♣, and East wins with Spadille, because West would hardly have led the King of trumps if he did not hold Manille, and probably Basto as well. East has no better return than 7♣, on which North plays the **Jack**. West allows it to win, by playing 4♣, because he is aware that North holds the more dangerous hand, and that sooner or later a trick in trumps must be lost to him. North must keep his top Diamonds and K♠, and he cannot safely lead a Heart. He, therefore, leads a Club. West wins with Basto, draws North's last trump with Manille, and continues with 5♣. It puts North on the spot. If he discards J♦, West will lead the suit and later win K♥ and a Diamond; if North discards 2♥ or K♠, West will win K♥, and continue with 3♥, so that he will either win Q♦, or North and East will divide their tricks three-two. Either way it is sacardo, and West scoops the pool.

Towie

Towie was originated by J. Leonard Replogle as a variation of bridge (see page 83). It may be played by any number of players, but is most acceptable as a game for three because only three take an active part in each deal.

Four hands of thirteen cards each are dealt in the usual way; the one to the quarter opposite the dealer is the dummy hand to be bid for. After dealing, the dealer chooses (without looking at them) six cards from the dummy hand, and faces them.

The players, beginning with the dealer, bid as in the parent game, but part scores are not reckoned and if the bidding ends without a game or higher contract being reached, there is a goulash deal, with further goulashes if necessary.*

When the bidding ends the player on the left of the declarer makes the opening lead. The dummy hand becomes the property of the declarer who sorts it, exposes it on the table, and plays it against the other two players in partnership, as in the parent game.

The scoring is the same as in bridge with the following differences:

1. In No-Trump contracts the trick score is 35 points a trick.
2. For winning a first game the declarer scores a bonus of 500 points and becomes vulnerable. For winning a second game—and with it the rubber—a player scores 1,000 points.
3. The declarer who makes a doubled or redoubled contract scores a bonus of 50 points if not vulnerable, and 100 points if vulnerable.
4. For undoubled overtricks the declarer scores 50 points each. If doubled or redoubled he scores for them as in the parent game.
5. The penalties for undertricks are:

   Not Vulnerable
   Undoubled: 50 points per trick
   Doubled: 100 points for the first and second tricks
               200 points for the third and fourth tricks
               400 points for the fifth and subsequent tricks

   Vulnerable
   Undoubled: 100 points for the first trick
              200 points for the second and subsequent tricks
   Doubled: 200 points for the first trick
              400 points for the second and subsequent tricks

   If the contract is redoubled the scores for doubled contracts are multiplied by two.

---

*For a goulash deal the players sort their cards into suits (the dealer sorts the dummy hand) and the hands are placed face downwards in a pile, one on top of the other, in front of the dealer. The cards are cut without being shuffled, and the same dealer deals the cards in bundles of five-five-three.

If there are more than three players participating in the game the inactive players are opponents of the declarer. They take no part in the bidding or play, but participate in the scoring, losing when the declarer makes his contract, and scoring the undertrick penalties when the declarer's contract is defeated.

At the end of a deal the declarer, whether he has won or lost his contract, retires from the table and his place is taken by one of the waiting players. The inactive players come into the game each in his turn, replacing the declarer of the previous deal. No vulnerable player, however, may re-enter the game if a non-vulnerable player is waiting to play.

The game ends when one player has won two deals.

Large penalties are not uncommon in towie because a player has no partner during the auction period and cannot do more than bid on the strength of his own hand, the six cards that he sees in dummy, and the seven cards that he expects to find there. Over-bidding is frequent, but risks must be taken, and the game is not for the chicken-hearted or cautious bidder. The play of the defence offers scope for skill, but, on the whole, the main object of a player must be to play the dummy, particularly when five are in the game.

The dummy hand after the face-down cards have been exposed

South and East were vulnerable, and South dealt. He bid a cautious One Spade, and, after a pass by West, East bid Three No-Trumps. South lacked the courage to bid Four Spades, and East, with dummy's cards opposite him, had an easy ride for his contract.

Auction Pitch

Auction Pitch, commonly known as Pitch and sometimes as Set Back, is a variation of all fours (see page 28). It is at its best and most popular when played by four players, each playing for himself.

As in the parent game, the cards rank in the usual order from Ace (high) to 2 (low), and six are dealt to the players in two bundles of three each. No card, however, is turned up to determine the trump suit.

The player on the left of the dealer bids first, and each player, in his turn, may either make a bid or pass. A bid must be for at least two points, and for more than the preceding bid, except for the dealer, who is entitled to buy the hand for the same number of points as the preceding bid. The maximum number of points in a deal is 4, and a player who expects to win them bids Smudge. The dealer cannot take the declaration from him.

The successful bidder is known as the maker, and he pitches (leads) to the first trick. The card that he leads determines the trump suit.

At each trick a player must follow suit to the card led, if he can, otherwise he may discard or trump. The winner of a trick leads to the next.

As in the parent game, points are scored as follows:

High. The player who holds the highest trump scores 1 point.

Low. The player who holds the lowest trump scores 1 point.

Jack. The player who wins the trick that contains the Jack of the trump suit (if it is in play) scores 1 point.

Game. Counting the Ace as 4, the King as 3, the Queen as 2, the Jack as 1 and the Ten as 10, the player with the highest total in the tricks he has won scores 1 point. If there is a tie no-one scores the point.

Every player records what he scores, and if the maker fails to reach his bid he is set back by the full amount of it. He records the score and if it reduces him to a minus score he encircles it. A player with a minus score is said to be in the hole.

The game is won by the player who first reaches 7 points, and if the maker and one or more of the other players reach 7 points in the same deal, the maker wins. As between the other three players, the points are counted in the order High, Low, Jack, Game.

A player who smudges and wins all four points automatically wins the game regardless of his score, unless he was in the hole when he smudged. In this event he scores only 4 points.

Bridge

Modern Bridge, more precisely Contract Bridge, but the 'Contract' has for long been dropped, was developed out of Auction Bridge and introduced to card players in the early 1920s. It took firm root quickly, and made rapid progress, to become the most popular game in the whole history of card-playing. To-day, half a century after its *début*, it is played by millions, rich and poor, from peers to peasants, and it has attracted to itself a vast literature in most European languages.

Bridge is played by four players, two playing in partnership against the other two, and with a standard pack of fifty-two cards. The cards rank in the order Ace (high) to 2 (low), and the Ace, King, Queen, Jack and Ten of a suit are known as the honour cards. The suits rank in the order Spades, Hearts, Diamonds, Clubs; the Spade and Heart suits are known as the major suits: the Diamond and Club suits as the minor suits. Although only one pack of cards is necessary, it is customary to use two, of different design or colour, and while one is being dealt the other is shuffled by the partner of the dealer, in readiness for the next dealer.

To determine partners, a pack is spread-eagled on the table. The four players draw cards from it, and the two who draw the two highest cards play in partnership against the other two. If two players draw cards of equal rank, precedence is determined by the rank of the suits. The player who draws the highest card has choice of seats and cards, and deals first. Thereafter the deal passes round the table clockwise. His partner sits opposite to him; the other two partners sit one on each side of him.

It is convenient to divide the game into two periods. The bidding, during which the two partnerships compete against each other to establish which suit shall be made trumps or whether the hand shall be played without a trump suit. The playing, during which the player who has won the contract strives to make it, playing his own hand and that of his partner exposed on the table, against the other partnership striving to prevent him.

The dealer bids first, and the bidding continues round the table clockwise. When a player bids he states the number of tricks in excess of six that he undertakes to win, and in the denomination that he undertakes to play. The lowest bid, therefore, is a bid of One (a contract to win seven tricks) and the highest is a bid of Seven (a contract to win all thirteen tricks). As No-Trumps takes precedence over the suits, and the suits rank in the descending order Spades, Hearts, Diamonds, Clubs, the lowest possible bid is One Club, and the ascending scale is: One Club, One Diamond, One Heart, One Spade, One No-Trump, Two Clubs, Two Diamonds .... Seven Hearts, Seven Spades, Seven No-Trumps. A contract of Six (to win twelve tricks) is called a small slam; a contract of Seven (to win all thirteen tricks) is called a grand slam.

In turn each bid must name either a greater number of tricks than the previous one, or an equal number of tricks in a higher denomination. If a player has no wish to contract to win tricks he says 'No Bid', and if all four players do so, the hand is thrown in and the deal passes.

In his turn any player may double a bid made by an opponent. The effect of a double is to increase the score whether the contract succeeds or fails: and the partnership whose contract has been doubled may redouble thereby increasing the score, win or lose, still further. Doubling and redoubling, however, do not increase the size of a contract: *e.g.* a bid of Four Clubs is inferior to a bid of Four Diamonds and remains inferior to it even though it may have been doubled and redoubled.

The bidding period continues until the last and highest bid has been followed by three passes. The player who first mentioned the denomination in the final contract then becomes the declarer.

It is usual to denote the four players by the cardinal points of the compass, and if we assume that South deals, a sequence of bidding to illustrate some of the points mentioned might be:

South	West	North	East
1 ♦	No bid	1 ♥	1 ♠
1 No-Trump	2 ♠	3 ♦	No bid
3 No-Trumps	Double	No bid	No bid
4 ♦	No Bid	5 ♦	Double
Redouble	No Bid	No Bid	No Bid

The final contract, therefore, is Five Diamonds, and the hand will be played by South, because he was the first on his side to mention Diamonds as the trump suit.

The playing period begins by the player on the left of the declarer leading to the first trick. As soon as he has done so, the partner of the declarer places his cards face upwards on the table as dummy. He takes no further 'part in the play except that he has a right to draw his partner's attention to certain irregularities, such as asking him if he has none of a suit when he fails to follow suit, and warning him against leading out of the wrong hand. The declarer plays the dummy hand as well as his own.

The play follows the normal routine of trick-taking games: if a player is able to do so he must follow suit to the card led; otherwise he may either discard or trump. The trick is won by the player who plays the highest card of the suit led, or the highest trump. The player who wins a trick leads to the next. Plate 13 shows the playing period of the game in progress.

When all thirteen tricks have been played, the players record their scores, and those of their opponents, on a marker, or sheet of paper, as shown in the accompanying diagram.

When a player makes his contract, the score for tricks won is entered below the horizontal line. All other scores are entered above this line.

A game is won when a partnership scores 100 points below the horizontal line, either in one or more deals. If a partnership scores less than game in one deal, it is said to have a part-score and if the opponents then score game the part-score cannot be carried forward towards the next game. When a partnership wins a game a line is drawn across the score sheet below it, and both partnerships begin the next game from a love score.

A partnership that wins a game becomes vulnerable and is subject to higher bonuses if it makes its contract, and increased penalties if it fails. Vulnerability, however, does not affect the points for winning the tricks contracted for.

The main object of the game is to win a rubber, which is the best out of three games.

If a partnership has bid and made its contract, it scores;

In No-Trumps: 40 points for the first trick and 30 points for each subsequent trick.

In Spades and Hearts: 30 points for each trick.

In Diamonds and Clubs: 20 points for each trick.

The scores for winning tricks are doubled if the contract has been doubled, and quadrupled if the contract has been redoubled.

If a partnership has made tricks in excess of its contract, it scores:

If undoubled: trick value for each trick.

If doubled: 100 points for each trick if not vulnerable.
200 points for each trick if vulnerable.

If redoubled: 200 points for each trick if not vulnerable.
400 points for each trick if vulnerable.

If a partnership has failed to make its contract, it loses:

If undoubled: 50 points for each trick if not vulnerable.
100 points for each trick if vulnerable.

If doubled: 100 points for the first trick; 200 points for each subsequent trick if not vulnerable.
200 points for the first trick; 300 points for each subsequent trick if vulnerable.

If redoubled: 200 points for the first trick; 400 points for each subsequent trick if not vulnerable.
400 points for the first trick; 600 points for each subsequent trick if vulnerable.

If a partnership wins a rubber, it scores:

In three games 500 points.

In two games 700 points.

A partnership scores bonuses of:

1,500 points, if vulnerable, for bidding and making a grand slam, 1,000 points if not vulnerable.

750 points, if vulnerable, for bidding and making a small slam, 500 points if not vulnerable.

150 points if either partner holds all four Aces in a No-Trump contract, or all five honours in a suit contract.

100 points if either partner holds any four honours in a suit contract.

50 points if a partnership makes a doubled or redoubled contract.

Bridge is not a difficult game unless a player makes it so by ill-advised bidding. Its most important feature is that a player scores below the line, towards game, only for the tricks that he has contracted to win, and, by a logical extension, he scores the big bonuses for slams only if the necessary number of tricks has been contracted for. It follows that it is of paramount importance for the partners to estimate the trick-taking power of their combined hands, and not only must a player estimate as accurately as possible the position of the adverse high cards and distribution (as revealed by the bids of the other players) but convey by his bidding as much information as possible to his partner. In short, bidding may be defined as a conversation between the partners, and both must speak the same language.

Most modern players value their hands by means of the well-known Milton Work count of 4 for an Ace, 3 for a King, 2 for a Queen, and 1 for a Jack.

85

The player who opens the bidding with a bid of One of a suit, promises to make a further bid if his partner responds with One in a higher-ranking suit, or Two in a lower-ranking suit. For this reason a player should not open unless he can see a sound rebid in his hand over partner's most likely response.

The strength to justify an opening bid varies, but in general it may be said that a hand totalling at least 13 points should be opened. It is clear, however, that the more points a player holds the less length does he need in the trump suit, and the fewer points in the hand the greater must be the length in the trump suit. With less than 13 points in the hand the practice is to open an 11- or 12-point hand with a reasonable 5-card suit, and with only 10 points in the hand, sometimes less, a player needs a reasonable 6-card suit, or two 5-card suits.

Open One Heart. The hand totals only 11 points, but the Heart suit is worth showing and if it is not shown at once it may be too late.

Open One Spade. The hand totals only 11 points, but is strong by reason of its distribution. With two suits of equal length it is proper to bid the higher-ranking before the lower-ranking one.

Open One Spade. The hand totals a mere 10 points, but the 6-card Spade suit is too good to be held back.

There are 40 points in the pack and experience has taught that if the combined hands have a total of 25 points game will be made, if 33 the small slam, and if 37 the grand slam. There are, of course, exceptions, but in the long run the rule is to be relied on.

A bid of One No-Trump is advised with a total of 16 to 18 points. The bid should never step outside the stipulated range, because partner needs to rely on it for his response. With 9 points he will jump to Three No-Trumps; with 7 or 8 he will bid Two No-Trumps and leave it to the opener to pass with a minimum, but bid Three with a maximum. A NoTrump range of 16 to 18 points is known as a strong No-Trump. Some experienced players favour, particularly when not vulnerable, a range of 12 to 14 points. It is known as a weak No-Trump. Whether a strong or a weak No-Trump is played is a matter of personal choice, but it must be agreed between the partners before play begins, because if a weak No-Trump is played partner must increase his responses by 4 points.

In the same way, an opening bid of Two No-Trumps is advised on 20 to 22 points, leaving it to partner to raise to Three if he holds 5 points, and to pass with less.

Opening bids of One No-Trump and Two No-Trumps postulate a balanced distribution of 4-3-3-3 or 4-4-3-2. A bid of Three No-Trumps is tactical. It shows a hand containing a solid minor suit, and altogether a hand that has a reasonable prospect of winning nine tricks if partner has one or two top cards in the right places.

The hand qualifies for an opening bid of Three No-Trumps. There is every prospect of making the contract; if not it will not cost a lot and there is the consolation that it has probably stopped the opponents from bidding a game that would have been a greater loss.

The partner of the player who opens the bidding with No-Trumps raises on a very precise number of points. The number of points, however, may be reduced slightly if the responder holds a 5-card suit. Over a bid of One No-Trump, partner holds:

The hand totals 8 points and 9 points are normally necessary to jump to Three No-Trumps. Here, however, the jump to Three No-Trumps is justified on the length of the Spade suit, and the good intermediate cards. It is unwise to bid Spades because if it is assumed that partner holds a balanced 16-point hand he is just as likely to win nine tricks in No-Trumps as the responder is to win ten in Spades. If Three No-Trumps cannot be made there is no reason to suppose that Four Spades can.

A jump take out into a suit is a game force. It does not, however, promise a very strong hand: rather it means that the responder, who knows the precise strength of his partner's bid, can foresee game for the partnership but cannot tell whether the combined hands will play better in No-Trumps or in a suit.

West	East
♠ Q J 4 3	♠ K 10 9 7 2
♥ A Q 2	♥ J 6 4
♦ K 9 3	♦ A J 8 2
♣ A 7 6	♣ 8
Bidding	Bidding
1 No-Trump	3 ♠
4 ♠	No Bid

Over West's opening bid of One No-Trump (16 to 18 points) East who has 9 points has enough to jump to Three No-Trumps. He prefers Three-Spades, however, which West raises to game, because game in Spades can hardly fail, but in No-Trumps will be defeated if a Club is led.

Another important feature of responding to a No-Trump bid is the Stayman convention. It is a bid of Two Clubs over partner's One No-Trump, or Three Clubs over his Two No-Trumps, made, irrespective of the holding in the suit, to ask partner to bid his better 4-card major suit, or, if he lacks one, to bid Diamonds.

West	East
♠ K Q 2	♠ A J 4 3
♥ A J 6 2	♥ K Q 8 4
♦ Q 6 4	♦ 3 2
♣ A Q 4	♣ J 8 5
Bidding	Bidding
1 No-Trump	2 ♣
2 ♥	4 ♥
No Bid.	

Without the convention East, with 11 points, would have no alternative except to jump his partner's opening bid of One No-Trump (16 to 18 points) to Three. The combined total of 29 points is more than adequate for the bid, but Three No-Trumps may be defeated if a Diamond is led and Four Hearts can hardly fail.

There is a large range of bids which show weakness and that may be recognized as such by the logic of the situation.

West	East
1 ♠	2 No-Trumps
3 ♠	?

East's bid of Two No-Trumps shows a count of from 11 to 13 points, and over it West cannot do more than repeat his suit. His hand, therefore, cannot be strong, and his bid of Three Spades no more than the cheapest way of keeping his promise to rebid, which he made when he opened with One Spade.

In the same way, if the bidding is:

West	East
1 No-Trump	2 ♠
?	

West should pass. East's bid must be showing a weak hand that he considers will play better in a suit than in No-Trumps, otherwise, over an opening bid of One No-Trump, it would be impossible for partner ever to play in Two of a suit.

Or we may consider the following sequences:

West	East		West	East		West	East
1 ♥	2 ♥		1 ♥	2 ♣		1 ♣	1 ♥
3 ♣	3 ♥		2 ♥	3 ♦		1 ♠	2 ♥
			3 ♥			2 ♠	3 ♥

In all these sequences the bid of Three Hearts shows weakness. A player cannot be holding much of a hand when he cannot do better than rebid his suit at the lowest level, and it is particularly pronounced when he rebids it twice.

An opening bid of Three of a suit is also a weakness bid. It is made with a hand that has little, if any, defensive strength, offers small chance of success of game, and with one long suit that, if trumps, is unlikely to be defeated by more than two tricks if vulnerable and three if not vulnerable.

This type of hand qualifies for an opening bid of Three Spades if only because, even if doubled and partner has no support, it cannot cost more than 500 points (two down). It is a reasonable loss if the opponents have a game in one of the other suits.

There is also a range of strong bids. The strongest of all is an opening bid of Two Clubs. It is strictly conventional and may be made even if the player is void in the suit. The bid guarantees either five or more high cards and distributional strength, or 23 or more points and a balanced distribution. With one exception the bid is forcing to game. Partner must respond no matter how weak his hand is, and with a weak hand he bids Two Diamonds. Any other response by him shows an Ace and a King or two King-Queen combinations or the equivalent in high cards. The exception to the bid not being forcing to game occurs when the opener has bid Two Clubs with a balanced hand and, after the negative response of Two Diamonds, has rebid Two No-Trumps.

West	East
♠ K J 3	♠ Q 6 2
♥ A Q 6	♥ 9 7 4
♦ A K 4	♦ 8 5 3 2
♣ A Q J 2	♣ 7 4 3

Bidding   Bidding
2 ♣   2 ♦
2 No-Trumps No Bid

West, with 24 points, is too strong to open with any other bid than Two Clubs, and over East's negative response he cannot do better than rebid Two No-Trumps. East with only 2 points in his hand does well to pass, but another point in his hand would make a big difference and with 3 points or more he would bid Three No-Trumps.

The opening bid of Two in any other suit is forcing for one round, and shows a hand containing not fewer than eight playing tricks and at least one powerful suit.

This hand is best opened with Two Spades. If it is opened with One Spade there is no satisfactory way of coping with a response of Two Hearts.

A strong 2-suited hand also qualifies for an opening bid of Two. The higher-ranking suit is bid first.

A 1-suited hand may also be opened with a Two bid. This hand should be opened with a bid of Two Spades, and Three Spades should be bid over any response made by partner.

The responses to opening Two bids (of suits other than Clubs) are not so well-defined and clear-cut as the responses to an opening bid of Two Clubs. In general, if partner holds a biddable suit he should bid it at the lowest level. If he lacks a biddable suit, but has a total of from 10 to 12 points, he should bid Three No-Trumps. If he lacks a biddable suit and insufficient points to bid Three No-Trumps, but has adequate support (*i.e.* **x x x** or **Q x**) for partner's suit and a count of 5, he should give a simple raise in partner's suit. If he lacks a biddable suit, insufficient points for Three No-Trumps, and insufficient support for partner's suit, he should make the negative response of Two No-Trumps.

As well as an opening bid of Two Clubs there are several other bids that are forcing to game. The most frequent is a jump bid in a new suit.

West	East
♠ Q 8 4	♠ A K 6
♥ 9 2	♥ A Q J 10 6 4
♦ A J 3	♦ 8 2
♣ A K 9 3 2	♣ J 4
Bidding	Bidding
1 ♣	2 ♥

The situation is typical. East's bid of Two Hearts sets up a forcing situation. It is true that a bid of One Heart by East cannot be passed by West, but it is better for East to get the hand off his chest, and by bidding Two Hearts he makes certain that the bidding will not be dropped until a game level is reached.

It is much the same if the opener makes a jump in a new suit over his partner's response:

West	East
♠ K J 6	♠ A Q 9 2
♥ A K J 7 4	♥ 10 8 3
♦ 6	♦ K Q 9
♣ K Q J 7	♣ 10 6 3
Bidding	Bidding
1 ♥	1 ♠
3 ♣	

In this situation (or a similar one) West's bid of Three Clubs is a game force and East cannot pass it.

In many cases a forcing situation is set up by reason of the logic behind the bidding.

West	East
♠ A K 9 6 3	♠ Q 7 4 2
♥ K J 9 2	♥ Q 10 8 3
♦ A 8 4	♦ K 6 2
♣ 9	♣ 5 4
Bidding	Bidding
1 ♠	2 ♠
3 ♥	?

As West rebid at the level of Three, over East's weak response of Two Spades, and when there was no need for him to rebid, he must have a very strong hand, and East must make a further bid. He bids Four Hearts and West passes.

An inferential force is even more pronounced in a sequence such as:

West	East
1 ♥	1 ♠
2 No-Trumps	3 ♥
?	

West must not pass because East is very clearly inviting him to choose between playing the hand in Three No-Trumps or Four Hearts, whichever contract best suits him.

When the bidding of the partners shows that they hold between them the balance of strength, they should consider bidding a slam. As a guide it may be said that prospects of a slam are good when a player holds enough to make a positive response to a forcing bid; or when the point count of the combined hands totals at least 33; or when a player has enough for an opening bid opposite a partner who has opened with a bid of Two, or who has opened the bidding and made a jump rebid.

Before a slam can be bid with a measure of safety, it is essential for the partners to find out if they hold between them control of the vital suits. The Blackwood convention has been designed to enable the partners to learn how many Aces and Kings are held by the partnership.

When the trump suit has been agreed either directly by support or by implication, or if a forcing situation has been set up, a bid of Four No-Trumps by either partner asks the other to bid Five Clubs if he lacks an Ace or holds all four, Five Diamonds if he holds one Ace, Five Hearts if he holds two and Five Spades if he holds three. If the player who has bid Four No-Trumps, after his partner's response continues with a bid of Five No-Trumps, he is showing that he holds all four Aces and is asking his partner to bid Six Clubs if he lacks a King, Six Diamonds if he holds one King, Six Hearts if he holds two, Six Spades if he holds three and Six No-Trumps if he holds all four.

Bidding	Bidding
1 ♠	2 ♥
3 No-Trumps	4 ♠
4 No-Trumps	5 ♥
6 ♠	No Bid

Once East has shown that he has support for Spades, West, with support for Hearts, visualises a slam. His bid of Four No-Trumps asks East how many Aces he holds, and East's response of Five Hearts tells West that he holds two. It is important for West to bid the slam in Spades, because if East plays in Hearts and his two Aces are in Hearts and Clubs (as they are) the opening lead of a Diamond from South may break Six Hearts out of hand. When West plays in Six Spades, the King of Diamonds is protected against the opening lead and twelve tricks are assured.

As West knows that there is an Ace against the hand the grand slam is out of the question and West, therefore, has no need to bid Five No-Trumps to ask East how many Kings he holds.

The convention is a very useful one, but it must be used with discretion, because if partner lacks the necessary Aces the partnership may find itself carried out of its depth. As a rule, it may be said that if the final contract is to be in Clubs the bid of Four No-Trumps should not be made unless the bidder holds at least two Aces, and if the contract is to be in Diamonds he should hold at least one Ace.

A limit bid is a bid that informs partner of the precise strength of the hand, and so permits him to estimate the combined strength of the partnership, and drop the bidding if he can see no future for it.

No-Trump bids are limit bids because they are made on an agreed number of points in the hand. A single raise of partner's suit is a limit bid that shows moderate strength and support for the suit; a double raise of partner's suit shows that the hand is too good for a mere simple raise and invites him to bid game if his hand is above average; a triple raise is distributional, it promises good support for the suit and a few scattered points, but no more because with good support for the suit coupled with high-card strength it would be more in order to make a gradual advance to a possible slam.

When an opponent has bid a suit at the level of One, a player should enter the auction only if he can be reasonably sure that his bid, if passed out, will not be defeated by more than two tricks if vulnerable and three if not vulnerable. This general rule, however, must be accepted with some reservation. It would, for example, not be wrong for a player who holds

to bid One Heart over an opponent's One Diamond. The bid might prove costly, but not very often, and it is cowardly not to contest the part-score for fear of the worst happening. A player has a right to assume that even if his partner has a blank hand and only two or three low Hearts, the hand will win three tricks in Hearts and one in each of the black suits.

A jump overcall shows strength, and, though it is not forcing, partner is expected to take action if he holds the values that would justify a response to a bid of One.

An overcall should be based on a 5-card or longer suit, though it is reasonable to overcall with **A K Q x** or **K Q J x** at the level of One. It is nearly always very unwise to overcall with a broken suit.

93

In general, when an opponent has opened the bidding with a bid of One of a suit, it is better to counter it with a take-out double than with a weak overcall. A double in this situation shows weakness in the suit doubled and a total of about 13 or 14 points with a balanced hand and 11 or 12 with an unbalanced one. Postulating that the doubler's partner has not bid (if he has the double is for a penalty) the doubler invites partner to bid his best suit.

West	*East*
♠ K J 9 6 2	♠ 5 3
♥ K J 9 2	♥ A Q 8 3
♦ 6	♦ K 7 2
♣ A Q 7	♣ 10 8 6 2

If South has bid One Diamond, West should double. East bids Hearts and the good fit has been found. If West bids One Spade over South's One Diamond the Heart fit will never be found and a good result will be exchanged for a bad one.

If partner's best suit is the one that has been doubled, either he bids No-Trumps or passes for a penalty if he holds length in the suit.

A double of One No-Trump is made with a balanced hand and a count of about 2 points more than the No-Trump bidder's average. With a weak hand partner will take out into his best suit, but if the combined count totals 23 or more he will pass for a penalty.

A pre-emptive bid is defined as an opening bid at the level of Three or higher. It is a bid of great value because either it prevents the opponents from entering the auction or compels one of them to bid at a level that is dangerously high when he has no notion of what cards his partner may be holding. Postulating that the bid of Three is weak and that an opponent holds strength in the other three suits, the most practical way of countering the pre-empt is to bid Three Diamonds over Three Clubs and Three No-Trumps over Three Spades, Hearts or Diamonds. Either bid invites partner to bid his best suit.

When the bidding period ends, and the playing period begins, the player on the left of the declarer leads to the first trick. It is only after he has led that the partner of the declarer exposes his hand on the table as dummy. It follows, therefore, that the opening lead has to be made in the dark, since the player can see only his own hand and is left to judge the best lead from it, coupled with the information that he has obtained from the bidding. The opening lead must be chosen with care. It is of great importance, because quite often the choice of a good or bad lead will decide whether or not the declarer's contract will be made.

Against a No-Trump contract, if partner has bid a suit, leading it usually offers the best chance of defeating the contract, unless the player on lead holds only a singleton in the suit or he has a good suit of his own.

With two cards of partner's suit the higher should be led; with three cards the highest should be led, unless the suit is headed by the Ace, King, Queen or Jack, when the lowest should be preferred. With two honours in partner's suit the higher should be led; with a sequence (a combination of three or more cards of adjacent rank) the highest should be led. In all other cases the fourth highest should be led.

When a player leads his own suit, he should lead the fourth highest of his longest suit, unless he holds a sequence (when he should lead the highest), a long suit headed by the Ace and King and an entry in another suit (when he should lead the King), or an intermediate honour sequence *e.g.* **A Q J x** or **K J 10 x** (when the higher of the two touching honours should be led).

The reason for leading the fourth highest card of a suit is that if partner subtracts the number of the card from eleven, the remainder will be the number of higher cards held by the other three players. The Rule of Eleven.

Q 9 7

	Dummy		
5 led	W E		**K 10 8**
	Declarer		

West leads the 5. As $11 - 5 = 6$, and East can see six cards higher than the 5 in dummy and in his own hand, he will know that the declarer cannot hold a card higher than the 4, so that whichever card is played from dummy he can win the trick by playing the card just higher.

Against a suit contract it is usually best to lead partner's suit, if he has bid one. If he has not, and the player on lead has to lead from his own suit, he should give preference to leading the top card of an honour sequence. He should avoid leading a card that may cost a trick *e.g.* leading the King from **K Q x**, or a card that may enable the declarer to win a trick with a card that might have been captured *e.g.* leading the Ace from **A Q x**. The lead of a trump is a good lead if the bidding has suggested that the dummy will be able to trump side suits.

After the opening lead has been made, and the dummy hand exposed, it is of first importance for the declarer, before he plays a card from dummy, to take stock of the position and decide upon the best way to play the cards.

West   East

Against West's contract of Three No-Trumps, North leads the Queen of Spades. At first sight it may seem immaterial whether West wins the trick with the Ace in dummy or with the King in his own hand. In the event, it matters a lot in which hand he wins the trick. If West gives consideration to the position he will appreciate that he must win the first trick with the King of

Spades in his hand, win the King, Queen and Jack of Clubs, reach dummy, by leading the 4 of Spades to the Ace, to win dummy's Ace and 7 of Clubs, and finally the two red Aces in his own hand. If West wins the first trick with dummy's Ace of Spades, he will lose the contract if the adverse Clubs fail to divide 3-2, because he has left himself with no side entry to the Clubs.

When the declarer is playing a No-Trump contract, usually his first aim should be to establish his longest suit. In many cases, however, it is better to develop a short and strong suit rather than a long and weak one.

North leads a Club against West's contract of Three No-Trumps. Consideration shows that West's best play is to win with the King of Clubs and play on Spades to knock out the Ace. This way, West makes sure of his contract with three tricks in Spades, three in Hearts, one in Diamonds and two in Clubs. The Diamond suit is longer than the Spade suit, but West cannot develop East's Diamonds without first losing the lead twice. By then the opponents will have set up the Clubs and broken the contract; in any case, only three tricks in Diamonds will be developed for eight in all, which is not enough.

In a suit contract, it is usually the right play for the declarer to draw the adverse trumps at the first opportunity. Trumps, however, should not be drawn if the declarer can find a better use for them.

West plays in Four Hearts, and North leads a Club. West wins the first trick with the Ace of Clubs, and if he draws the trumps at once his contract will depend on the finesse of the Queen of Spades being successful. It is no more than an even chance. The contract is a certainty if West, after winning the first trick with the Ace of Clubs, leads either the 7 or 3 of the suit. It does not matter whether North or South wins the trick, or what card is returned. Declarer wins the next trick and trumps a Club in dummy. Now the adverse trumps may be drawn, and West comes to ten tricks with one Spade, five Hearts, two Diamonds and one Club by straight leads, and the ruff of a Club on the table.

A valuable weapon in the armoury of the declarer is the ability to manage a suit to make the most tricks out of it.

West	East
A 9 3 2	K Q 10 5 4

In this position it is vital to play the King first. Then, if either North or South is void of the suit, there is a marked finessing position over the Jack, and five tricks in the suit will be made.

The unthinking player who first plays the Ace, on the assumption that it does not matter which high card he plays first because the outstanding cards will normally divide 3-1 or 2-2, will lose a trick in the suit whenever North is void and South holds J 8 7 6. It will occur about five times in every hundred.

West	East
A K 10 5 3	9 7 6

If West cannot afford to lose more than one trick in the suit, his play is to win either the Ace or King; if both opponents follow suit, he enters East's hand in a side suit, leads the 7 from the table and if South plays the 8, plays the 10 from his own hand. This protects him against losing two tricks in the suit if South started with **Q J 8 x**.

There is a percentage play or a safety play for almost every combination of a suit, and it may be found by analysing the division of the remaining cards in the suit.

West	East
♠ A K 4 2	♠ 5 3
♥ A 9 7	♥ 10 6 2
♦ A 9 4	♦ K 8 7
♣ K 7 6	♣ A 10 5 4 3

Against West's contract of Three No-Trumps, North leads a Spade. West can make his contract only if he wins four tricks in Clubs. After winning the first trick with the King of Spades, the right play is for West to win the King of Clubs. If North and South both follow suit, West continues with the 7 of Clubs and plays the 4 from dummy if North plays an honour, but the 10 if North plays a low card. If South follows suit, there is only one more outstanding Club and it will fall under East's Ace. If North shows out on the second round of Clubs, then South started with **Q J x x** of the suit and West cannot do anything about it. The directed play, however, guarantees that he will win four tricks in the suit if North originally held **Q J x x** of the suit.

Most important of all, however, is an ability to count the cards. It is not all that difficult, and, in the main, is largely a matter of drawing deductions from the bidding and previous play of the cards, coupled with training oneself to think along the right lines.

West deals at love all, and the auction is:

West	North	East	South
1 ♣	No Bid	1 ♦	1 ♥
2 ♦	2 ♥	2 ♠	4 ♥
No Bid	No Bid	No Bid	

West leads Diamonds and East wins the first two tricks with the Ace and King of the suit. A third round of Diamonds is ruffed by South with the 8 of Hearts.

As South has lost two tricks, it would seem that his contract is doomed, because West, by reason of his opening bid and lacking either the Ace or King of Diamonds, must surely be holding the Kings of Hearts and Clubs.

South, however, has a partial count of the hand that will enable him to make his contract if he knows how to take advantage of it. On the assumption that West almost certainly started with three Diamonds and probably five Clubs, he cannot have more than five cards in Spades and Hearts. South, therefore, wins the Ace of Hearts (in case the King is singleton) and when the King of Hearts does not come down, he leads a Spade to dummy's King, a Spade from dummy to the Ace in the closed hand, and then trumps his last Spade with dummy's 10 of Hearts. As West played the 7 of Hearts under South's Ace and followed to the three rounds of Spades, South may reconstruct the position as:

Now, by leading the Queen of Hearts from dummy, West is put on lead with the King, and as he must return a Club, South wins two tricks in the suit.

The play of the defenders is more difficult than that of the declarer, because a defender has to combine his hand with that of the unseen one held by his partner. They have the slight advantage of a partnership language that enables them to exchange information and advice, but, for the most part, success in defence comes mainly from drawing the right deductions from the bidding, and the cards that have been played to previous tricks.

To lead the highest card of a sequence, to win with the lowest, and to follow suit as the situation dictates, is a general rule that does not need to be enlarged on. Most of the general rules for defence play, however, have been handed down from the days when whist was the fashionable game. At bridge reservations have to be made, because the bidding and the exposed dummy hand allow for modifications of what were only broad generalities in the first place.

To return the suit that partner has led is not always the best play. Sometimes it is more important to take time by the forelock.

South deals and opens the auction with One No-Trump (12 to 14 points) and North jumps him to Three.

West leads the 3 of Hearts and East wins with the Ace. If East returns a Heart, South has no difficulty in making nine tricks, because dummy's 10 of Hearts protects the Jack in the closed hand and the defenders cannot win more than one trick in Spades and three in Hearts. With the 2 of Hearts on the table, East should appreciate that his partner cannot hold more than four Hearts and that they cannot be better than **K Q 9 3**, because if they were **K Q J 3** he would have led the King and not the 3. As once East gives up the lead he can never regain it, he must take advantage of the time factor, the tempo, and lead the Queen of Spades. The only chance of defeating the contract is to find West holding the Ace of Spades, and as South's bid of One No-Trump postulates a maximum of 14 points, East, who holds 7 points and can count 10 on the table, can count West with just enough room in his hand for the Ace of Spades as well as for the King and Queen of Hearts.

To cover an honour with an honour may be good play in many cases, but it is not when the honour has been led from a sequence.

The Queen is led from dummy. If East covers with the King, the declarer will win four tricks in the suit by winning with the Ace and returning the suit to finesse against West's 10. East, therefore, should not cover. The Queen will win, but now the defenders will always win a trick in the suit because if the declarer continues with dummy's Jack, the lead is no longer from a sequence and East covers it with the King. With **K x** only, East should cover the Queen, otherwise the declarer, after winning dummy's Queen may continue with a low Spade (not the Jack) from the table and East's King will be wasted.

Second hand plays low; third hand plays high, is another general rule that has been handed down from the past. It is, perhaps, a rule worth remembering, because exceptions when second hand should play high are few and far between, and when third hand sees only low cards on his right, there are virtually no exceptions to his playing high.

8 3 2

J led

K 6 4

West leads the Jack. East should play the King like a man. He knows that the declarer holds the Queen (otherwise West would have led it in preference to the Jack) and if declarer holds the Ace as well the King is doomed. East, therefore, must play on the chance that West has led from **A J 10 x** and that declarer holds **Q x x**.

A very important weapon in the armoury of the defenders is the echo or peter, sometimes called the come-on or high-low signal. Reduced to its simplest terms, when a defender plays a higher card followed by a lower one of the same suit, it is a request to partner to play the suit. In many cases a defender can afford to play the suit only once. In such a case to play a 7 or a higher card is an encouragement to partner, and, by contrary, to play a lower card is a discouragement to him. Against a trump contract, the high-low play in a side suit shows that a doubleton is held and that the third round can be trumped. If the play is made in the trump suit itself, it shows that three trumps are held. Against a No-Trump contract, the echo shows length in the suit, usually four cards.

The defenders are frequently compelled to discard, and nearly always discarding presents them with a problem. The general rules to follow are not to retain the same suit as partner; not to discard from a suit in which you have the same length as dummy or suspect the declarer has in his hand; and never to discard so that the declarer is given information.

Counting the cards is, of course, as important to the defenders as it is to the declarer. In some ways, however, the defenders have it a bit easier. If the declarer is in a No-Trump contract he will have limited his hand to an agreed number of points. It follows, therefore, that if the declarer's limit is 16 to 18 points and he has shown up with 15 points, the defenders know that he has left in his hand no more than a King or its equivalent. In much the same way, in a suit contract the declarer and his dummy will rarely hold less than eight trump cards between them. It follows, therefore, that if a defender holds three trumps, he knows that his partner is probably holding not more than two.

In conclusion, it may be said that good defence consists in playing those cards that give as much information as possible to partner, and making things as easy as possible for him; by contrary, in playing those cards that give as little information as possible to the declarer and making things as difficult as possible for him. Whenever it is possible to do so, a defender should play the cards that the declarer knows are in his hand, and retain those of which he knows nothing. If all this comes as a counsel of perfection – the best bridge players are perfectionists.

Brint

Brint was originated by J. B. Chambers in 1929. It is a hybrid of bridge (see page 83) and vint, the national card game of Russia. It has been described as bridge with vint scoring, because the score that counts towards game, and recorded below the line, depends entirely upon the level to which the bidding has been carried. No-Trumps and the suits retain their rank, but each trick (over six) at the level of One is worth 10 points, at the level of Two 20 points, and so on up to Seven when each trick is worth 70 points.

The full scoring table is:

		When the Declarer is Not Vulnerable		
		Undoubled	**Doubled**	
When the Contract is at the level of:	**Each Odd-trick (whether Doubled or not) is worth:**	**Penalty for each Undertrick**	**Bonus for Contract and each Overtrick**	**Penalty for each Undertrick**
One	10	50	50	100
Two	20	50	50	100
Three	30	50	50	100
Four	40	100	100	200
Five	50	150	150	300
Six	60	200	200	400
Seven	70	250	250	500

The score for tricks made is unaffected by a double, but if a doubled contract is redoubled the trick score, as well as the bonus and penalty for a doubled contract, is doubled. The bonuses and penalties are increased by 100 points each if the player is vulnerable.

A game is won by the pair that first reaches a trick score of 160 points.

The bonuses for bidding and making slams and games, and for holding honours, recorded above the line as at bridge, are:

For a successful bid of Seven – 1000 points
For a successful bid of Six – 500 points
For a successful bid of Five – 250 points
For a successful bid of Four – 500 points if vulnerable
                                250 points if not vulnerable
In a No-Trump contract for four Aces in one hand – 150 points
In a Suit contract for *five* honours in one hand – 200 points
In a Suit contract for *four* honours in one hand – 100 points
They are unaffected by vulnerability, doubling and redoubling.

Calypso

Calypso was invented by R. W. Willis of Trinidad: it dates from the mid-1950s, and though designed on entirely new lines, inevitably borrows some of the best features of bridge (see page 83) and canasta (see page 105).

The game is played with four packs of cards (with identical backs) shuffled together, but the cards are shuffled only at the start of a game, and a player holds only thirteen of them at a time.

Four players take part, and it is a novel feature of the game that each player has his own trump suit. Spades and Hearts play in partnership against Diamonds and Clubs. The players cut for seats and trump suits. The highest has choice of both, and his partner takes the corresponding suit and sits facing him. The choice of a trump suit conveys no advantage; it is purely a matter of personal preference.

Thirteen cards are dealt to each player, and the dealer places the rest of the pack to his left, ready for the next dealer after the hand has been played.

The player on the left of the dealer leads to the first trick. Thereafter the lead is made by the player who wins a trick. When playing to a trick a player must follow suit if he can; otherwise he may either discard or trump by playing a card of his own trump suit.

A trick is won by he who has played the highest card of the suit led, or by he who has trumped it, or over-trumped it by playing a higher trump of his own trump suit. If two or more players play identical cards, the first played takes priority for the purpose of winning tricks, and perhaps the most important feature of the game is that if a player leads a card of his own trump suit, he wins the trick automatically unless it is trumped by another player or over-trumped by still another player. To illustrate:

North ♣	East ♠	South ♦	West ♥
8 ♥	J ♥	10 ♥	3 ♥

North has led the 8 of Hearts, and East wins the trick because he has played the highest Heart.

4 ♦	6 ♠	7 ♦	3 ♦

North has led the 4 of Diamonds, and East wins the trick because he has trumped. South has merely followed suit to North's lead.

3 ♥	4 ♠	6 ♦	J ♥

North has led the 3 of Hearts, and South wins the trick, because although East has trumped, he has over-trumped. West has merely followed suit to North's lead.

9 ♣	J ♣	6 ♣	5 ♣

North has led the 9 of Clubs and wins the trick because Clubs is his own trump suit. That East has played a higher Club does not score.

North ♣	East ♠	South ♦	West ♥
6 ♣	7 ♠	9 ♦	5 ♣

North has led the 6 of Clubs, East has trumped, but South wins the trick because he has over-trumped.

6 ♥	Q ♥	Q ♥	10 ♥

North has led the 6 of Hearts, and the trick is won by East as his Queen of Hearts was played before South's.

The object of the game is to build calypsoes. A calypso is a complete suit (from Ace to 2) in a player's trump suit.

When a player wins a trick, he leaves exposed on the table, in front of him, any cards that will help him to build a calypso, passes to his partner any cards that will help him to build a calypso, and discards the others, face downwards, on his right.

North (whose trump suit is Clubs) leads the 4 of Clubs and wins the trick:

4 ♣	6 ♣	J ♣	6 ♣

North places the 4 ♣, 6 ♣ and J ♣ face upwards on the table in front of him, and discards the second 6 ♣. He then leads the 8 ♣ and the trick is:

8 ♣	J ♣	7 ♣	8 ♦

Again North wins the trick. He keeps the 7 ♣ and 8 ♣ for his calypso, passes the 8 ♦ to his partner for his calypso, and discards the J ♣ because he already has one.

The play continues until all thirteen tricks have been played; the next player then deals another hand of thirteen cards each.

A player may build only one calypso at a time, but once a calypso has been built the player may begin another. He may use any cards in the trick with which a calypso has been completed, but he cannot use any cards from his discard pile. These cards are dead.

The game ends when each player has dealt once. The score is then made up as follows:

For the first calypso—500 points.
For the second calypso—750 points ⎫ When obtained by
For any subsequent calypso—1,000 points ⎭ the individual players.
For each card in an incomplete calypso—20 points.
For each card in the discard pile—10 points.

The two partners add their totals together, and stakes are paid on the difference between the totals of the two sides.

A serious view is taken of revoking. A revoke does not become established until a player of the offending side has played to the next trick, and a revoke made in the twelfth never becomes established, but if established a revoke suffers a penalty of 260 points.

SOLO CALYPSO is played by four players but each plays for himself. The play is more or less identical with the parent game, the main difference between the two is that, in solo calypso, the players draw cards for choice of seats and trump suits; the highest has first choice, the lowest takes what is left.

CALYPSO FOR THREE PLAYERS is played with three packs of cards and one complete suit (it does not matter which) removed from all three packs. The game consists of three deals. Each player plays for himself.

Canasta

Canasta is a variation of rummy (see page 139) that was developed in South America as an independent game. It may be played by any number of players from two to six, but is at its most skilful when played by four. If two or three play each plays for himself; if four they play as two partners against the other two, the partners sitting facing each other; if five they play two against three, but of the three only two play at a time and rotate so that at each deal a different player sits out; if six play they play as three partners against the other three, the partners sitting alternately around the table.

The game is played with two 52-card packs and two Jokers to each pack. The four Jokers and the eight 2s are wild cards: they may be named as any other card.

The dealer deals eleven cards to each player * and the rest of the pack (the stock) is placed face downwards in the centre of the table. The top card is turned face upwards and placed alongside it. It is known as the up-card, and is the start of the discard pile. If it is a wild card or a red 3 it is covered with the next card of the stock, and if this also is a wild card or a red 3 it is covered with the next card of the stock, and so on.

The red 3s are bonus cards that count for or against the side to which they fall. They do not form part of a player's hand, and at his turn to play he who holds a red 3 must place it face upwards on the table in front of him and refill his hand by drawing the top card of the stock. If a red 3 is taken in the discard pile, it is similarly faced, but the player does not refill his hand from the stock.

The object of the game is to form melds of three or more cards of the same rank, with or without the help of wild cards. Sequences are not recognized as melds.

The player on the left of the dealer plays first. Thereafter play continues clockwise round the table. A play consists of a player drawing a card, melding (optional), discarding. A game in progress is shown in Plate 14.

The Draw The player takes either the top card of the stock or the up-card of the discard pile provided he can meld with it. In the latter case, however, he must take with it the whole of the discard pile subject to its not being frozen. At the beginning of the game the discard pile is frozen until a side has made its first meld; it is then unfrozen for that side only. Even for a side that has melded the discard pile is frozen at any time that a red 3 or a wild card is the up-card. It remains frozen until it is taken by a player, because the fresh discard pile is not frozen unless the player starts the fresh pile with a wild card. If a player plays a black 3 to the discard pile it is frozen for the next player only.

---

* If two play each is dealt fifteen cards; if three play each is dealt thirteen cards.

The Meld A meld is valid if it contains at least two 'natural' (*i.e.* not wild) cards of the same rank, and not more than three wild cards. Black 3s, however, may not be melded unless the player melds out in the same turn. Wild cards may not be melded separately from natural cards. A meld must be placed face upwards on the table, and the melds of the two partners are placed in front of only one of them. A player may add one or more cards of the same rank, or wild cards, to a meld previously faced by his side. A player may make as many melds as he chooses, including the addition of cards to melds made by his side; also he may not add cards to the melds of his opponents. Wild cards, once melded, cannot be replaced with natural cards.

A canasta is a meld of seven or more cards, and may be built up from an initial meld of three or more cards. If a canasta contains no wild cards it is a natural canasta; if it is formed with one, two or three wild cards it is a mixed canasta. Wild cards may be added in any number to a canasta, but other melds are limited to three (see illustration).

Natural canasta

Mixed canasta

Meld of 50 points

Meld of 90 points

Meld of 120 points

Every card melded has the following point value:

Jokers – 50 points each.

Aces and 2s – 20 points each.

Kings, Queens, Jacks, 10s, 9s and 8s – 10 points each.

7s, 6s, 5s, 4s, and black 3s – 5 points each.

These points count to the credit of a side if the cards are melded when a deal ends, and to its debit if they are not melded.

The red 3s have a value of 100 points each, unless a side holds all four of them, when each has a value of 200 points. At the end of the deal a side that has made any meld scores all its red 3s as a plus bonus: a side that has made no meld deducts the value of its red 3s from its score.

The first meld is governed by a strict rule. If the score of a side is under 1500 points the first meld must total at least 50 points; if the score is between 1500 and 2995 points it must total at least 90 points; and if the score is 3000 points or more it must total at least 120 points. There is no minimum total for a side that has a minus score.

The Discard. After a player has made a draw and melded if he has chosen to, he must play a card to the discard pile. The card must be played from hand and not from a meld on the table. The discard, however, is optional when the player melds every card in his hand (called melding out). It sometimes happens that a player is able to meld all his cards in one turn, he not having melded previously. It is known as melding out blind, and the bonus is doubled. Either way, however, a player must have, or be able to complete, a canasta, and as melding out may not suit partner he should first always ask him: 'May I go out?' Partner's reply to the question must be a simple 'Yes' or 'No', and, whichever it is, is binding on the partnership. Indeed, if the partner says 'Yes' and the player cannot, after all, meld out he suffers a penalty of 100 points.

The side that goes out totals the point values of the cards in its melds; adds a bonus of 100 points for melding out (200 points if it has melded out blind); 100 for each red 3 (800 points if the partnership holds all four red 3s); 500 points for each natural canasta and 300 points for each mixed canasta. From this is subtracted the total point value of the cards left in the hand of the partner.

The score of the side that did not meld out is determined in the same way, and it is deducted from that of the side that melded out. If it has not made a meld the value of its red 3s are deducted from, instead of added to, its total.

The game is won by the side that first reaches a total of 5,000 points, or the higher total if both sides pass 5,000 in the same deal.

The chief aim of a player must be to make canastas. If there is a choice, it is best to begin as many melds as possible, because each is a start towards a canasta. One should take advantage of the fact that, to fulfil the minimum count, a player may take two or more different melds at the same turn. At the same time, it is unwise to meld every meldable card as soon as you can. It depletes the hand and leaves you at the mercy of the opponents until you are able to go out. A good general rule is that it is unwise to make a first meld if it reduces the hand to less than six cards. A first meld should always be made if it can with the minimum number of cards.

A player should always try to retain at least one wild card in his hand, and, except to help complete a canasta, he should not add unnecessarily to a meld when there is the risk that the opponents will go out.

Nearly always it is unwise to discard Aces; they pull more weight when melded.

Since black 3s have no constructive value there is a tendency to discard them at the first opportunity. It is not bad play to do so, and it has the advantage of freezing the pack for one's left-hand opponent. In general, however, it is better to retain a black 3 until one is faced with the problem of finding a safe discard.

As the two partners hold between them only eleven cards, it stands out that at best they are unlikely to make more than one canasta out of them. There are, however, sixty-four cards that have not been dealt to the four players. Clearly, therefore, taking the pack must be to a player's advantage, because he can make so many more canastas out of it.

If your side wins the first pack, do not reduce your hand unnecessarily. Do not be frightened to discard from your longest holdings. By contrast, if your side loses the first pack your only defence is to play to go out. There is a very important difference between attacking and defending play.

When the pack is frozen, try to build up a hand in pairs. Pairs are very valuable, because every meld must contain at least two cards of the same suit—a pair that is.

THREE-PACK CANASTA, or Samba, may be played by any number of players from two to six, but is a satisfactory game only for six playing in three partnerships of two each. One player sits between two opponents, one of each of the other partnerships.

Three 52-card packs with two Jokers each are used. Thirteen cards are dealt to each player. Game is 10,000 points, and when a side reaches 7,000 its minimum count for its first meld is 150 points. Five red 3s have a value of 1,000 points; six 1,200 points. A side must have two canastas to meld out.

Euchre

Euchre, a game always more popular in the New World than in the Old, and made famous by Bret Harte's witty *Plain Language from Truthful James*, has several variations. The standard game is suitable for from two to six players, but is best for four, two playing in partnership against the other two.

The game is played with the 32-card or short pack, that is the regular pack from which the 6s and lower cards have been removed. The cards rank in the order from Ace (high) to 7 (low) with the exception that the Jack of the trump suit (Right Bower) takes precedence over all other trump cards, and the Jack of the suit of the same colour (Left Bower) ranks as the second highest trump.

There is some advantage in dealing. The players, therefore, must draw cards to decide who shall deal. The highest takes first deal, which, thereafter, passes round the table clockwise.

The dealer gives five cards to each player either in bundles of two then three, or three then two. It does not matter which, but he must be consistent throughout the game. The rest of the pack is placed face downwards in the centre of the table, and the top card is turned face upwards. It is the potential trump suit, and, beginning with the player on the left of the dealer, each player in turn has the option of either refusing or accepting it.

To accept it as the trump suit the opponents of the dealer say: 'I order it up'; the dealer's partner says: 'I assist'; and the dealer himself says nothing, but accepts by making his discard. To refuse the card as the trump suit, the opponents and partner of the dealer say: 'I pass'; the dealer signifies refusal by taking the card from the top of the pack and placing it, face upwards, partly underneath the pack.

If all four players pass on the first round, there is a second round. Beginning with the player on the left of the dealer, each player in turn may now either pass, or name any suit he likes (other than that of the turned up card) as trumps. If all four players pass on the second round, the hand is abandoned and the deal passes.

When the trump suit has been settled, the player who has named it (the maker) has the right to go it alone, but he must announce his intention to do so before a card has been led. His partner places his cards face downwards on the table, and takes no active part in the hand. The maker (he is the only one of the four who can go alone) plays his hand against the two opponents in partnership. If he wins the march (all five tricks) he scores 4 points; if he wins three or four tricks he scores 1 point; if he is euchred (*i.e.* fails to win at least three tricks) the opponents score 2 points each.

Euchre is a trick-taking game. The player on the left of the dealer (or the player on the left of the maker if he is going it alone) leads to the first trick. Thereafter the player who wins a trick leads to the next. A player must follow suit to the card led if he can, if not he may either discard or trump.

If the partnership that made the trump suit wins the march it scores 2 points; if it wins three or four tricks it scores 1 point; if it is euchred the opposing side scores 2 points. It is customary for each side to keep the score by using a 3 and a 4 (cards not needed in the game) as shown in the illustration. The side that is first to score five points wins.

| 1 point | 2 points | 3 points | 4 points |

TWO-HANDED EUCHRE is played in exactly the same way as the parent game except that the pack is reduced to twenty-four cards by removing the 8s and all lower cards, and, obviously, there is no declaration of going it alone.

THREE-HANDED EUCHRE is played in the same way as the parent game except that the maker of the trump suit plays against the other two in partnership. If the maker wins the march he scores 3 points; if he wins three or four tricks he scores 1 point; and if he is euchred each of his opponents scores 2 points.

CALL-ACE EUCHRE is a variation that may be played by four, five or six players, each playing for himself. It is played in the same way as the parent game with the exception that the maker has the option of either playing for himself or of calling for a partner by saying: 'I call on the Ace of . . .' and he names a suit. The player who holds the Ace of this suit then plays in partnership with the maker against the other players, but he does not reveal himself. It follows, therefore, that until the Ace is played, and it may not be in the deal, everyone except the holder of the Ace (if it is in play) is left to guess where his interest lies.

The scoring is rather different to that of the other variations as fundamentally the game is all against all. For winning the march a lone player scores 1 point for every player in the game; in a partnership hand the score is 2 points each if three or four players are in the game, and 3 points each if five or six players are in the game. For winning three or four tricks a lone player scores 1 point; in a partnership hand both players score 1 point. If a lone player or a partnership is euchred the other players score 2 points each.

Hearts

Hearts and its several variations is very similar in principle to black maria (see page 74) because the object of the game is to avoid taking tricks that contain certain specified cards. The play itself follows the general principles of trick-taking games: the player on the left of the dealer leads to the first trick, and thereafter the winner of a trick leads to the next; a player must follow suit to the card led if he can, and if he cannot he may discard any card that suits him.

The game may be played by any reasonable number of players, but it is at its most interesting and skilful as a game for four, each playing for himself. *

The Queen of Spades and all cards of the Heart suit are penalty cards. Every deal is a separate event, and the usual method of settling is to debit he who wins the Queen of Spades with 13 points, and those who win Hearts with 1 point for each card.

A revoke is heavily penalized. A player may correct a revoke if he does so before a card is led to the next trick; otherwise the revoke is established, the hand is abandoned, and the revoking player is debited with all 26 points.

The game is not a difficult one, but it calls for an ability to count the cards, read the distribution and visualize possibilities. It is instructive to consider the play in the deal below if West has to make the opening lead and assumes that the best lead is the 2 of Hearts because one of the other players will certainly have to win the trick.

*When the game is played by three players or by more than four, low cards are removed from the pack to reduce it to a number that allows every player to be dealt the same number of cards.

Against West's opening lead of the 2 of Hearts the play will be short and sharp, and West will come off worst of all because good play by his opponents will saddle him with the Queen of Spades.

West	North	East	South
2♥	4♥	3♥	8♥
6♥	7♥	10♥	9♥
Q♥	K♥	J♥	A♦
A♥	5♥	Q♠	Q♦

A more experienced West would have kept off leading a Heart. It is probable that his best lead is the singleton Diamond, because he has nothing to fear in the Spade suit, and, once he has got rid of his Diamond, he gives himself the best chance to get rid of the dangerous Ace and Queen of Hearts.

In **DOMINO HEARTS** the players are dealt only six cards each, and the rest of the pack is placed face downwards in the centre of the table. The player on the left of the dealer leads to the first trick, and the game is played in the same way as the parent game except that if a player cannot follow suit to a card that has been led he must draw a card from the stock, and continue to do so until he draws a card of the suit led. Only after the stock has been exhausted may a player discard from his hand if he cannot follow suit to a lead.

Play continues until all the cards have been taken in tricks, each player dropping out as his hand is exhausted. If a player wins a trick with the last card in his hand, the next active player on his left leads to the next trick. The last player to be left in the game retains all the cards left in his hand, and takes into it any cards that may be left in the stock.

The Queen of Spades is not a penalty card; only cards of the Heart suit are, and 1 point is lost for each one taken in a trick or left in the hand of the surviving player.

In **GREEK HEARTS**, as in black maria (see page 104) each player, before the opening lead is made, passes three cards to his right-hand opponent and receives three from his left-hand opponent.

As in the parent game the penalty cards are the Queen of Spades and all cards of the Heart suit, and the penalties for winning them are the same; if, however, a player wins all the Hearts and the Queen of Spades, instead of losing 26 points, he receives 26 points from each of the other players.

The game calls for some considerable skill, because, before passing on his cards, a player has to decide whether he will take the easy road and play to avoid winning penalty cards, or try for the big prize by winning all. The decision is never an easy one, because by discarding a high Heart one may be helping an opponent to a better score, and oneself lose a good score if one receives the Queen of Spades and a couple of high Hearts from one's left-hand opponent.

HEARTSETTE is played in the same way as the parent game, but with a widow hand. If three or four take part in the game the 2 of Spades is removed from the pack, and if five or six take part the full pack is used.

When there are three players, each is dealt sixteen cards, when four, twelve cards, when five, ten cards and when six, eight cards. The remaining cards are placed face downwards in the centre of the table.

The player on the left of the dealer leads to the first trick and whoever wins it takes the widow and discards from his hand to reduce it to the proper number of cards. No-one else sees the widow nor the cards that have been discarded.

The play continues in the same way as in the parent game with the same penalty cards and penalties for winning them.

OMNIBUS HEARTS or Hit the Moon, combines most of the features that have been added to the parent game. Like it it is at its best when played by four, each playing for himself.

Thirteen cards are dealt to each player, and before the opening lead is made each player passes three cards to his right-hand opponent and receives three from his left-hand opponent.

The play is the same as in the parent game. All the Hearts and the Queen of Spades are penalty cards, but a novel feature is that the 10 of Diamonds is a bonus card. A player loses 1 point for every Heart that he wins and 13 points if he wins the Queen of Spades. By contrary, he wins 10 points if he takes the 10 of Diamonds, and if he wins all the Hearts, the Queen of Spades and the 10 of Diamonds (known as hitting the moon—no longer such a feat as it once was) he wins 26 points instead of losing 16.

The game is won by the player who has the highest plus score, or lowest minus score, when one player reaches a score of -100.

The game calls for skill both in discarding to the right-hand opponent and in the play. Good discarding is dictated by the fact that only the Club suit is neutral and harmless. Every Heart is a liability and top Spades are dangerous (unless adequately supported by low cards) though top Diamonds are advantageous the low ones may be liabilities.

In play it is necessary to aim at forcing the lead into the hand of the least dangerous opponent. All the time temporary partnerships must be formed. If the score stands at: North -83, East -41, South $+32$, West $+47$, it is obvious that West will be doing his best to win the game by driving North to -100 as quickly as possible. A skilful South, therefore, will enter into a tacit partnership with North to try and save him by prolonging the game and so give himself more time to pull ahead of West. The strategy is perfectly proper because both players are acting in their own interests.

PIP HEARTS is played in the same way as the parent game, but the Queen of Spades is not a penalty card and the penalty for winning a Heart is increased to the pip value of the card, the court cards counting Jack 11, Queen 12, King 13 and Ace 14.

Pinocle

(see footnote page 63)

Pinocle has much in common with bezique (see page 30) and originated in Europe. It has, however, long since crossed the Atlantic, and, if we exclude the ubiquitous bridge (see page 83) it shares with poker (see page 133) the honour of being the national card game of the U.S.A.

In its original form, pinocle is a game for two players and is described on page 63. American card-players, however, have developed a number of variations suitable for more than two. The most popular is Auction Pinocle, a rather remarkable game because though fundamentally a game for three it makes a better game when played by four.

In every deal only three players take an active part. If four play the dealer deals no cards to himself; and if five wish to take part the dealer deals no cards to the second player on his left as well as none to himself. The inactive players, as they are called, take no part in the bidding and play, but participate in the settlement.

The pinocle pack consists of forty-eight cards, namely the A 10 K Q J 9 (in that order) of each suit, duplicated. The dealer deals fifteen cards face downwards to the active players, either in five bundles of three each, or in three bundles of four each and one of three, and after the first round, three cards face downwards to the table as a widow-hand.

A bid is a contract to score either by melds, by cards won in tricks, or by both, the number of points named, and the player on the left of the dealer makes the first bid which must be at least 300. After this, each player in turn may either pass or make a higher bid. Bids must be in multiples of ten, and once a player has passed he cannot re-enter the auction. When two players pass a bid the player who made it becomes the bidder, his bid the contract, and the other two players his opponents.

If the opening bid of 300 is passed by the other two players the bidder may concede defeat by throwing in his cards without looking at the widow. He pays 3 units to the kitty (but nothing to his opponents) and the deal passes to the next player.

If the bid is for more than 300, or if the bidder does not wish to concede defeat, he shows the widow to his opponents and takes the cards into his hand. He then names the trump suit, and places on the table in front of him his melds. They are scored for as follows:

Class A
A 10 K Q J of the trump suit = 150 points
K Q of the trump suit (royal marriage) = 40 points
K Q of a plain suit (common marriage) = 20 points

Class B
Pinocle (Q ♠ and J♦) = 40 points
Dis (**9** of the trump suit) = 10 points

Class C

Four Aces – one of each suit = 100 points
Four Kings – one of each suit = 80 points
Four Queens – one of each suit = 60 points
Four Jacks – one of each suit = 40 points

No card may be used twice in melds of the same class, but the same card may be used in two or more melds of different classes. Only the bidder melds. He then discards face downwards (buries) three cards from his hand in order to reduce it to fifteen cards: later the cards that he discards will be counted for him as won in a trick. The discards must be made from the cards in his hand, not from those in his melds, but before he leads to the first trick he may change the cards that he has discarded, change the melds and the trump suit.

When the bidder and his opponents have agreed on the value of the melds and how many more points (if any) he needs to fulfil his contract, the bidder leads to the first trick. If, however, he thinks he will not be able to make his contract he may concede defeat (called *single béte*) and pay to the players, active and inactive, the value of his bid.

When playing to a trick a player must follow suit if he can, and if he cannot he must play to win the trick by trumping or over-trumping it. Only if he has no card of the suit led and no trump card may he discard. If a trump is led, the subsequent players must try to win it. A trick is won by the highest card of the suit led or the highest trump if the led card has been trumped. If two identical cards are played the one first to be played wins the trick, if the trick is to be won by the card.

When all the tricks have been played, the players score for each Ace 11 points, each Ten 10 points, each King 4 points, each Queen 3 points, each Jack 2 points, and for winning the last trick 10 points. It gives a total of 250 points to be won in tricks.

Every deal is a separate event and settlement is made before the next deal begins. It is usual to reduce the contract to units on which payment is made.

Contract	Unit Value	
300–340	3	
350–390	5	If Spades
400–440	10	are trumps
450–490	15	the unit
500–540	20	values are
550–590	25	doubled.
600 and more	30	

The bidder pays double (called *double béte*) if his score for melds and cards taken in tricks fails to equal his contract; he receives if his score equals or exceeds his contract, but he does not receive more than the unit value of his contract.

Payment is made to and from all players, active and inactive, and to and from a kitty if the contract is for 350 or more.

The kitty is a separate account and is the common property of the players. They make good any deficiency if it owes, and divide any surplus when the game breaks up.

As the name implies **PARTNERSHIP PINOCLE** is played by four players two playing in partnership against the other two. The partners face each other.

The 48-card pinocle pack is used. The dealer gives each player twelve cards in bundles of three each, and turns up the last card dealt to himself to determine the trump suit. In turn, beginning with the player on the left of the dealer, any player who holds the dis (9 of the trump suit) may exchange it for the turned-up card, and if the dealer turns up the dis as the trump card he scores 10 points. Each original holder of a dis, whether or not he exchanges it with the turned-up card, scores 10 points for it.

The players expose their melds on the table in front of them, and in addition to the melds for auction pinocle (page 160) melds and the scores for them are as follows:

Double Trump Sequence **A 10 K Q J**	1,500 points
Double Pinocle	300 points
All Eight Aces	1,000 points
All Eight Kings	800 points
All Eight Queens	600 points
All Eight Jacks	400 points

When the players have shown their melds and scored for them, they return them to their hands. No meld, however, finally counts unless the partnership wins a trick, and when a trick is won both partners score for their melds.

The player on the left of the dealer leads to the first trick, and the play continues as in auction pinocle.

When all twelve tricks have been played, the players count 10 points for every Ace and 10 won, 5 points for every King and Queen, and 10 points for winning the last trick. As in auction pinocle the total is 250 points.

The game is won by the partnership that first wins 1,000 points in melds and cards won in tricks, but if both partnerships reach 1,000 or more points in the same deal the game continues to 1,250 points, and, if it happens again, to 1,500 points, and so on.

At any time during the game a player may claim that he has scored 1,000 points or more and won the game. Play is brought to an end and the claim is verified. If the claim is found to be correct his partnership wins the game; if the claim is found to be wrong his partnership loses the game. In either case, what the opposing side has scored makes no difference to the result.

PARTNERSHIP PINOCLE FOR MORE THAN FOUR PLAYERS is played with two 48-card pinocle packs shuffled together. Six players form two partnerships of three players each sitting alternately at the table: eight players form two partnerships of four players each sitting alternately.

The dealer gives 16 cards to each player in bundles of four each and turns up the last card dealt to himself to denote the trump suit.

The game is played in the same way as partnership pinocle, but in addition to the melds opposite, melds and the scores for them are as follows:

Triple Trump Sequence **A 10 K Q J**	3,000 points
Double Trump Sequence **A 10 K Q J**	1,500 points
Four Kings and Four Queens of the same suit	1,200 points
Three Kings and Three Queens of the same suit	600 points
Two Kings and Two Queens of the same suit	300 points
Quadruple Pinocle	1,200 points
Triple Pinocle	600 points
Double Pinocle	300 points
Fifteen Aces, Kings, Queens and Jacks	3,000 points
Twelve Aces	2,000 points
Twelve Kings	1,600 points
Twelve Queens	1,200 points
Twelve Jacks	800 points
Eight Aces	1,000 points
Eight Kings	800 points
Eight Queens	600 points
Eight Jacks	400 points

FIREHOUSE PINOCLE is played as a partnership game for four, two playing in partnership against the other two. Twelve cards are dealt to each player. As in auction pinocle the trump suit is bid for; the player on the left of the dealer bids first; each player has only one bid or pass, and the minimum bid is 200. The bidder makes the trump suit and leads to the first trick. Game is won by the partnership that first reaches 1,000 points. The score of the bidder's side is counted first, and the game is played to the end. A partnership cannot concede defeat.

CHECK PINOCLE was developed some say in Texas, out of firehouse pinocle, and is considered one of the best and most skilful of all partnership games, not excluding bridge.

The game is played by four players, two playing in partnership against the other two, with the regular 48-card pinocle pack.

Twelve cards are dealt to each player in bundles of three at a time, and each player in turn, beginning with the player on the left of the dealer, must either bid or pass. The lowest bid is 200, subsequent bids must be made in multiples of ten, and once a player has passed he may not re-enter the bidding. None of the first three players may make a bid unless he holds a marriage (King and Queen of one suit) but if all three pass the dealer must bid at least 200 and he does not need a marriage to do so; if, however, he wishes to make a higher bid than 200 he must hold one. The bidding ends when a bid has been passed by the three other players, and the bidder then names the trump suit.

The players then expose their melds on the table. The melds and the scores for them are the same as in auction pinocle (page 114) and the partners add the values of their melds together and record the total as a single score.

Some melds have what is known as a check (chip) value; a Trump Sequence (**A 10 K Q J**) and Four Aces each of a different suit are each worth 2 checks, Four Kings, Four Queens, Four Jacks each of a different suit, and Double Pinocle are all worth 1 check. Check values are paid across the table as the game procedes.

The players return the melds to their hands, and the play is the same as in partnership pinocle. When all twelve tricks have been played a partnership scores 10 points for every Ace and 10 that it has won, 5 points for every King and Queen, and 10 points if it has won the last trick.

The bidding side adds these points to those that it has already scored for its melds, and if the total is at least equal to the bid the contract has been made and the partnership scores for everything that it makes; if its total is less than its bid the amount of its bid is deducted from its score. In all cases the opposing side scores for everything that it makes.

The game is won by the partnership that first scores 1,000 points. The score of the bidding partnership is counted first, and as the game is over when it reaches 1,000 points, the opposing partnership scores nothing in the final deal.

At the end of each deal a partnership is entitled to checks on the following scale:

Contract	If Made	
200–240	2 checks	If the contract is
250–290	4 checks	defeated the
300–340	7 checks	bidding partnership
350–390	10 checks	pays double checks
400–440	13 checks	to the opposing
and 3 added checks for		partnership.
each series of 50 points.		

A partnership that wins all twelve tricks in a deal receives 4 checks; for winning the game it receives 7 checks and 1 check for each 100 points (or part thereof) by which the score of the winning partnership exceeds that of the losing partnership; and if the losing partnership has a net minus score, the winning partnership receives an additional 4 checks.

Polignac

Polignac is sometimes played as a party game with the 52-card pack. It is, however, better as a serious game for four, playing all against all, with the 32-card pack – the 6s and lower cards removed.

Eight cards are dealt face downwards to each player. The player on the left of the dealer leads to the first trick. Thereafter the player who wins a trick leads to the next. A player must follow suit to the card led, if he can, otherwise he may discard.

The object of the game is to avoid taking tricks that contain a Jack, and 1 point is lost for every Jack taken, with the exception of the Jack of Spades (Polignac) which costs the winner 2 points.

The usual method of scoring is to play a pre-arranged number of deals (that should be a multiple of four) and he who loses the least number of points is the winner.

It is a very simple game, but some skill is called for particularly in choosing the best card to lead after a trick has been won, correct discarding when unable to follow suit, and deciding whether or not to win a trick when the choice is available.

Slobberhannes

If we may judge by its name, Slobberhannes is either of Dutch or German origin. It is a very simple game that is played in exactly the same way as polignac (see above). The only difference is that a player loses 1 point if he wins the first trick, 1 point if he wins the last, 1 point if he wins the trick containing the Queen of Clubs, and a further 1 point (making 4 points in all) if he wins all three tricks.

Solo Whist

Solo Whist, more commonly called Solo, is one of the classical games for four players. It is played with the full pack of fifty-two cards. Thirteen cards are dealt to each player in three bundles of three cards each, and the last four cards singly. The dealer turns up the last card to indicate the trump suit.

Each player in turn, beginning with the player on the left of the dealer, must either pass or make a bid. The bids (declarations) are:

Proposal. The player who makes a Proposal asks for a partner with the object of making eight tricks in partnership with him against the other two players. In turn, any other player may Accept, and the two play as partners from the seats in which they are sitting. The declaration of Proposal and Acceptance is usually called Prop and Cop.

Solo is a declaration to win five tricks against the other three players.

Misère is a declaration to lose all thirteen tricks. The hand is played without a trump suit.

Abundance is a declaration to win nine tricks against the other three players; the declarer chooses his own trump suit. A player who wishes to play abundance with the turned-up suit as trumps may overcall with Royal Abundance, but the stake value of the bid remains unchanged.

Open Misère is a declaration to lose every trick, and after the first trick has been played with his cards exposed on the table in front of him. There is no trump suit.

Declared Abundance is a declaration to win all thirteen tricks with a trump suit of his own choice.

Every bid must be higher than the previous one, and with the exception of the player on the left of the dealer, who may accept a proposal after passing, no player may re-enter the bidding once he has passed. The bidding ends when a bid has been passed by the other three players.

If the final bid is Declared Abundance, the declarer leads to the first trick. Against any other declaration the opening lead is made by the player on the left of the dealer. The play follows the general principles of trick-taking games: a player must follow suit if he is able to, otherwise he may either discard or trump, and the winner of a trick leads to the next.

Stakes are scaled to the value of the bids:

Proposal and Acceptance = 2 units *   Abundance = 4 units
Solo = 2 units   Open Misère = 6 units
Misère = 3 units   Declared Abundance =
                                                      8 units

---

*Proposal and Acceptance does not carry equivalent stakes to Solo because they are paid by and received from two players, whereas in Solo (and higher declarations) they are paid to and received from three players.

Solo is a combination of whist and nap(oleon). It is a fairly simple game, and by far the simplest of the declarations is Proposal and Acceptance. As no player will propose without some strength in trumps, the partnership hardly ever fails to make eight tricks. It is a notoriously dull contract, therefore, and most modern players reject it.

The declaration of Solo is another that is-fairly easy to win, though it must never be forgotten that the player has to compete against three. It is unwise to bid Solo without a good trump suit, and the dealer is in the ideal position to bid it with success because he plays last to the first trick: it gives him the best chance to win it and make an immediate attack on the trump suit.

Misère is not such an easy declaration as it may seem. A 5-card suit, unless it contains the 2, is likely to spell defeat. If a player holds **7 6 5 4 3** of a suit he will usually be defeated if another holds four of the suit including the 2.

Abundance should not be attempted without a very good trump suit, and Declared Abundance is best avoided by any except an experienced player.

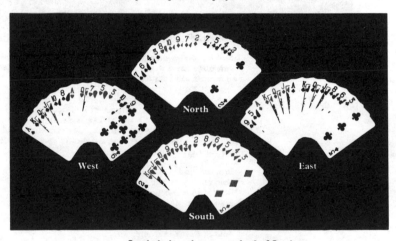

North

West

East

South

South deals and turns up the 2 of Spades.

West	North	East	South
Solo	Misère	Abundance	Open Misère
Pass	Pass	Pass	

West's Solo is the obviously correct bid. He cannot fail to win less than five tricks and it is too much to expect the Hearts to develop three tricks to make Abundance a good call.

North's Misère is optimistic. Had he been left to play it, the opening lead of a Heart would have broken him out of hand.

East's Abundance is a certainty with eleven tricks (and him needing only nine) for the taking of them.

South's Open Misère is not to be advised. As already pointed out a 5-card suit missing the 2 is a danger spot. As it happens it is the Heart suit that proves his downfall.

West leads the 10 of Clubs, and the play is:

West	North	East	South
10 ♣	7 ♣	J ♣	K ♥
9 ♣	5 ♣	A ♣	J ♥
A ♠	4 ♣	3 ♣	10 ♥
A ♥	8 ♥	A ♦	6 ♥

The position is down to:

South is doomed because West wins the 7 ♥ and 5 ♥ (on which South plays the 4 ♥ and 2 ♥) and continues with the 3 ♥ which South must win with the 9 ♥.

As solo is limited to a mere handful of declarations, the variation known as **AUCTION SOLO** is much to be preferred, because it permits of a larger number of declarations and, therefore, makes a more interesting and skilful game. In ascending order the declarations are:

Proposal and Acceptance.
Solo of Five in own suit.
Solo of Five in trump suit.
Solo of Six in own suit.
Solo of Six in trump suit.
Solo of Seven in own suit.
Solo of Seven in trump suit.
Solo of Eight in own suit.
Solo of Eight in trump suit.
Misère.
Abundance of Nine in own suit.
Abundance of Nine in trump suit.
Abundance of Ten in own suit.
Abundance of Ten in trump suit.
Abundance of Eleven in own suit.
Abundance of Eleven in trump suit.
Abundance of Twelve in own suit.
Abundance of Twelve in trump suit.
Open Misère.
Declared Abundance with no trump suit (bidder has the lead).
Declared Abundance in the original trump suit (bidder does not have the lead).

Such, at least, are the declarations in the original version of the game, but modern players do not recognize all of them. Proposal and Acceptance are nearly always omitted, so also are Solo of Five in own suit, and Declared Abundance in the original trump suit.

Once the players have agreed on which declarations are admissible and which not, the game is played in the same way as the parent game.

Settlement is made in the following way:

Proposal and Acceptance
> For success: receive 6 units each plus 1 unit for each overtrick.
> For failure: pay 6 units each plus 1 unit for each undertrick.

Solo
> For success: receive 6 units from each player plus 3 units for each overtrick.
> For failure: pay 6 units to each player plus 3 units for each undertrick.

Misère
> For success: receive 12 units from each player.
> For failure: pay 12 units to each player.

Abundance
> For success: receive 18 units from each player plus 3 units for each overtrick.
> For failure: pay 18 units to each player plus 3 units for each undertrick.

Open Misère
> For success: receive 24 units from each player.
> For failure: pay 24 units to each player.

Declared Abundance
> For success: receive 36 units from each player.
> For failure: pay 36 units to each player.

The stake-values of Solo and Abundance are unchanged whether the contract is for five, six, seven or eight, or nine, ten, eleven or twelve tricks, overtricks and undertricks count from the number of tricks that are contracted for.

The method of scoring appears to encourage underbidding. In practice, however, it is not so and as first bidder a player would be well advised to declare his full strength at once, especially if his hand is worth no more than six tricks. With six tricks in a plain suit a player should bid it at once, no matter what his position at the table, but if the tricks are in the original trump suit it is reasonable to bid only a Solo of Five: he may get away with it, and, if not, a Solo of Six in the trump suit will overcall an opponent's Six in a plain suit. The penultimate player should make it a rule always to bid his hand to the limit; if he does not the last player will and then there may be no second chance.

Whist

Whist developed out of the sixteenth-century game of triumph. At first its practice was confined to the lower classes, but in 1718 it was taken up by a party of gentlemen, Lord Folkestone among them, who met at the famous Crown Coffee House, and they, with the help of Edmond Hoyle, introduced the game to fashionable society. At this time the game was known as whisk: soon after it was changed to whist in order to underline the silence in which it was proper to play the game.

During the eighteenth and nineteenth centuries it was by far the most popular card game of the English-speaking nations, but at the close of the nineteenth-century it lost much of its popularity due to the introduction of bridge (see page 83). It is, however, still extensively played.

In principle whist is a very simple game, played by four players, two playing in partnership against the other two. The partners sit facing each other. Thirteen cards are dealt singly to each person, and the dealer exposes the last card to denote the trump suit. He takes it into his hand after he has played to the first trick.

The player on the left of the dealer leads to the first trick. Thereafter the player who wins a trick leads to the next. A player must follow suit to the card led if he can, if not he may either discard or trump.

The object of the game is to win a rubber (best out of three games), and a game is won when one side has won 5 points. The first six tricks (the book) do not count for scoring: a side scores 1 point for each trick that it wins over six. The Ace, King, Queen and Jack of the trump suit are known as honours, and any side that is dealt all four of them scores 4 points, and any three 2 points. If, however, at the beginning of a deal a side has a score of 4 points it cannot score for honours.

The deal passes in a clockwise rotation.

Skill at whist is largely a matter of playing in close collaboration with one's partner, and estimating from the cards held and those that have been played, the most likely position of those that remain to be played.

To this end, there are a number of recognized plays which should be departed from only under special circumstances, to be learnt by experience. It is, for example, good tactics for second player to play low and third high; a player should not finesse against his partner; and if an opponent plays an honour it is usually profitable to play a higher honour on it.

A player who holds five or more trumps in his hand should make it a rule to lead one; and if a player fails to lead a trump and wishes his partner to do so, he calls for the lead of one by first playing an unnecessarily high card in a suit and following it with a low card in the same suit.

The lead is a good opportunity for a player to give his partner information about his hand, and the leads listed in the table opposite are standard practice and should be known to all players.

In plain suits:

Holding	1st Lead	2nd Lead
A K Q J	**K**	**J**
A K Q	**K**	**Q**
A K x and more	**K**	**A**
A K	**A**	**K**
K Q J x	**K**	**J**
K Q J x x	**J**	**K**
K Q J x x x and more	**J**	**Q**
A x x x and more	**A**	4th best of remainder
K Q x and more	**K**	4th best of remainder
A Q J	**A**	**Q**
A Q J x	**A**	**Q**
A Q J x x and more	**A**	**J**
K J 10 9	**9**	**K** (if **A** or **Q** falls)
Q J x	**Q**	
Q J x x and more	4th best	

In the trump suit:

Holding	1st Lead	2nd Lead
A K Q J	**J**	**Q**
A K Q	**Q**	**K**
A K x x x x x and more	**K**	**A**
A K x x x x	4th best	

Lacking any of these combinations the fourth highest of the longest suit should be led.

In the deal below the mechanics of the game are illustrated.

South deals and turns up the 4 of Spades to denote trumps. West leads the 5 of Diamonds, and the play is:

West	North	East	South
5 ♦	J ♦	A ♦	3 ♦

West leads the fourth highest of his longest suit, commonly called fourth-best. East wins with the A ♦. It would be finessing against his partner if he played the Q ♦. In the event it makes no difference, because East has no better play than to return his partner's suit, and it is proper to lead the highest from an original holding of three.

2 ♦	7 ♦	Q ♦	K ♦

South, therefore, wins the second trick, instead of the first, with the K ♦

West	North	East	South
5 ♣	3 ♣	A ♣	K ♣
8 ♣	6 ♣	7 ♣	Q ♣

East has no better lead than the 7 ♣. He knows that South holds the Q ♣, because without it South would not have led the K ♣ at the previous trick, but it offers a chance of trumping if West can take the lead early in the play.

10 ♦	5 ♠	4 ♦	9 ♦
6 ♠	A ♠	3 ♠	2 ♠
10 ♠	K ♠	8 ♠	4 ♠
J ♣	9 ♣	2 ♥	2 ♣

North has no better lead than the 9 ♣.

8 ♦	3 ♥	J ♠	4 ♣
6 ♦	7 ♠	Q ♠	9 ♠

East pulls the remaining trumps.

K ♥	A ♥	J ♥	Q ♥

The end position has come down to:

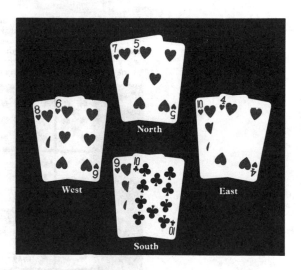

North

West

East

South

It is North's lead. North and South have won six tricks, East and West five tricks. North, therefore, leads the 5 ♥. If East wins with the 10 ♥ his side will win the odd trick as West will win the last trick with the 8 ♥. North's only hope is that East will make the mistake of playing the 4 ♥, because then South will win with the 9 ♥ and the last trick with the 10 ♣.

6 ♥	5 ♥	10 ♥	9 ♥

East makes no mistake.

8 ♥	7 ♥	4 ♥	10 ♣

East and West, therefore, have won the odd trick and score 1 point. There is no score for honours as both sides held two.

Brag

Brag is almost certainly the ancestor of poker (see page 133) and itself probably derived from the Spanish game of primero, the popular card game of Tudor England and, so far as we can trace, the first card game to be played scientifically in this country.

The game is played with the full 52-card pack, and by any number of players from five to eight. The general principle of the game is quite simple. The players stake on the respective merits of their cards, and the best hand is determined by certain arbitrary rules. Bluffing is an important feature of the game. The Ace of Diamonds, Jack of Clubs and 9 of Diamonds are known as braggers, and rank as Jokers or wild cards.

In **SINGLE-STAKE BRAG** the dealer puts up a stake to the agreed limit, and deals three cards face downwards to each player. In turn, beginning with the player on the left of the dealer, each player must either drop out of the game for the round in progress, or put up a stake at least equal to that of the dealer's. If he chooses he may raise the stake, in which event, any player coming into the

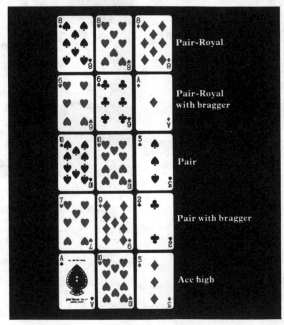

Pair-Royal

Pair-Royal with bragger

Pair

Pair with bragger

Ace high

The classes of brag hands, the highest at the top

game, or already in the game, must raise his bet to as much as the highest individual stake, or drop out of the game and lose what he has already staked. If no-one meets the dealer's stake he withdraws it, and receives an agreed amount from the other players. The deal then passes to the next player.

Unlike at poker, there is no discarding and drawing more cards. When all those who wish to play have raised their bets to an equal amount, the cards are shown and the player with the best hand collects all the stakes.

Flushes and sequences are of no value. The best hand is a Pair-Royal; it consists of three cards of equal rank (the Aces high the 2s low) and a hand of three natural cards takes precedence over one with braggers. The next best hand is a Pair, with a preference for a natural pair over one with a bragger, and if two players have equal pairs the one with the higher third card wins. If no player holds either a Pair-Royal or a Pair, the player with the highest single card wins and if two players hold exactly equal hands the winner is he who was first to stake.

In **THREE-STAKE BRAG** the game begins by each player putting up three separate stakes; the dealer then deals two cards face downwards and one card face upwards to each player.

The first stake is won by the player who is dealt the highest face-upwards card. For this round of the game the braggers take their normal position in the pack, and if two or more players are dealt cards of equal rank, precedence is determined as in the single-stake game.

The hand is next played as in single-stake, and the winner takes the second stake. If no-one bets, the hands are exposed and the highest hand wins.

Finally, the players expose their cards and the third stake is won by the player whose cards most nearly total 31 (over or under) the Aces counting 11, the court cards 10 each and the other cards at their pip values. A player whose hand totals less than 31 may draw a card from the remainder of the pack, but if his total then exceeds 31 he automatically loses the game.

Coon Can

In the U.S.A. Coon Can is known as Double Rum. It is no bad name for it because it is a variation of rummy (see page 139) played with two packs of cards shuffled together with two Jokers.

The game may be played by any number of players up to eight; each plays for himself.

Ten cards are dealt face downwards to each player. The rest of the pack (the stock) is placed face downwards in the centre of the table, and the top card of it is turned face upwards and placed alongside it to start the discard pile.

The object of the game is to get rid of all the cards held, by melding them face upwards on the table, either in sets of three or more of the same rank, or in sequences of three or more of the same suit, the Ace either high or low but not round-the-corner. A Joker may be used to represent any card that the holder chooses.

Each player, beginning with the one on the left of the dealer, plays in turn. He is under no obligation to meld, but he must take into his hand either the top card of the stock or the top card of the discard pile, and discard a card to reduce his hand to ten cards. If he chooses to meld he must do so between drawing a card and discarding one, and as well as melding, at the same time, he may add cards to melds that he has already made, and to those of his opponents.

A Joker may be moved from one end of a meld to the other, provided the player has the natural card to replace it. If, for example, a sequence is: **6 ♠ 7 ♠ 8 ♠ Joker**, a player who holds a **9 ♠** may play it in room of the Joker and transfer the Joker to represent the **5 ♠**. Once moved, however, a Joker cannot be moved a second time and a player who holds a **5 ♠** cannot play it in room of the Joker and place the Joker elsewhere. Nor can a Joker be moved if it is in the interior of a sequence, as in **4 ♠ 5 ♠ 6 ♠ Joker 8 ♠**. The Joker cannot be replaced by a **7 ♠**. When a Joker cannot be moved it is customary to place it cross-wise, as a reminder to the other players.

The game is won by the player who is first to meld all his cards. The remaining players pay him the same number of units as the pip value of the unmelded cards left in their hands—a Joker counting 15, an Ace 11, the court cards 10 each, and all other cards their pip values.

Rarely it happens that the stock will be exhausted before the game has been won. In this event the game continues and the players draw cards from the discard pile, discarding a different card to that drawn. If this proves insufficient to finish the game, the pip values of the hands are counted and placed into a pool to be scored by the winner of the next hand.

Napoleon

Napoleon, usually called Nap, is one of the simplest of all card games. It is played with the full pack of fifty-two cards, by any number of players up to six, each playing for himself.

Each player is dealt five cards, and, beginning with the player on the left of the dealer, every player in turn must either pass or declare to win a specified number of tricks in the ascending order: Two, Three, Four and Nap (a declaration to win all five tricks).

The player who has contracted to win most tricks leads to the first trick and the card that he leads determines the trump suit. Play follows the usual routine of trick-taking games: a player must follow suit if he can, otherwise he may discard or trump, and the player who wins a trick leads to the next.

Stakes are paid only on the number of tricks contracted for. Those won above, or lost below, the number contracted for are ignored. The usual method of settlement is by means of a level-money transaction:

Declaration	Declarer wins	Declarer loses
Two	2 units	2 units
Three	3 units	3 units
Four	4 units	4 units
Nap	10 units	5 units

Payment is made to, and received from, all players at the table.

Nap(oleon) is such an elementary game that in some circles interest is added to it by introducing a number of extraordinary declarations:

Misery is a declaration to lose every trick. It ranks between the declaration of Three and Four, and though normally it is played without a trump suit, some play it with a trump suit, determined as in the parent game by the opening lead. It pays and wins 3 units.

Wellington is a declaration to win all five tricks at double stakes. It cannot be declared, however, except over a declaration of Nap.

Blücher is a declaration to win all five tricks at triple stakes. It cannot be declared, however, except over a declaration of Wellington.

Peep Nap sanctions the player who has declared Nap (or Wellington or Blücher if these declarations are permitted) to exchange the top card of the pack for a card in his own hand.

Purchase Nap sanctions each player before declaring to exchange any number of cards in his hand for fresh cards, by paying into a pool 1 unit for every card exchanged. The pool is carried forward from deal to deal and taken by the first player to win Nap (or Wellington or Blücher if these declarations are permitted).

SEVEN-CARD NAPOLEON is a variation of the parent game in which seven cards are dealt to each player, and a player cannot contract to win less than three tricks. There is no Wellington and no Blücher. Misery is optional and, if permitted, ranks between Nap and Six.

Apart from these amendments, the game is played in the same way as the parent game.

Settlement is made as follows:

Declaration	Declarer wins	Declarer loses
Three	3 units	3 units
Four	4 units	4 units
Nap (five tricks)	10 units	5 units
Misery (if played)	10 units	5 units
Six	18 units	9 units
Seven	28 units	14 units

Payment is made to, and received from, all players at the table

Poker

Poker is not a difficult game to learn, but by no means an easy one to play well because skill at the game is born only of experience coupled with some knowledge of arithmetic. Fundamentally, poker is a game of calculating chances.

The parent game, commonly called straight poker, but more correctly straight draw poker, is played with the 52-card pack by any reasonable number of players: five, six or seven is considered the ideal number.

Each player is dealt five cards face downwards, and the object of the game is to make the best hand by an exchange of cards, and then bet on it against the other players.

The cards rank in the order from Ace high to 2 low, suits are equal and in ascending order the nine classes of poker hands, together with the approximate odds against their being dealt to a player, are:

Highest Card: any five odd cards. Evens.

One Pair: two cards of the same rank and three odd cards. 15 to 11.

Two pairs: two cards of the same rank, two other cards of the same rank and an odd card. 20 to 1.

Threes: three cards of the same rank and two odd cards. 46 to 1.

Straight: any five cards in sequence, not of the same suit; An Ace may be either high or low. 254 to 1.

Flush: any five cards of the same suit. 508 to 1.

Full House: three cards of the same rank and two other cards of the same rank. 693 to 1.

Fours: four cards of the same rank and an odd card. 4,164 to 1.

Straight Flush: a sequence of five cards all of the same suit: an Ace may be either high or low. 64,973 to 1.

Examples of each hand are illustrated. They are valued on the highest combination, and if the combination of two or more players is equal, by the highest odd card. In the event of two or more players holding exactly equal hands the stakes are divided.

The player on the left of the dealer begins the game by putting up an agreed amount, known as the ante. For convenience we will assume that it is 1 chip. The player on his left then puts up a straddle of 2 chips.*

The dealer now deals, face downwards, to each player five cards. After looking at his cards, the player on the left of the straddle has the option of playing or not. If he decides not to play he throws his cards face downwards towards the centre of the table, and takes no further interest in the deal in progress. If he decides to play he puts up 4 chips. The player on his left now has the choice of

---

* Throughout the game every player puts his chips on the table in front of him.

The classes of poker
hand, the highest at
the bottom. The
numbers of possible
ways in which each
hand can be made up
are as follows:
highest card:
          1,302,540
one pair: 1,098,240
two pairs: 123,552
threes: 54,912
straight: 10,200
flush: 5,108
full house: 3,744
fours: 624
straight flush: 40

throwing in his hand, coming into the game for 4 chips, or doubling (*i.e.* coming into the game for 8 chips). In the same way, in turn, every player has the choice of throwing in his hand, coming into the game, for the same stake as the previous player, or raising the stakes until the agreed maximum is reached.

When staking reaches the ante and straddle, they can either throw in their hands and sacrifice what they have already put up, or come into the game by raising their stakes to the appropriate amount.

If no player comes into the game, the straddle recovers his 2 chips and takes the 1 chip put up by the ante.

Staking continues for some little time, because if a player has come into the game and a subsequent player has doubled, it is open to those who have already staked to increase their stakes, and this progressive staking continues until no-one increases the stakes or the agreed limit is reached.

When all have staked, those left in the game have the chance to improve their hands by exchanging cards. The dealer ignores those who have already thrown in their hands, but gives all the other players in turn as many cards as they wish after they have discarded those cards that they do not wish to retain. A player may discard any number of his cards, but no experienced player would remain in the game to exchange four cards, and only one who has taken leave of his senses will do so to exchange all five cards. Most players will exchange one, two, or three cards.

When cards have been exchanged, the player who was first to come in begins the betting. Either he throws in his hand (sacrificing the stake he has already made to come in) checks (signifies his intention to remain in the game without increasing his stake) or raises (increases his stake to any amount up to the agreed limit).

If he checks, all the players who follow him have, in their turn, the same choice. If no-one raises those left in the game show their cards and the player with the best hand takes all that has been staked. If a player raises, the subsequent players, in turn, have the option of throwing in their hands, putting up sufficient chips to meet the raise, or raise still further.

In this way the betting continues until the final bet is either called or not. If the final bet is called, the players left in the game show their cards and the player with the best hand wins all that has been staked: if the final bet is not called, the player whose bet has not been called wins all that has been staked with no need to show his hand.

Poker falls naturally into two parts: the staking and the betting. The staking is the easier part of the game because it is open to a precise arithmetical analysis. We may suppose that a player is dealt:

$$10 \spadesuit \quad 6 \spadesuit \quad 5 \spadesuit \quad 2 \spadesuit \quad 9 \heartsuit$$

Since a pair of 10s is of small value, the player's aim must be to discard the 9 of Hearts hoping to draw a Spade to fill the flush.

There are 47 cards from which to draw, and of them only 9 are Spades, the other 38 are non-Spades. It follows, therefore, that the odds against drawing a Spade are 38 to 9, or approximately $4\frac{1}{4}$ to 1. If three players have come into the game with 4 chips each, making 15 chips on the table with the ante and straddle, it is not worth while playing because it costs 4 chips to come in so that the table is offering odds of 15 to 4 ($3\frac{3}{4}$ to 1) and the chance of improving is $4\frac{1}{4}$ to 1. If, however, four players have come in it will be just worth while coming into the game, because now there will be 19 chips on the table so that the table is offering odds of $4\frac{3}{4}$ to 1, which is better than the odds against improving.

Poker players should study very carefully the mathematical chances, because the whole theory of staking may be summed up by asking oneself two questions: What are the chances of improving my hand? What odds are the table laying me? Then, if the answer to the first question is greater than to the second the player should come in, if it is not he should throw in his hand.

The betting is the more difficult part of the game because it is largely psychology. At the same time, a player has to be gifted with the quality that we call judgement because his betting must be dictated by the manner in which the other players are betting, and how they, on their part, will interpret his betting. Particular note should be taken of the number of cards drawn by each of the other players and deductions drawn from the information gained. The subsequent betting should go a long way towards confirming whether the deductions are correct or not, and whether the player has improved on the draw.

A good poker player is inscrutable and unpredictable, because he varies his game to make the most with his good hands and lose the least with his bad ones. He profits by the advice of Saint Matthew—'let not thy left hand know what thy right hand doeth'—and he is always imperturbable, because there is no future in gloating over a win and wailing over a loss. If he thinks that he holds the best hand he bets on it boldly: if he thinks that he is beaten he throws in his cards and cuts his losses.

Pot-Deals, commonly called Pots, are widely played, and are an important feature of all variations of the game. When a pot is played there is no ante and no straddle; instead every player contributes an agreed amount to a pot, or pool, that is independent of the staking and betting. The player on the immediate left of the dealer has first decision whether to open the game by staking or not. If he does not open, the option passes to the player on his left, and so on.

The essence of a pot is that a player is debarred from opening the game, by putting up a stake, unless his hand qualifies him to do so by a pre-arranged standard. If no player opens, the deal passes, and the players sweeten the pot, by adding to it, for the next deal. If the pot is opened, other players may come in even if their hands are below standard, and he who wins the deal also wins the amount in the pot as well as all the stakes put up by the other players. The player who opened the game must show that his hand qualified for opening.

In a *Jackpot* a player must have a pair of Jacks, or better, to qualify for opening.

In a *Progressive Jackpot*, if no-one opens the first deal, the second deal is a Queenpot, and if no-one opens it the next is a King-pot, and so on. Some stop at Acepots, others continue to two pairs before beginning again at a Jackpot if no-one has opened the game.

In a *Freak Pot*, sometimes called Deuces Wild, all the 2s are wild cards and may be used to represent any cards that the holder chooses. Fives (five cards of the same rank) is now a possible hand, and it is classed above a straight flush, but is beaten if the straight flush is headed by an Ace.

In a *Double Pot*, or Legs, any type of pot is chosen, but a player must win it twice before he may take his winnings.

WILD WIDOW is a variation of the parent game, but, after four cards have been dealt to each player, a card is turned face upwards in the centre of the table and is left there for the duration of the deal. The dealer then gives each player one more card, and the game is played with the three other cards of the same rank as the exposed card wild.

In **SPIT IN THE OCEAN** only four cards are dealt to each player. A card is then dealt face upwards in the centre of the table. Each player considers this card as the fifth card of his hand. It is a wild card, as also are the other three cards of the same rank.

STUD POKER is a variation of the parent game the main feature of which is that some of the cards are dealt face upwards and some face downwards. There are several ways of playing the game.

In *Five-card Stud* there is no ante unless agreed on. The dealer gives each player a card face downwards (it is known as the hole card) and then a card face upwards. The deal is then interrupted for a betting interval. After the betting interval the dealer gives each active player another three cards face upwards, and after each there is a betting interval. If two or more players remain in the game after the last betting interval, they turn up their hole cards and the player with the best hand wins.

Each betting interval begins with the player who holds the best combination of cards exposed, and if two or more players have equal combination the one nearest to the dealer's left bets first. At the first betting interval the player who opens must make a bet; at subsequent intervals he may check. Any player who drops out of the game must turn his exposed cards face downwards.

Seven-card Stud, sometimes called Down the River, or Peek Poker, is played in the same way as five-card stud, except that the dealer first deals to each player two cards face downwards and one card face upwards. There is a betting interval, and, after this, the active players are dealt three cards face upwards and one face downwards, with the deal interrupted for a betting interval after each round of dealing. At the showdown, a player exposes his hole cards and selects five of his seven cards to form his hand.

WHISKY POKER is so called because it was originally played in the American lumber camps to decide who should pay for the drinks.

Every player contributes an agreed amount to a pool. The dealer deals an extra hand (widow) to the centre of the table, immediately before dealing cards to himself. The player on the left of the dealer, after looking at his cards, may either exchange his hand for the widow, pass (in which case the option of taking the widow passes to his left-hand neighbour) or indicates, by knocking the table, that he will play with the cards dealt to him.

If the player on the left of the dealer (or any subsequent player) takes the widow, he puts his own cards face upwards on the table as a new widow. The player on his left may now either take the whole of the exposed widow in exchange for his own hand, take one or more cards from it in exchange for cards in his hand, or knock. A player, however, cannot draw cards from the widow and knock at the same turn, and the option to exchange the widow or cards with it, continues until a player knocks. As soon as a player does so, the remaining players have one turn each to exchange their hands or cards for it. After the player on the right of the knocker has had his turn, the players expose their cards and the best hand wins the pot.

If no-one takes the widow before it is the turn of the dealer, he must either take the widow or turn it face upwards on the table. Even if he decides to knock, without making an exchange, he must still turn up the widow.

In **KNOCK POKER** every player puts up an ante. The dealer gives every player five cards, as in the parent game, and the rest of the pack (the stock) is placed face downwards in the centre of the table. The player on the left of the dealer draws the top card of the stock and discards a card from his hand. Thereafter each player in turn draws either the top card of the stock or the top card of the discard pile, and discards a card from his hand.

At any time after drawing a card and before discarding one, a player may knock the table. He then discards a card from his hand. The other players have one more turn each to draw and discard a card, or drop out of the game by paying the knocker the amount of the ante. After the player on the right of the knocker has drawn and discarded, or dropped out of the game, all players remaining in the game show their cards and settlement is made as follows:

1. If the knocker has the best hand, all who are in the game pay him twice the ante.
2. If the knocker and one or more other players have equal hands they divide the winnings except for the amount paid to the knocker by those who dropped out of the game.
3. If the knocker does not have the best hand he pays twice the ante to every player remaining in the game, and the player with the best hand wins the antes.

HIGH-LOW POKER. Any variation of poker may be played high-low. As a rule the hand is played as a pot. The player plays his hand for either high or low, but does not have to announce which until the last card is dealt. The highest and the lowest hands divide the pot between them. An Ace is always high and cannot be counted as a low card except as part of a sequence in the high hand.

In **STRIP POKER** the dealer deals five cards, face downwards, to each player. There is no ante and no straddle. After an exchange of cards (as in the parent game) the players expose their cards and the one with the worst poker hand pays the table by removing an article of clothing.

The game, with all its voluptuous prospects, is said to be at its best in mixed company during a heat wave!

Rummy

Rummy, the name is frequently truncated to Rum, is one of the most popular of all card games. It is played with the full 52-card pack, and is suitable for any number of players up to five or six, each playing for himself. More than six players should prefer coon can (see page 130) or the variation known as continental rummy.

Ten cards are dealt to each player if only two play; seven cards if three or four play; and six cards if five or six play. The rest of the pack (the stock) is placed face downwards in the centre of the table, and the top card of it is turned face upwards and laid alongside it to start the discard pile.

Each player in turn, beginning with the one on the left of the dealer, must take into his hand either the top card of the stock or the top card of the discard pile, and discard a card from his hand, but if he has drawn the top card of the discard pile he must not discard it in the same turn.

The object of the game is to make sets of three or more cards of the same rank, or sequences of three or more cards of the same suit (the Ace being low) and declare them by exposing them on the table, after drawing a card from the stock or discard pile and before discarding a card from the hand. At the same time a player may add one or more proper cards to sequences and sets already declared either by himself or the other players.

If the stock is exhausted before any player declares all his hand, the discard pile is turned face downwards and becomes the stock.

The player who is first to declare all his cards wins the hand, and the other players pay him for every court card left in their hands 10 points each, for every Ace 1 point, and for every other card its pip value. If a player declares all his cards in one turn he scores rummy and is paid double.

Rummy is a very simple game that has lent itself to a number of improvements.

In **BOATHOUSE RUMMY** a player may draw the top card of the stock; or he may draw the top card of the discard pile and then either the top card of the stock or the next card of the discard pile. He may, however, discard only one card from his hand.

In a sequence the Ace may be either high, low, or round the corner.

The play does not come to an end until a player can declare his entire hand in one turn.

A losing player pays only for the unmatched cards in his hand, but Aces are paid for at 11 points each.

CONTINENTAL RUMMY is a variation of the parent game that is suitable for any number of players up to twelve. If two to five play two packs with two Jokers are used; if six to eight play three packs with three Jokers are used; and if nine to twelve play four packs with four Jokers are used.

Each player receives fifteen cards. A player may not declare until all fifteen of his cards are melded either in five 3-card sequences, or in three 4-card sequences and one 3-card sequence, or in one 5-card, one 4-card and two 3-card sequences. Sets of three or more cards of the same rank are of no value. A Joker may be used to represent any card. The Ace may be high or low, but not round the corner.

There are many ways of scoring, but generally the winner collects from all the other players 1 unit from each for winning, and 2 units from each for every Joker in his hand.

GAMBLER'S RUMMY is so called because it is the variation of the parent game that is most frequently played for high stakes.

Only four players take part and each is dealt seven cards. The Ace is low and, as in the parent game, counts only 1 point in the settlement. A player is not allowed to declare all his hand in one turn. He must declare it in at least two turns, but he is not debarred from going out second turn even if on his previous turn he played off only one card on another player's declaration.

The stock is gone through only once. When it is exhausted the players must draw the top card of the discard pile, and the game ends when a player refuses it.

KNOCK RUMMY, or Poker Rum, is played in the same way as the parent game, but a player does not declare his sequences and sets by exposing them on the table. Instead, after drawing a card, he knocks on the table, and then discards. Play comes to an end. The players separate their matched cards from their un-matched ones, and each announces the count of his unmatched cards, as reckoned in the parent game. The player with the lowest count wins the difference in counts from all the other players. If a player ties with the knocker for the lowest count he wins over the knocker. If the knocker does not have the lowest count he pays a penalty of an extra 10 points to the player with the lowest count. If the knocker goes rummy (has all his cards matched when he knocks) and wins, he receives an extra 25 points from all the other players.

Stock — Discard pile

The player should take the 5 ♠ and discard 9 ♣, as 5 ♠ offers alternative chances of melding: either with 5 ♥ or 6 ♠

Scotch Whist

Scotch Whist, sometimes called Catch the Ten because one of the objects of the game is to win the trick that contains the 10 of the trump suit, is played with a pack of thirty-six cards. The 2s, 3s, 4s, and 5s are removed from the standard pack. The cards rank from Ace (high) to 6 (low) with the exception that the Jack of the trump suit is promoted above the Ace.

The game is suitable for any number of players from two to eight, but, as every player must begin with the same number of cards, if five or seven players take part the 6 of Spades is removed from the pack, and if eight take part all four 6s are. If two, five or seven play, each plays for himself. If four, six or eight play they may either play each for himself, or form into partnerships.

Dealing varies with the number of players taking part in the game. If two play each receives eighteen cards that are dealt in three separate hands of six cards each, to be played independently; if three play each receives twelve cards that are dealt in two separate hands of six cards each, to be played independently; if four or more play the cards are dealt in the normal clockwise rotation. In every case the dealer turns up the last card to indicate the trump suit.

The player on the left of the dealer leads to the first trick. Thereafter the player who wins a trick leads to the next. Play follows the usual routine of trick-taking games: a player must follow suit, if he can, to the suit led, if he cannot he may either trump the trick or discard on it.

The object of the game is to win tricks containing the five top trump cards, and the player, or partnership, that does scores 11 points for the Jack, 4 points for the Ace, 3 points for the King, 2 points for the Queen, and 10 points for the Ten. Over and above this, each player, or partnership, counts the number of cards taken in tricks, and scores 1 point for every card more than the number originally dealt to him, or it.

The game ends when a player, or partnership, has reached an agreed total, usually 41 points.

It stands out that a player must direct his play towards winning tricks that contain the top cards of the trump suit, particularly that which contains the 10, since the Jack can only go to the player to whom it has been dealt, and usually the luck of the deal determines who will win the tricks that contain the Ace, King and Queen.

In a partnership game the player who has been dealt the 10, either singleton or doubleton, would be well advised to lead it. It gives a good score if his partner is able to win with the Jack; if an opponent wins the trick the partnership must hope to recover by aiming to win as many tricks as possible. If the game is being played all against all, the player who has been dealt the 10 should try and get rid of all the cards in his shortest suit, so that he can win the 10 by trumping with it.

Spoil Five

Spoil Five, sometimes called Forty-five, is an excellent game for any reasonable number of players, but is best for five or six, as it calls for some show of skill.

It is played with the full pack of fifty-two cards, but that it is rarely, if ever, played outside its native Ireland may be ascribed to the eccentric order of the cards. The 5 of the trump suit is always the highest trump, the Jack of the trump suit is the second highest, and the Ace of Hearts the third highest. Thereafter, if a black suit is trumps the cards rank in the order **A K Q 2 3 4 6 7 8 9 10** and if a red suit is trumps in the order **A** (if Diamonds are trumps) **K Q 10 9 8 7 6 4 3 2**. In plain suits, the black suits rank in the order **K Q J A 2 3 4 5 6 7 8 9 10**; the red suits in the order **K Q J 10 9 8 7 6 5 4 3 2 A** (except in Hearts). It is concisely expressed as 'highest in red; lowest in black', but even with this help it is all rather involved.

Five cards are dealt to each player either in bundles of two then three, or three then two. The next card is exposed to determine the trump suit. A pool is formed to which every player contributes an agreed amount, and it is usual to fix a maximum and, after the first deal, only the player whose turn it is to deal contributes to the pool.

The object of the game is to win three tricks, and, at the same time, prevent another player from winning them.

The player who wins three tricks takes the pool; and if no-one wins three tricks (a spoil) the deal passes to the next player. When a player has won three tricks the hand ends and the deal passes, unless the player who has won them declares 'Jinx'. It is an undertaking to win the remaining two tricks. Play then continues and if he fails to win the two tricks he loses the pool; on the other hand, if he wins the two tricks not only does he take the pool but the other players each pay him the amount that they originally contributed to the pool.

The player on the left of the dealer leads to the first trick. Thereafter the winner of a trick leads to the next. The rules of play are precise and peculiar to the game:

1. If the card turned up to denote the trump suit is an Ace, the dealer may rob. He may, that is, exchange the Ace for a card in his hand, but he must do so before the player on his left leads to the first trick.

2. Any player who has been dealt the Ace of the trump suit may exchange any card in his hand for the turn-up card, but he need not do so until it is his turn to play.

3. If a trump is led a player must follow suit if he can, but the 5 and Jack of the trump suit and the Ace of Hearts are exempt from following suit to the lead of a lower trump. It is called reneging. It means that the 5 of the trump suit need not be played if the Jack of the trump suit is led, and the Jack of the trump suit need not be played if the Ace of Hearts is led; if, however, the 5 of the trump suit is led no trump can renege.

4. If a plain suit is led a player may follow suit or trump as he

chooses, but he must not discard from another plain suit if he is able to follow suit or trump.

5. If a player misdeals the deal passes to the next player.

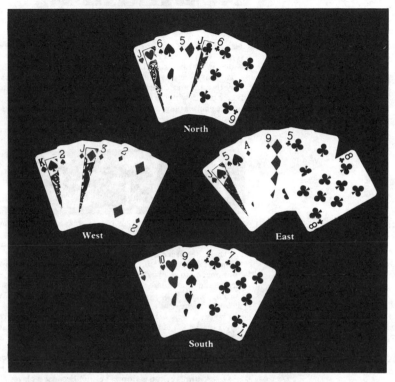

East is dealt the 8 ♣, but exchanges it for the 9 ♦

In a 4-handed game, South deals and turns up the **9 ♦**.

West leads the **J ♦**. North may renege the **5 ♦**, but it would hardly be good play not to use it to win the second highest trump, so he plays it. East, who holds the **A ♦**, robs by exchanging the 8 ♣ for the **9 ♦** and, of course, plays it. West who started with the hope of a jinx is now not so sure that he will win even three tricks. His prospects, however, improve when South, perforce, plays the **A ♥**. At least South cannot hold another trump.

North leads the **J ♣**, East plays the **5 ♣**, South the **7 ♣**, and West wins with the **2 ♦**.

West leads the **K ♠**, North plays the **6 ♠**, and East sees the possibility of himself winning three tricks. He trumps with the **A ♦**, and South plays the **9 ♠**. With any luck East should be able to win the last two tricks with the **J ♠** and **5 ♠**.

As it happens, however, East's play has enabled West to win three tricks, because when East leads the **J ♠**, West wins with the **3 ♦** and the last trick with the **2 ♠**.

143

Newmarket

Newmarket is a modern variation of the old game of pope joan (opposite) and is known by a number of other names – Boodle and Stops in England; Chicago, Michigan and Saratoga in America.

It is an excellent game for from three to eight players that is easy to learn and contains an element of skill that guarantees the better player winning in the long run.

The game is played with a full pack of fifty-two cards, and an Ace, King, Queen and Jack (each of a different suit) from another pack. These four extra cards are known as the boodle cards, and are placed, face upwards, in a row in the centre of the table.

Before the deal each player has to stake an agreed number of chips (usually, but not necessarily, 10) on the boodle cards. He may stake his chips as he pleases, but he must not stake more nor less than the agreed number.

The dealer then deals the cards one at a time to each player in rotation, and to an extra hand or dummy. As the players must each receive the same number of cards, any over-cards are dealt to the dummy hand which remains face downwards on the table throughout the deal.

The cards rank in the order from Ace (high) to 2 (low) and the player on the left of the dealer makes the first lead. He may lead a card from any suit, but it must be the lowest card that he holds in the suit. The players do not play in rotation round the table. The next play is made by the player who holds next higher cards in the suit, then the next higher card is played by the player who holds it, and so on, until the run is stopped either because a player plays the Ace of the suit, or the next higher card is in the dummy hand. Either way, the player who played the last card leads the lowest card of another suit, and if he has no other suit the lead passes to the player on his left.

When a player plays a card that is identical with one of the boodle cards he collects all the chips that have been staked on it.

The object of the game, however, is not only to win the chips that have been staked on the boodle cards, but to get rid of all one's cards, because the player who is first to do so receives one chip from each of the other players. If no player gets rid of all his cards, the one who holds the fewest number of cards wins the hand, and if two players are left with an equal number of fewest cards they divide the winnings.

If when a deal comes to an end the chips on one or more of the boodle cards have not been claimed, because the corresponding cards to the boodle cards are in the dummy hand, they are carried forward to the next deal.

PopeJoan

Pope Joan is a very old card game that at one time was exceptionally popular in Scotland. The 9 of Diamonds is given the name of Pope, and as the Pope was the Antichrist of Scottish reformers, there is reason to think that it was for this reason that the nickname of Curse of Scotland became attached to the card.

The game is played with a standard pack of fifty-two cards from which the 8 of Diamonds is removed. Originally a special board, consisting of a circular tray divided into eight compartments, and revolving about a central pillar, was used with counters. To-day these boards are museum pieces, and modern players must make do with eight saucers labelled: *Pope* (9 ♦), *Ace, King, Queen, Jack, Matrimony, Intrigue, Game,* placed in the centre of the table.

Each player begins with the same number of counters of an agreed value, and the dealer places six in the saucer labelled Pope (9 ♦), two each in Matrimony and Intrigue, and one each in Ace, King, Queen, Jack and Game. It is called dressing the board.

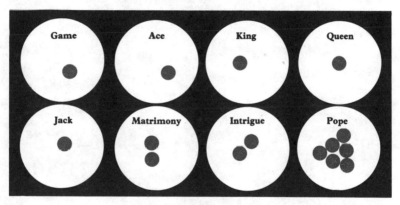

Cards are then dealt to the players and to an extra hand (widow) in the centre of the table. The number of cards dealt to each player and the widow depends on the number of players in the game. The players must each hold the same number of cards, so any over-cards go to the widow. The last card is turned face upwards to denote the trump suit, and if it is either the Pope (9 ♦) or an Ace, King, Queen or Jack, the dealer wins the counters in the corresponding saucer.

The player on the left of the dealer leads to the first trick. He may lead any card he chooses, and at the same time he announces it. Suppose it is the 6 of Clubs. Then the player who holds the 7 of Clubs plays it and announces it, the player who holds the 8 of Clubs plays it and announces it, and so on, until the run comes to an end.

The four Kings are stop cards, and in the Diamond suit the 7 is as well, because the 8 has been removed from the pack. In practice, of course, any card may be a stop card on account of the cards in the widow hand, and because the next higher card may already have been played.

When a run comes to an end, the player of the stop card starts a fresh run by leading any card he likes. In this way the game continues until one of the players has played all his cards. He is then entitled to the counters in the Game saucer, and, in addition, he receives from each player 1 counter for every card left in his hand. The player who is left with the Pope (9 ♦), however, is exempt from paying the winner so long as he holds the card in his hand. If he has played it in the course of the game he loses this advantage.

During the course of the game, any player who plays the Ace, King, Queen or Jack of the trump suit, or the Pope (9 ♦), wins the counters in the corresponding saucers; if the same player plays the King and Queen of the trump suit he wins the counters in matrimony, and if the same player plays the Queen and Jack of the trump suit he wins those in Intrigue.

The deal passes round the table clockwise, and any counters that have not been won in a deal are carried forward to the next.

Ranter Go Round

Ranter Go Round is an old Cornish game with the rather more appropriate alternative name of Cuckoo.

It may be played by any reasonable number, with a standard pack of fifty-two cards. The cards rank in order from King (high) to Ace (low); the suits have no rank. Each player begins with an agreed number of units, usually three. The dealer deals one card face downwards to each player. The object of the game is to avoid being left with the lowest card.

The player on the left of the dealer begins the game. He may either retain his card or offer it to his left-hand neighbour with the command 'Change'. There is no choice about it. The player so commanded must exchange cards with his right-hand neighbour unless he holds a King, when he says 'King', and the game is continued by the player on his left.

When an exchange has been made, the player who has been compelled to do so may pass on the card he has received in the same way, and so on, clockwise round the table, until the card is brought to a halt either by a King or by a player receiving a high card in exchange, so that he has nothing to gain by passing it on.

Any player giving an Ace, 2 or 3, in obedience to the command 'Change', must announce the rank of the card.

The dealer is last to play, and if he wishes to exchange his card, he does so by cutting the remainder of the pack and taking the top card of the cut.

If in doing this he draws a King he loses the hand and contributes one unit to the pool. If he does not draw a King, all the players expose their cards and the one with the lowest contributes one unit to the pool. If two or more tie for lowest card, all contribute to the pool.

When a player has contributed all his units to the pool, he retires from the game. The others continue, and the game is won by he who is left with at least one unit in hand.

Red Dog

Although in Red Dog, or High-card Pool, players stake on their cards, it is usually accepted as a party game, rather than a banking game, because the players stake against a pool and not against a banker.

The game may be played by any number up to ten, with the standard pack of fifty-two cards, ranking from Ace (high) to 2 (low). The suits have no rank.

The players contribute to the pool an agreed number of units, and each player is dealt five cards (only four cards if nine or ten players are in the game). Beginning with the player on the left of the dealer, each in turn stakes a minimum of one unit and a maximum that must not exceed the number of units in the pool, that he holds a card that is higher than, and in the same suit as, the top card of the stock when it is his turn to play.

The dealer faces the top card of the stock. If the player can beat it, he shows his card and is paid out of the pool. His remaining cards are not seen. If he cannot beat it, his stake is added to the pool and his cards are shown to the other players.

If at any time a player's winning bet takes all in the pool, a new pool is started as at the beginning of a game.

Widow   A   B

Rockaway

Rockaway or Go Boom is a game that may be played by any reasonable number of players.

Two packs of cards are shuffled together, and the dealer deals seven cards, face downwards, to each player. The next card (the widow) is placed face upwards in the centre of the table, and the rest of the pack (the stock) is placed face downwards on the table.

In turn, and beginning with the player on the left of the dealer, each player covers the widow either with a card of the same rank, of the same suit, or with an Ace, drawn from his hand. If he has no card in his hand to comply with the rule he draws a card from the stock and continues to draw one until he draws a card that permits him to cover the widow.

The card that covers the widow then becomes the widow for the next player, and so on, round the table in a clockwise direction.

When the stock is exhausted, the players play out the cards in their hands, and a player who cannot cover the widow misses his turn.

The hand comes to an end when a player has exhausted the cards in his hand. The remaining players expose their cards, which are scored against them: an Ace counting 15 points, a court card 10 points, and all other cards their pip value.

The deal passes round the table in a clockwise direction, and the game comes to an end when every player has dealt an equal number of times, by arrangement before the game begins.

E dealt. A, therefore, leads first, and the play is:

A	B	C	D	E
6 ♣	2 ♣	2 ♦	K ♦	A ♠

As an Ace counts 15 points against a player who is left with it, E plays A ♠ rather than one of his Diamonds.

10 ♠	9 ♠	J ♠	8 ♠	?

As E has no Spade, no 8 and no Ace in his hand, he must draw from the stock, and continue to do so until he draws a playable card.

It can be seen that E was foolish to play his Ace first round. As no opponent can go out in less than seven rounds, E would have been wise to keep his Ace for six rounds at least. He would not then have found himself in such a bad position on the second round. Usually, an Ace should not be played if another choice is available.

Spinado

Top: **matrimony**
Centre: **intrigue**
Bottom: **spinado**

Spinado is a less complicated version of pope joan (see page 145). No board is necessary (if you could find one) and there are only three pools: Matrimony, Intrigue and Game.

Before dealing, the dealer contributes 12 counters to the Matrimony pool, and 6 each to the Intrigue and Game pools. The other players contribute three counters each to the Game pool.

Matrimony is the King and Queen of Diamonds: Intrigue is the Queen and Jack of Diamonds.

The four 2s and the 8 of Diamonds are removed from a standard 52-card pack, and the dealer deals the cards to the players and to an extra hand (widow). As the players must each hold the same number of cards, over-cards go to the widow hand.

The player on the left of the dealer starts the game by playing any card that he chooses, and the other players continue by playing the next higher cards in succession until a stop is reached. The player who plays the stop card then starts a new run by playing any card that he chooses.

The Ace of Diamonds is known as Spinado, more usually truncated to Spin, and whoever holds it may play it at any time that he chooses provided that he accompanies it with the proper card, and announces that he is playing Spinado. It constitutes a stop, and he receives 3 counters from each of the other players.

During the game, the player who plays the King of Diamonds receives 2 counters from each of the other players, and if he plays the Queen of Diamonds as well he wins the Matrimony pool. The player who plays the Queen of Diamonds and the Jack of Diamonds wins the Intrigue pool, and those who play the Kings of Spades, Hearts and Clubs receive 1 counter from each of the other players.

The game is won by the player who is the first to play all his cards. He takes the counters in the Game pool and is exempt from contributing to the pools in the next deal, unless it is his turn to deal.

A player who is left with Spinado in his hand pays the winner of the game double for each card he is left with.

Spinado, therefore, should not be kept back too long. On the other hand, it is not always advisable to play it with one's first card. If, for example, a 10 is led, and the player who holds Spinado also holds the King and Jack, it is an error of judgement to play Spinado with the Jack, because if the Jack proves to be a stop there was no need for the play of Spinado, and the King is the natural stop if another player follows with the Queen.

It is better to hold up Spinado to be played with some card that is not known to be a stop.

Thirty-One

Thirty-one may be played by any number of players up to fifteen. It is played with the full pack of fifty-two cards, the Aces ranking high the 2s low.

Before each deal the players contribute an agreed amount to a pool.

Three cards are dealt face downwards to each player, and three cards are placed face upwards in the centre of the table. It is known as the widow hand.

In turn each player, beginning with the one on the left of the dealer, must exchange one of his cards with a card from the widow. He cannot pass, nor can he exchange more than one card. Counting the Ace as 11, the court cards as 10 each and all the other cards at their pip values, the object of the game is to hold three cards of the same suit which will add up to 31. Next in value is a hand that contains three cards of the same rank. Failing either, the pool is won by the player who holds the highest total in any one suit.

Widow   Hand

The player might be advised to exchange his 5 ♦ with the 7 ♥ and rap, since 25 is not a bad score

The exchange of cards with the widow-hand continues until a player has obtained a 31-hand. When a player holds such a hand he exposes it on the table, claims the pool, and the deal passes. At any stage of the game, however, a player who thinks he has a hand good enough to win, may rap the table. The other players now have the right, in turn, either to stand pat with the cards that they hold, or exchange one more card with the widow. The players then expose their cards and the one who holds the best hand wins the pool.

Baccarat

Baccarat, more correctly Baccarat Banque, is a game of chance that is played in casinos everywhere.

The game may be played by any number up to thirty or more. The banker sits midway down one of the sides of a long, oval table (opposite), and the players sit in equal numbers on both sides of him. Those for whom there is no room to sit, stand behind them.

Six packs of cards are shuffled together, in Las Vegas eight packs are used, cut and placed in an open-ended box known as a shoe, designed to release only one card at a time. The court cards rank in value at 10 points each; all other cards at their pip values.

The banker, who is also the dealer, puts his stake on the table in front of him, and any player who wishes to bet against the whole of it, calls 'Banco'. If two or more call, the one nearest to the banker's left makes the bet. If no-one calls, the players combine their bets to equal the stake put up by the banker.

The banker then gives a card face downwards to the player on his right, a card to the player on his left and a card to himself. He repeats the operation so that the three of them have two cards each.

The object of the game is to form in two or three cards a combination counting as nearly as possible to 9. In counting the total, ten is disregarded; if, for example, a player's two cards total 15 it counts as a point of 5.

The banker looks at his two cards and if he has a point of 8 or 9 he shows his cards and wins the hand. If he has not got a point of 8 or 9, he announces that he will give and the player on his right looks at his cards. If he has a point of 8 or 9 he shows his cards and announces his natural. If he has not got a point of 8 or 9 he may ask for one more card which the banker gives to him face upwards. The player on the left of the banker goes through the same performance, and then the banker may, if he chooses, take one more card. Finally, the banker wins or loses to each player according to whose point is nearer to 9; equality neither wins nor loses.

To illustrate. The banker holds 10 ♠ and A ♥, making a point of 1, and he, therefore, must give. The right-hand player holds 5 ♣ and 3 ♣. He faces his cards, announces his natural point of 8, and must win. The left-hand player holds 9 ♠ and 4 ♣, making a point of 3. He must draw and the banker gives him 8 ♦, reducing his point to 1. For the moment, however, the left-handed player does not announce his point. The banker faces his cards, and, as he holds no more than a point of 1, he draws a card. It is the 8 ♣, which raises his point to 9.

The banker, therefore, wins from the left-hand player, but loses to the right-hand player because though the banker has a point of 9, against the point of 8 held by the right-hand player, a natural beats any point made by the addition of a drawn card.

The rules of play are strict. They should never be deviated from because the player who is holding the cards is playing for all on his side of the table. If he deviates from the rules, and thereby loses the hand, he is liable to make good all losses incurred through his error. A player must not look at his cards until the banker has either announced that he holds a natural or that he will give cards. When a player looks at his cards, if he holds a natural he must expose his cards and declare his natural at once. If a player does not hold a natural, he must draw a card if he holds a point of 4 or less, stand if he holds a point of 6 or 7, and use his discretion to draw or stand only if he holds a point of 5.

The layout of the staking table used in baccarat and *chemin de fer*

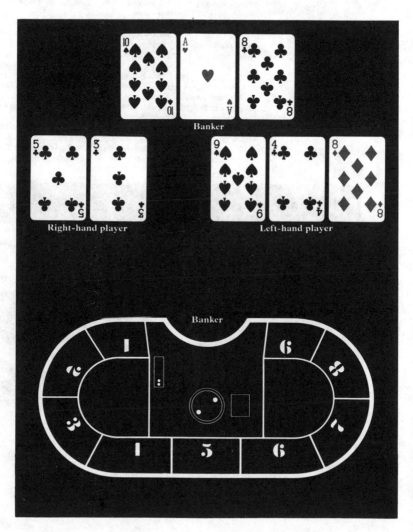

Banker

Right-hand player

Left-hand player

Banker

Blind Hookey

Blind Hookey may be played by any number of players with a single pack of fifty-two cards.

After the pack has been shuffled by one player and cut by another to the banker, it is passed to the player on the left of the banker, who removes a few cards (not less than four) from the top of the pack, and places them in a pile face downwards on the table in front of him. He then passes the pack to his left-hand neighbour who does the same thing, and so on until all the players (the banker last) have placed a small pile of cards in front of them.

Without looking at the cards, all the players (except the banker) stake to an agreed limit and turn their piles face upwards to expose the bottom card. The banker wins from all whose exposed card is lower than or equal with his and loses to all whose card is higher. By agreement, the Ace may be high or low.

Play continues with the same banker if he wins more than he loses, but passes to the next player if the banker loses more than he wins.

Banker

The banker wins from A, B, C and F and loses to D, E and G. Overall he loses 3 units and, therefore, the bank passes to the next player

Another way of playing the game is for the banker to cut the pack into three piles. The players place their stakes on either of two piles, and the third pile is taken by the banker. The three piles are turned face upwards and the players receive from the banker or lose to him according to whether the bottom cards of their piles are higher or lower than the bottom card of his pile.

Chemin de Fer

Chemin de Fer, nearly always called Chemmy, is the same game as baccarat (see page 152) modified for social play, because in all games of chance the banker has an advantage to a greater or lesser degree, and his advantage at *chemin de fer* is nothing like what it is at baccarat because he plays against one hand instead of against two.

For all practical purposes the difference between baccarat and *chemin de fer* is that at the latter game the bank passes in rotation round the table, the banker holding the bank until he loses a coup when it is passed to the player on his left; and the banker deals only one hand, not two, to the players, the hand being held by the one who has made the largest bet.

As the banker plays against only one hand, he may not use his judgement whether to draw or stand. The rules for play are precise and strict:

1. If his point is 8 or 9 he declares a natural.
2. If his point is 7 he stands whether the player draws any card or stands.
3. If his point is 6 he draws if the player draws a 6 or a 5, but stands if the player draws any other card or stands.
4. If he holds a point of 5 he draws if the player draws a 7, 6, 5, 4, 3, or stands, but stands if he draws any other card.
5. If he holds a point of 3 or 4 he draws if the player draws a 7, 6, 5, 4, 3, 2, or Ace or if he stands, but stands if he draws any other card.
6. If he holds a point of 0, 1 or 2 he draws whether the player draws any card or stands.

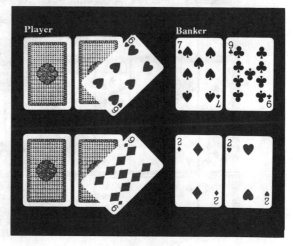

Banker's point is 6. Player has drawn a 6, so banker must draw

Banker's point is only 4, but as player has drawn a 9 he must stand

EasyGo

Easy Go is a very simple game of chance played by any number up to nine with a single pack of fifty-two cards.

The banker deals five cards face upwards to every player, except himself. He now faces a card and any player who holds a card of the same rank pays into a pool 2 units if it is the same colour and 1 unit if it is different. In all the banker faces five cards in turn, and for the second card the players pay into the pool 3 units if the cards are of the same colour and 2 if they are different; for the third card they contribute 5 units if the cards are of the same colour and 4 if they are different; for the fourth card they contribute 9 units if the cards are of the same colour and 8 if they are different; for the fifth card they contribute 17 units if the cards are of the same colour and 16 if they are different.

There is now a second show of five cards by the banker, but this time the players take out of the pool at the same rate as they paid into it.

After this, anything left in the pool is taken by the banker, but if there is not enough in the pool to meet the requirements of the players he must make it good.

The bank passes clockwise round the table.

Overall result of this game of easy go:
A wins 1 unit;
B wins 5 units;
C wins 3 units;
D wins 2 units;
E loses 3 units;
banker loses 8 units

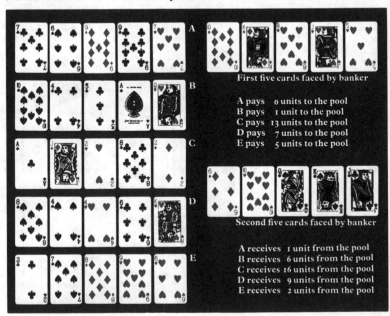

First five cards faced by banker

A pays   0 units to the pool
B pays   1 unit to the pool
C pays   13 units to the pool
D pays   7 units to the pool
E pays   5 units to the pool

Second five cards faced by banker

A receives   1 unit from the pool
B receives   6 units from the pool
C receives   16 units from the pool
D receives   9 units from the pool
E receives   2 units from the pool

Hoggenheimer

Hoggenheimer, or English Roulette, is played with a pack of cards from which the 2s, 3s, 4s, 5s and 6s have been removed, and the Joker (or one of the rejected cards) added.

After the pack has been shuffled and cut, the banker deals the cards, face downwards, in four rows of eight cards each, and places aside, also face downwards, the thirty-third card. Great care must be taken when dealing that no-one sees the face of any of the cards.

The top row is for Spades, from Ace to 7; the second row for Hearts, from Ace to 7; the third row for Diamonds, from Ace to 7; the bottom row for Clubs, from Ace to 7.

The players now stake their money. They may stake on a single card being turned up (even chance), or two touching cards being turned up (2 to 1 chance), or all four cards in a column or any group of four touching cards being turned up (4 to 1 chance), or all eight cards in a row being turned up (8 to 1 chance).

Hoggenheimer in progress. Stake 1 is on 10 ♠ being turned up; Stake 2 on 9 ♠, 8 ♠; Stake 3 on all four Queens; Stake 4 on 10 ♦ , 9 ♦ , 10 ♣, 9 ♣; Stake 5 on all Clubs; Stake 6 on 7 ♥ and 7 ♦

When the players have placed their bets, the banker picks up the thirty-third card and shows it. If it is the Joker he wins all the money on the table and there is a redeal. If, as is more likely, it is another card, he places it in its appropriate place in the layout, exposes the card that it replaces and transfers this card to its appropriate place in the layout; and so on until the game is brought to an end when the banker exposes the Joker.

The banker then collects the money on those chances that have not materialised in full, and pays out on those chances that have.

Lansquenet

Lansquenet, of German origin, is a game of pure chance that derives its name from the seventeenth-century German mercenary (*landsknecht*) with whom the game is said to have been popular.

Any number may play. The banker places the two top cards of the pack (hand cards) face upwards on the table. He then deals a card face upwards to himself, and one face upwards to the players. If either card is of the same rank as one of the hand cards it is put with them and another card dealt in its place.

First card drawn from pack: Q ♠. The card is placed on the table and players may bet on it. Second card drawn: 8 ♠. The card is added to the hand card pile. Third card drawn: K ♥. The banker wins the two units staked on K ♦

The players place their bets, and the banker covers them. He then draws cards from the pack, face upwards, one at a time. If he draws a card of the same rank as the players' card he wins bets on it; if he draws a card of the same rank as his own card he loses all the bets on the other card; and if he draws a card that matches neither card nor the two hand cards it is placed on the table and the players may bet on it.

When the players' card is matched the banker withdraws both cards and deals another card to the players. Cards that match the hand cards are placed with them. The game ends when the pack is exhausted unless the banker matches his own card first.

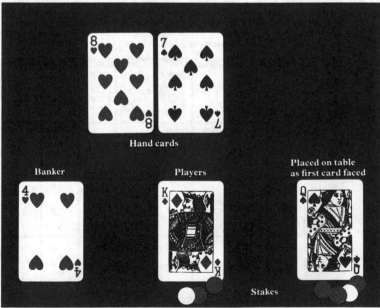

Hand cards

Banker

Players

Placed on table
as first card faced

Stakes

Monte Bank

In principle Monte Bank is a game of chance that is very similar to lansquenet (opposite).

It is played by any number of persons, with a pack of cards from which the 8s 9s and 10s have been removed.

After the cards have been shuffled and the pack cut by one of the players, the banker draws the two cards from the bottom of the pack and places them face upwards on the table (the bottom layout), and then the two cards from the top of the pack and places them face upwards on the table (the top layout).

The players place their bets up to an agreed maximum on whichever layout they choose. The banker then turns the pack face upwards and if the exposed bottom card (known as the gate) is of the same suit as any of the four cards in the layouts, he pays all bets on that layout, and collects all bets on a layout that shows no card of the same suit as the gate.

The layouts and gate are then discarded, and the game is continued with new layouts and gate. The bank passes after five coups.

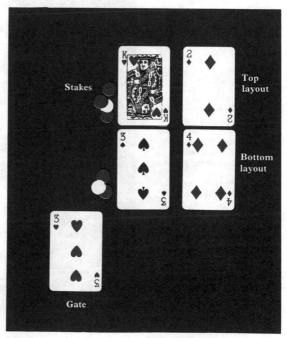

Banker pays four units to players who stake on the top layout and collects the three units on the bottom layout. If the gate had been a Diamond, all players would have won; if a club all would have lost

Stakes

Top layout

Bottom layout

Gate

Racing

Racing is played with the standard pack of fifty-two cards. The four Aces are placed in a row on the table. The remainder of the pack is shuffled and cut, and the banker draws the top seven cards from the pack and lays them in a vertical column immediately below the Aces, so that the lay out takes the form of a T (see illustration).

The banker deals the remaining cards one at a time, and each time that the card of a suit is dealt the Ace of the same suit is moved one card forward, the winner being the Ace that is first to pass the seventh card.

Players place their stakes on whichever Ace they choose. The race ends when the first Ace passes the seventh card.

Racing layout. The banker might offer evens on a suit if there are no cards in the layout, 2-1 if there is one card (as with Clubs and Hearts here), 3-1 if there are two cards (Diamonds here), 5-1 if there are three cards (Spades here) and 10-1 if there are four cards. If there are five or more cards of a suit in the layout, it is impossible for that suit to win, and there must be a redeal

Slippery Sam

Slippery Sam or Shoot, as it is sometimes called, may be played by any number from two upwards, but the game is best for from six to eight players. It is probably the only banking game which favours the player rather than the banker, because the player has the advantage of seeing his cards before he bets and, therefore, can calculate whether the odds are in his favour or against him. Provided he bets with intelligence he should come out a winner.

The game is played with the standard 52-card pack, the cards ranking from Ace (high) to 2 (low).

The banker places an agreed sum in a pool and then deals three cards, one at a time, face downwards, to each player. The remainder of the pack (the stock) he places face downwards on the table in front of him and topples it over to make it easier to slide off the top card.

The player on the left of the dealer, after looking at his cards, bets that at least one of them will be in the same suit as, and higher than, the top card of the stock. He may bet all that is in the pool or any part of it, but he may not bet less than an agreed minimum. When he has made his bet, the banker slides the top card off the stock and exposes it. If the player has won his bet he exposes his card and takes his winnings out of the pool. If he has lost his bet he pays the amount that he betted into the pool and does not expose his card. The four cards are then thrown into a discard pile, and the opportunity to bet passes to the next player.

Meanwhile: a player must not look at his cards until it is his turn to bet; if the pool is exhausted the bank immediately passes to the next player, otherwise the banker holds the bank for three full deals round the table, and then he may either pass the bank to the player on his left or hold the bank for one more, but only one more, deal round the table.

Since the player wins if a red card or a Club lower than the 10 is exposed, and loses only if a Spade or the Ace, King, Queen or Jack of Clubs is exposed, he has 32 chances of winning and 17 of losing: he should stake heavily

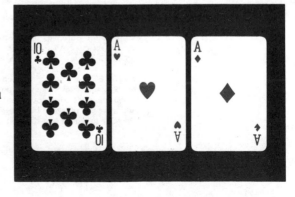

Trente et Quarante

Trente et Quarante, or *Rouge et Noir*, is a game of pure chance and, like baccarat (see page 152) is essentially a casino game. It is played on a long table, each end marked as in the accompanying diagram. The banker sits midway down one of the sides, the players sit, and some stand behind them, at each end.

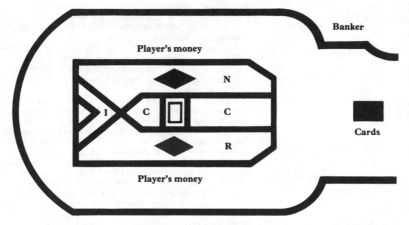

Six packs of cards are shuffled together, cut, and – with the Ace counting as 1, the court cards 10 each, and other cards their pip values – the banker deals a row of cards until the total exceeds 30. He then deals a second row immediately below it in a similar manner. The top row is *noir* (black) the lower *rouge* (red) and whichever row adds up to the lesser total wins. Apart from these two chances the players can bet on whether the first card dealt will be the same colour as the winning row (*couleur*) or the opposite colour (*inverse*). All four are even chances, but if both rows add up to 31 it is a *refait* (drawn game) and the player may either halve his stake with the bank, or allow the whole of it to be put in prison. He has the right to choose between the red and black prisons, and if his stake wins on the next deal he withdraws it.

All other identical totals end in the deal being declared void, and leave the player at liberty to withdraw his stake or leave it on the table to win or lose the next deal.

Vingt-et-Un

Vingt-et-Un, or Twenty-one, is a leading game in the casinos of America where it is known as Black Jack. Although it is a game of chance, in which the odds on winning are heavily in favour of the banker, in Great Britain it is far more of a social pastime and, under the name of Pontoon (almost certainly an easy corruption of punting) it was exceptionally popular in the trenches during the war of 1914–1918.

The game is played with a standard 52-card pack, by any number of players up to ten: if more than ten take part two packs of cards shuffled together should be used.

The banker deals one card face downwards to each player and to himself, and the players, after looking at their cards, stake any amount up to the agreed maximum.

The object of the game is to obtain a total of 21, or as near to it as possible, but without exceeding it. For this purpose an Ace counts 11 or 1 (at the option of the holder) a court card 10, and any other card its pip value.

When the players have made their bets, the banker looks at his card, and has the right to double. In this event the players must double their bets.

The banker then deals another card, face downwards, to all the players and to himself. If a player holds a pair he may announce his intention to split. He stakes the same amount as his original bet on both cards, and the banker deals a second card to each. The player plays both hands separately. The banker may not split pairs.

If the banker holds a natural (an Ace and a court card or a 10) he turns the two cards face upwards and receives from the players double what they have staked, except that if a player also holds a natural he loses only his original stake. The hands are thrown in, and the banker deals another hand.

If the banker does not hold a natural, but a player does, the banker pays him double his stake, and, after the deal has been completed, the bank passes to him. The bank, however, does not pass on a split natural. If two or more players hold naturals, the one nearest to the banker's left takes the bank.

When all naturals (if any) have been declared and settled, the banker asks each player in turn (beginning with the one on his left) whether he wants more cards or not. The player has three options. He may *Stand*; that is he elects to take no more cards. He may *Buy*; that is he increases his stake for the advantage of receiving a card face downwards. He may *Twist*; that is he does not increase his stake and receives a card face upwards. The rules to be observed are:

1. A player may not stand if he holds a count of 15 or less.
2. A player may not buy for more than his original stake.
3. If a player has twisted a third card he may not buy a fourth or fifth, though a player who has bought a third card may twist subsequent cards.
4. A player may not increase, though he may decrease, the amount

for which he bought a previous card.

5. If a player has received four cards he may not buy a fifth if the total of his four cards is 11 or less.

Five cards is the most that a player may hold, and if they total 21 or less the banker pays him double, unless the banker also holds five cards that total 21 or less when the banker wins.

The player who makes a total of 21 with three 7s, receives from the banker triple his stake. The banker does not have this privilege.

When the total of a player's cards exceeds 21 he turns his cards face upwards and the banker wins all that he has staked.

When all the players have received cards, the banker turns his two cards face upwards and deals himself as few or as many cards as he chooses. If.when doing so he exceeds a total of 21 he pays the players their stakes. At any time, however, he may elect to stand and agree to pay those players who have a higher total and receive from those who have a lower or equal total.

Banker pays B (double), C, E and F Banker wins from A and E Banker loses 9 units on deal

Board
and Tile Games

Chess

The game of chess as played today has an interesting if somewhat obsure history. Originally evolved as a game for four players, various changes have taken place over a period of many centuries and it is generally agreed by modern players that the game as played today can hardly be improved upon.

Most authorities attribute invention of the game to the Hindus but no precise date can be given. It was probably devised during the fifth century A.D. and during the next hundred years spread from India to Persia. In the course of time it reached North Africa, Italy, Spain and by the tenth century most of Europe. England has the Norman Conquest to thank for the introduction of the game and the earliest chess book to be published here was Caxton's *The Game and Playe of the Chesse* which is dated 1474.

Originally called *Chaturanga* the pieces used represented the four divisions of an Indian army–elephants, mounted horsemen, horse-drawn chariots and footsoldiers. Originally the game was played with a dice which decided the piece a player should move. In course of time this was dropped and it was generally agreed that the player must decide which piece had best be moved to effect a Checkmate.

A number of changes have taken place during the centuries that the game has been played. The Queen was once a male figure in the shape of some sort of minister or adviser to the King. When chess reached the European Continent this piece became a Queen and much greater powers were conferred upon her. Whereas the male adviser to the King was limited to one square at a move the newly crowned Queen was granted the sweeping powers of both Bishop and Rook. This piece could now move across the board as far as the player wished using ranks, files or diagonals.

The rook has had many different shapes and forms in the past. Sometimes a chariot, sometimes an elephant, it is today represented as a castle turret. Bishops too have had changes of form and power. Once an elephant, the piece became a Bishop when chess reached England. In France however the change was to that of a court jester and the piece became 'le fou'.

Knights seem always to have been associated with cavalry and today the piece is represented by a horse's head. When Nathaniel Cook designed the pieces most of us play with today he persuaded his friend the eminent chess player Howard Staunton to allow the set to be named after him. The Knight in the Staunton set is a horse's head said to have been based on the famous Elgin marbles.

Pawns were foot soldiers in the original game and they appear as such in many chess sets today. The Staunton pieces represent the Pawn as a small ball on a bell-shaped base.

When learning to play chess it is best to use Staunton pieces because these are now used in chess clubs and at all chess tournaments throughout the world.

The Board and the Pieces
Chess is played on a board of 64 squares of which 32 are White and 32 are Black. It is very important that players ensure that the board is the right way round before they set up the pieces. Each player should have a White square at his right hand corner.

The squares are coloured light and dark – usually White and Black but sometimes Cream and Brown or even White and Green. They are not identified by letters or numbers except in theory. To be able to record games both letters and numbers have been given to the squares and the item on notation explains the two main systems. It is possible to play the game without knowing either of them but a player wishing to improve his play would do well to master both because not all books use the same system.

Object of the Game
The object of the game is for a player to defeat his opponent by capturing his King. In fact the King is not removed from the board, but as soon as he is manoeuvred into a position from which he cannot escape, the game is over and the player who has made the capture has won.

Players move alternately and, except when making a special move called 'castling' which will be explained later, only one piece is moved at a time. A piece can be moved to a vacant square or to one occupied by a hostile piece which is then removed from the board in this same move.

The player who has the White pieces has a slight advantage and decision as to who plays White is decided by lottery. It is usual for one of the players to hold a Pawn of each colour in his closed hands and for his opponent to point to or touch one of the hands. Whichever colour he has selected he plays in the first game and thereafter the players alternate.

Value of the Pieces
The rules of chess decree that not all pieces move in the same way and therefore some pieces are stronger than others. A player should

know the value of the pieces he is using or he will very soon find that, even if he knows the moves and can play a game, he will have difficulty in winning.

You need not remember the following points which experts have agreed should be awarded to the pieces, but you should be able to list the pieces in your mind in descending order of value. Here are the values:

Queen   9 points
Rook   5 points
Bishop   3 points
Knight   3 points
Pawn   1 point
King   ?

Clearly the Queen is your strongest piece and then come your Rooks. If your opponent has a Queen and King left on the board at the end of the game, and you have two Rooks and a King, then theoretically you have the edge on him—by one point.

Bishops and Knights come next and are equal in value in the early part of the game but the position of pieces in the end game may give the advantage to one or the other of these pieces.

Pawns have the least value but players should not underestimate them. After all each one qualifies for exchange to a Queen if they can reach the opponent's back row! Furthermore a well positioned Pawn in the end game may tip the scales to victory for a player.

It is not really possible to give a reliable point value to a King. He is not a powerful piece but he is valuable. If you lose your Queen you can still play on. Lose your King and you lose the game!

Check and Checkmate

Your opponent's King is said to be in Check if, having made a move you find you are able to capture the King in your next move. It is required that the player say 'Check' so that his opponent is aware that some action must be taken to save the threatened King. If a player finds that his King is in Check and that there is no way of saving the King then that is Checkmate and the game is over.

The Figures

The figures in this article have been designed to show the movements of the various pieces and, for simplicity, only those pieces involved in the move with the hostile King are shown. In a game of chess there would probably be many more pieces on the board but it was thought that these, if shown, would only confuse or distract the reader.

Notation

There are two different ways of recording chess games and it will repay the reader to master both. Neither is difficult to learn and once the shorthand is understood a player can record his own games and, just as important, play out on his own board the games played and recorded by the experts.

The system in common use in the English speaking countries is known as Descriptive Notation (or English Notation) but most other countries use what is called Algebraic Notation.

Descriptive Notation

A very simple code is used to designate the pieces. Each is referred to by its initials as follows:

King–K
Queen–Q
King's Bishop–KB
Queen's Bishop–QB
King's Knight–KKt or KN
Queen's Knight–QKt or QN
King's Rook–KR
Queen's Rook–QR

The Pawns are named after the piece they stand before, thus:

King Pawn–KP
Queen Pawn–QP
King's Bishop Pawn–KBP
Queen's Bishop Pawn–QBP
King's Knight Pawn–KKtP or KNP
Queen's Knight Pawn–QKtP or QNP
King's Rook Pawn–KRP
Queen's Rook Pawn–QRP

Now for the board. Each square has a number for White and a number for Black. White's squares are numbered from the bottom of the board on all illustration figures and Black's from the top. The numbers run from 1 to 8 in each file and the files are identified by the names of the pieces which occupy them at the start of a game. Hence you get K1 and Q1 in the centre of the back rank and K1 goes to K8 up the board for White. K1 for Black runs down the board to K8. The same applies to all the other files.

BLACK

QR1 / QR8	QKt1 / QKt8	QB1 / QB8	Q1 / Q8	K1 / K8	KB1 / KB8	KKt1 / KKt8	KR1 / KR8
QR2 / QR7	QKt2 / QKt7	QB2 / QB7	Q2 / Q7	K2 / K7	KB2 / KB7	KKt2 / KKt7	KR2 / KR7
QR3 / QR6	QKt3 / QKt6	QB3 / QB6	Q3 / Q6	K3 / K6	KB3 / KB6	KKt3 / KKt6	KR3 / KR6
QR4 / QR5	QKt4 / QKt5	QB4 / QB5	Q4 / Q5	K4 / K5	KB4 / KB5	KKt4 / KKt5	KR4 / KR5
QR5 / QR4	QKt5 / QKt4	QB5 / QB4	Q5 / Q4	K5 / K4	KB5 / KB4	KKt5 / KKt4	KR5 / KR4
QR6 / QR3	QKt6 / QKt3	QB6 / QB3	Q6 / Q3	K6 / K3	KB6 / KB3	KKt6 / KKt3	KR6 / KR3
QR7 / QR2	QKt7 / QKt2	QB7 / QB2	Q7 / Q2	K7 / K2	KB7 / KB2	KKt7 / KKt2	KR7 / KR2
QR8 / QR1	QKt8 / QKt1	QB8 / QB1	Q8 / Q1	K8 / K1	KB8 / KB1	KKt8 / KKt1	KR8 / KR1

Fig. 1   **WHITE**

Figure 1 shows the numbering for both White and Black. When recording movements always use the minimum shorthand. For example, if White's King Pawn opens the game by moving two squares forward this is written as P–K4. There is no point in identifying the Pawn as KP because it is the only one that can move to this square at this stage of the game. The dash (–) indicates 'moves to'. Other shorthand you should know is equally simple. The letter x = captures.

Therefore P x P simply means Pawn takes Pawn and this would apply if there is only one Pawn that can take another. If two Pawns have the option of capturing a hostile Pawn the one making the move should be identified such as BP x P (Bishop Pawn captures Pawn) or QP x P (Queen Pawn captures Pawn).

There are a few other simple symbols you should know about. Any move by any piece which puts the hostile King in jeopardy–that is to say a move which means that the King could be captured in the next move–is one that puts the King in Check. The player who has made this move must announce this by saying Check. It is recorded as simply ch after the move (example Q–R8 ch. The Queen has been placed in the eighth rank and in her next move could capture the King).

The move known as castling which will be fully explained later is recorded as O.O if made on the King's side of the board and O.O.O if on the Queen's side. The only other shorthand you need to know is the ! normally put after a good move by an analyst (example

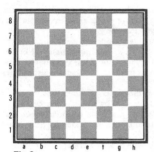

Fig. 2

QxR ch ! which simply means Queen captures Rook and puts the King in Check, a good move) and ? which implies a move of doubtful worth, or a bad one. Sometimes one gets a combination of these last two such as RxB !? which means Rook captures Bishop–a daring move of doubtful wisdom depending on further moves by both players.

Algebraic Notation

Many players and especially chess writers prefer this system which is popular on the Continent. There is much to be said in its favour but; until it is more widely used in the English speaking countries, the reader would do well to master Descriptive Notation.

Algebraic Notation is easy to follow. The board is (in theory but not in practice) numbered from 1 to 8 up the files and from a to h across the ranks as shown in Figure 2. The history of this system goes back to Medieval times and was reintroduced about the middle of the 18th century.

The pieces with the exception of the Pawns are represented by their initials as in Descriptive Notation. The eight files have the letters a to h. The eight ranks have the numbers 1 to 8 starting from White's first rank. Black's first rank therefore is No. 8. The squares are therefore identified by a combination of letter and number.

A move is written as the initial of the piece plus the identification of the square it leaves and the square to which it moves. As in Descriptive Notation the act of moving a piece is shown as a hyphen or dash. To capture is shown as x.

Descriptive Notation gives the Ruy Lopez opening as follows:

	White	Black
1)	P–K4	P–K4
2)	Kt–KB3	Kt–QB3
3)	B–Kt5	and so on

Algebraic Notation of these moves is as follows:

1)	e2–e4	e7–e5
2)	Kt–g3	Kt–c6
3)	B–b5	and so on.

Very few chess books in the English language use Algebraic Notation so the reader may think it best to concentrate on Descriptive Notation first.

Kings

Each player has a King. He is not the most powerful piece on the

PAWNS   QUEEN KING   PAWNS
     BISHOP   BISHOP
   KNIGHT   KNIGHT
ROOK   ROOK

QUEEN'S   KING'S
SIDE   SIDE

ROOK   ROOK
   KNIGHT   KNIGHT
     BISHOP   BISHOP
PAWNS   QUEEN KING   PAWNS
Fig. 3

board but he is certainly the most valuable. This is explained by the fact that you may lose any other piece or pieces and carry on playing, but, if your King is captured, you lose the game.

Movement of the King is restricted to one square at a time except when making a special move known as castling which will be explained later. For the present, regard your King as valuable, slow moving and vulnerable. Take heart from the fact that this also applies to your opponent's King.

A King can use ranks, files or diagonals provided that he moves no further than one square in a move. Why should a player wish to move his King? The answer is that if a King is under attack and *can be taken* in the next move then the player under pressure must do one of four things. He must:

1) Move his King to a square which is not under attack – which explains why you might want to move him, or

2) the player must capture his opponent's attacking piece with his King. This he may not be able to do because the attacking piece may not be on a square adjacent to that of the King so he might

3) move another piece to place it between the attacking piece and the beseiged King. Alternatively the player whose King is attacked may be able to

4) remove the attacking piece with one of his other pieces.

If any of these moves can be made the game goes on. If not the King is Checkmated and the game is over.

Pawns

Each player has eight Pawns and these are placed directly in front of the other pieces as shown in Figure 3. For recording the movements of a game Pawns take the name of the piece they stand in front of and reading from left to right they are as follows: Queen's Rook Pawn (QRP), Queen's Knight Pawn (QKtP), Queen's Bishop Pawn (QBP), Queen's Pawn (QP), King's Pawn (KP), King's Bishop Pawn (KBP), King's Knight Pawn (KKtP) and King's Rook Pawn (KRP).

The rules governing Pawn movements are quite simple and apply to all Pawns. They always move forward and, except when making a capture, they always keep to the file in which they are placed at the beginning of the game. A Pawn is always moved one square at a time except in its first move when the player has the option of moving it two squares.

Pawns capture diagonally and this they can only do if there is a

Fig. 4

Fig. 5

Fig. 6

hostile piece on the square ahead of them in the left or right adjacent file. Look at Figure 4. White has moved his Queen Pawn two squares forward as his first move and Black has replied with the same move P–Q4. The result is that both Pawns are blocked and can make no further move until one is captured and removed or makes a capture. Suppose that White now decides to move his King Pawn and to take advantage of the rule allowing a Pawn being moved for the first time to go forward two squares. Figure 5 shows his move P–K4. It is Black's move and because Pawns capture diagonally he takes White's Pawn as shown in Figure 6. If White had moved his King Pawn only one square it would not have been taken. Furthermore it would have been one square diagonally behind his Queen Pawn guarding it. In other words the King Pawn could capture any piece which took the Queen Pawn.

Pawns can capture any hostile piece in this way except the King but they can threaten the King. A Pawn can put a King in Check.

Promoting Pawns

There is one other very important thing you must know about Pawns. Although they are the least powerful pieces on the board, every one of them is a potential Queen. To achieve this promotion it is necessary for a player to get a Pawn to his opponent's back rank. This is never easy because there are so many hostile pieces waiting to attack any advancing Pawn. It is worth trying to achieve a second Queen because, as we shall shortly see, a Queen is more powerful than any of the other pieces and to have two on the board means almost certain victory. A strong player may well achieve this if playing against a beginner but good players of equal strength usually ensure that advancing Pawns are dealt with before they become eligible for promotion.

It should be mentioned that a Pawn reaching the eighth rank does not automatically become a Queen. The player can elect to exchange it for any other piece he cares to choose except, of course, a King.

Most sets of chessmen do not contain more than one Queen for each player so that if a Pawn is exchanged for a second Queen the player must improvise. If there is a Rook off the board at the time it is usual to use this with a Pawn balanced on top of it. More often than not a Pawn becomes a Queen late in the game when the player's Queen has been captured and is already off the board. She can now be taken back into service and is placed on the square which the successful Pawn reached.

Fig. 7

Fig. 8

Fig. 9

Rooks

The movements which a Rook may make are very easy to learn. In a way it is the most straightforward piece on the board. A Rook can travel as far across the board as the player wishes provided that it is kept to a rank or a file. In other words the Rook can be moved forwards or backwards in a file or to the left or right in a rank. A Rook can put the hostile King in Check from the other side of the board. Look at Figure 7. The Black King is not in Check from the Rook because he cannot be captured in White's next move. Suppose White moves his Rook to the square shown in Figure 8 (R–K1). Now the Black King *is* in check and Black's next move must be to rescue his King. The arrow shows the path White Rook would take to capture the King.

Rooks can capture any hostile piece on the board by moving along the ranks or files and removing the piece from the square they travel to. Look at Figure 9. Black Rook can travel across the rank and capture White Bishop as shown by the arrow. If Black makes this move then White Pawn can capture Black Rook! This was a bad manoeuvre for Black because Rooks are more valuable than Bishops. This is where tactics come into chess. Only make a capture if it is really to your advantage to do so. Be sure you understand the relative values of the pieces and do not sacrifice a strong piece for the capture of a piece relatively weaker! If the protecting Pawn had not been in the position shown and the Bishop had been isolated, then the Rook capture would have been worthwhile.

Bishops

The movements which a Bishop is allowed to make are as simple as those of the Rook. The difference is simply that Bishops are confined entirely to the diagonals on the board. They move across the corners but never across ranks or up and down files. Like the Rook a Bishop can be moved as far as the player wishes provided that his path is unobstructed. Bishops capture by occupying the square of a hostile piece which is removed from the board.

One of your Bishops starts, and remains throughout the game, on a White square and the other on a Black square. This, of course, also applies to your opponent's Bishops.

As long as he is kept to diagonals a Bishop can advance or retreat provided the way is clear. When he takes a piece he occupies the square on which he made the capture and he remains on that square until moved again – or until he is captured.

Fig. 10   **Fig. 11**

In Figure 10 the White Bishop is in a position to capture either the Black Knight or the Black Pawn. The Black Knight is protected by another Black Pawn so that if the Bishop does take the Knight he will be captured by Black Pawn. On the other hand if the player elects to capture the lone Black Pawn the Bishop is still safe. This would normally be the better move. It is a capture rather than an exchange.

In some circumstances an exchange would be the better move. In Figure 11 the White Bishop has the same choice of victims and elects to capture the Knight. If Black Pawn captures the Bishop the pathway is clear for White Rook to capture Black Queen and call Check. In fact, it is Checkmate because the Black King cannot escape from the back row. He is hemmed in by his own Pawns. White has made the sacrifice of a Bishop to win the game.

Knights

The movements of the pieces so far described have been simple to describe and should be easy to learn. The movement of a Knight does call for a little concentration because it is not quite so straight-forward in its mode of progress across the board. A Knight moves two squares forward and one to the side every time it moves. It cannot elect to go one or two squares and then stop. It must make this L-shaped move or not move at all. Knights can advance or retreat and the movement across the squares can be two across a rank and one up a file or two up a file and one across a rank. Figure 12 shows a Knight moving out from its starting position and the arrow shows the square to which the player has elected to move it. Note

Fig. 12   **Fig. 13**

Fig. 14   **Fig. 15**

that from this starting position there is one other square available to it and this is marked with a cross. Figure 13 shows a Black Knight in one of the centre squares. From this position the Knight can move to capture any one of the White Pawns round him. It should be remembered that Knights are the only pieces on the board which are allowed to hop over other pieces – and this applies to your own or those of your opponent.

Queens
Each player starts the game with a Queen. She is the most powerful piece on the board and the good player will ensure that, whatever move he makes throughout the game, his Queen is safe from capture. There are positions in which it may pay the player to sacrifice his Queen in order to ensure a Checkmate, but we will deal with this later.

Now for the movements a Queen is allowed to make. She combines the movements of both Rook and Bishop. That is to say a Queen may use ranks or files like a Rook or, if the player wishes she may use diagonals like a Bishop. She may be moved backwards or forwards across the board. Queens capture pieces in the same way as Bishops, Rooks or Knights. They occupy the square of the hostile piece and the latter is removed from the board. It should be mentioned that the Queen cannot make the Knight move. She is confined to ranks, files or diagonals.

In Figure 14 the White Queen is in a position to capture Black Rook or Black Knight as the arrows show. If the player elects to capture the Knight the game could go on with Black moving to get out of his difficulties. On the other hand if White Queen captures the Black Rook it is Checkmate. The Black Knight is not in a position to capture the White Queen and Black King cannot take her because if he did he would be moving into Check from the White Rook. The only escape square which might have been available to him is covered by the White Bishop.

If a Queen is in a position to make a capture always watch closely to ensure she does not put herself in jeopardy. In Figure 15 the Black Queen can capture White Rook and in the same move put White King in Check. Not a good move this because White Knight would then very promptly capture Black Queen! It is usually considered bad play to bring a Queen out into the open early in the game. She is powerful but like any other piece the Queen is vulnerable too.

Fig. 16   **Fig. 17**

Special Moves

There are two special moves a player should know about before he starts to play a game. The first of these is the En Passant move which is seldom made but nevertheless it should be understood perchance the player has the opportunity of making it.

En Passant

Stated briefly it is simply this. Any Pawn on the board when making its first move can go two squares forward but it cannot escape capture if it moves alongside a hostile Pawn. In Figure 16 White Pawn is about to be moved for the first time and there is a Black Pawn which in this position cannot capture White. If White takes advantage of the rule which allows him to go forward two squares then Black can capture White as if White had moved only one square. Figure 17 shows the move White Pawn has made and an arrow shows the square to which Black Pawn can now go and at the same time White Pawn is removed from the board. The result is a Pawn capture for Black as if White Pawn had moved forward only one square. The En Passant move does not crop up very often but the other special move does and the player should master it before starting to play. This is known as castling and it is usual for both players to make this move early in the game.

Castling

Each player is allowed to castle once during a game and experienced players usually aim to do it by about the tenth move – or soon after. In the one move the King is placed at the side of the back rank and a Rook is brought towards the centre of this rank. The object is to get the King to a place of greater safety and, at the same time, bring a powerful piece into active play towards the centre of the board. A player may castle on either side of the board depending on whether or not the way is clear for him to do so.

On the King's side the Bishop and the Knight must have vacated their squares before the player can castle. On the Queen's side the Queen herself must also have left her starting square. Figure 18 shows White ready to castle on the King's side and the arrows indicate the move about to be made. Note that after the move there is one White square at the corner. When castling is completed on the Queen's side there is both a White and Black square in the back rank corner. Figure 19 shows White ready to castle on the Queen's side (the arrows show the move). Figure 20 shows the move completed.

Fig. 18

Fig. 19

Fig. 20

A player cannot castle if his King is in Check, nor can he do so if either the King or the Rook have already made a move in the game. He cannot castle if the square he is to occupy or the one he crosses is under attack from a hostile piece. In other words he cannot move into or across 'Check'. The illustrations show the moves for the White pieces and exactly the same applies to the Black pieces.

Openings

There are many different ways of opening a game and a beginner would do well to study some of the well-known and well-tried variations. Games are named after the manner in which players use their pieces in the first few moves and have sometimes acquired the names from players who have introduced the opening or who were well-known for their use of it. Sometimes the place of origin gives its name to an opening and in some cases the name indicates the type of play expected. The Ruy Lopez opening is named after a sixteenth century Spanish priest who published an early textbook on the game and who was patronised by Philip II. The Spanish King invited Lopez to his court for games of chess. The Vienna Opening dates back to the Vienna Chess Congress of 1873 when it was used in tournament play and thereafter became popular with chess masters from Vienna. Examples of openings which anticipate the likely course of the game are Queen's Gambit Accepted and Queen's Gambit Declined. There are many variations on these openings and the beginner cannot be expected to master more than one or two openings to start with.

It is however worth studying the first few moves of some of the standard openings and some of these are given here.

Ruy Lopez

This is probably the most widely used opening of all. The moves start as follows:

White	Black
1) P–K4	P–K4
2) Kt–KB3	Kt–QB3
3) B–Kt5	

and depending on Black's third move the variations have additional titles such as Bird's Defence, Classical Defence and so on.

Examine carefully the first two moves for each player. White opens with a centre Pawn and Black replies with this same move P–K4 to stop the advance of White and give himself equality in the centre squares. White's second move Kt–KB3 is a threat to Black's Pawn and whereas Black could make a similar threat by copying White's move he in fact brings out his Queen's Knight. This is a defending move which shows White that Black will capture White's Knight if White dares to take the Pawn. Exchanging a Knight for a Pawn is a very poor move for White so he now goes B–Kt5. This is a threat to Black's Knight though the Knight is protected by two Pawns. If White Bishop captures Black Knight then Black Pawn takes White Bishop. Black's third move could be P–R3 (Morphy's Defence) which would drive the Bishop away or Kt–Q5 (Bird's Defence) which is an escape for the Knight and gives him a centre square.

For readers who would like to pursue further the Ruy Lopez opening here are some variations to try out.

Ruy Lopez Classical Defence

	White	Black
1)	P–K4	P–K4
2)	Kt–KB3	Kt–QB3
3)	B–Kt5	B–B4
4)	P–B3	KKt–K2
5)	P–Q4	P×P
6)	P×P	B–Kt5 ch
7)	B–Q2	B×B ch
8)	Q×B	P–Q4
9)	P×P	Kt×P
10)	B×Kt ch	P×B

The eleventh move could be for both players to castle. In terms of material captured, the players are equal. They both have more or less equal domination of the centre of the board. There is still room for development for both.

Ruy Lopez Morphy Defence

	White	Black
1)	P–K4	P–K4
2)	Kt–KB3	Kt–QB3
3)	B–Kt5	P–QR3
4)	B–R4	Kt–B3
5)	O–O	Kt×P
6)	P–Q4	P–QKt4
7)	B–Kt3	P–Q4

8)	PxP	B–K3
9)	Q–K2	Kt–B4
10)	R–Q1	P–Kt5

This would follow on with (11) White B–K3, Black KtxB and (12) RPxKt for White. Here again the material captured gives equality to both players and domination of the centre squares is about equal. White has the advantage of having castled but the disadvantage of doubled Pawns in his Queen Knight file.

English Opening

This opening acquired its name because it was used on various occasions by the famous British nineteenth century player Howard Staunton. Its usual feature is that White opens with a Bishop Pawn leaving Black the opportunity to play for centre domination in the early moves. In theory White can counter this and by opening with a Bishop Pawn he is able to strengthen his position by quick development of his pieces. Here is one of the English openings:

English Opening   Four Knights' Variation

	White	Black
1)	P–QB4	P–K4
2)	Kt–QB3	Kt–KB3
3)	Kt–B3	Kt–B3
4)	P–Q4	P–K5
5)	Kt–Q2	KtxP
6)	KKtxP	KtxKt
7)	KtxKt	B–Kt5 ch
8)	B–Q2	BxB ch
9)	QxB	Kt–K3

In the first nine moves each player has captured a Knight, a Bishop and a Pawn. Black has put White in Check twice and is already in a position to castle. Note that in the fourth move White offered a Pawn which Black refused and Black pressed on to threaten White's Knight. Having driven Black's Knight back, White must now continue development of his other pieces. It is anybody's game.

There are many other openings to study and readers who intend to take the game seriously should obtain a copy of one of the many books on chess openings.

Middle Game

This is the most difficult area to cover as far as instruction and

Fig. 21

Fig. 22

advice are concerned. There are so many different positions in which pieces may be placed on the board that it is only possible to give general guidance relating to a few common dangers to avoid. The beginner must always watch his Queen. Whatever move is contemplated he should look at it in the light of how does it leave his Queen when the move is made. He should also anticipate the next move of his opponent and make sure that, if it is an attack on the Queen, she can be saved before it is too late. This, of course, is in addition to safeguarding his King!

Pins

A piece which cannot or should not be moved is said to be pinned. Figure 21 shows a White Rook which is pinned by a Black Bishop. If White moved his Rook he would put his own King in Check which the rules do not allow. Figure 22 shows a White Knight pinned by a Black Bishop. If White moves his Knight, which he is allowed to do, he would lose his Queen to the Bishop.

A player who has a piece pinned should consider the following possible action:
1) capture the piece which is causing the pin.
2) move the piece which is being guarded to free the pinned piece.

Forks

If a piece is in a position from which it can capture either one of two pieces it is said to have them in a fork. Figure 23 shows a White Queen which in one move has put the Black King in Check and has forked Black Knight and Rook. When Black moves his King out of

Fig. 23

Fig. 24

Fig. 25

Fig. 26

Fig. 27

Check White Queen can capture either the Knight or the Rook.

A particularly deadly fork is a Knight attack on King and Queen as shown in Figure 24. Black must move his King and then White captures Black's Queen.

Skewers

A skewer is an attack on one piece which, when moved to avoid capture leaves the attacker in a position to take another piece. In Figure 25 White Bishop has put Black King in Check. The King must move and then Bishop captures Black Queen. From this example it is clearly dangerous play to position your King in front of your Queen. Sometimes it is possible to force a King into this position. Figure 26 shows a Black Rook about to force the White King to move from the Rook file. Figure 27 shows that Black's second Rook can now Check Black King forcing it to move again so that Black Rook can capture White Queen. A skewer can take place on a diagonal, a rank or a file.

End Game

The final stages of a game offer opportunities to the beginner for worthwhile study. It is disappointing to capture material, avoid pins forks and skewers but fail to effect a Checkmate. Study the simple mates to start with. If a Queen can safely occupy a square adjacent to that of the hostile King when he is at the edge of the board then that is a certain mate. Figure 28 shows that White King is not in Check but it is Black's move. Figure 29 shows the winning move. White King cannot capture Black Queen because he would

Fig. 28

Fig. 29

Fig. 30

Fig. 31

Fig. 32

move into Check from the Bishop. There is no escape square to which he can now move.

A simple mate is often effected with two Rooks. The hostile King must be driven to the edge of the board. Figure 30 shows Black King in Check from one White Rook and he must move. The only rank available to him is the back rank because the second White Rook stops him coming forward. Figure 31 shows that he has retreated and now White moves his second Rook to the back rank and this is mate. Figure 32 shows the move.

It has been stressed that players should always keep a wary eye on their Queens to ensure that these are not captured. In the part dealing with Queen movements it was stated that in some positions a player may decide to sacrifice his Queen to ensure a Checkmate. Here is an example which is worth playing out on your board. The game has reached the 17th move (Figure 33). White goes P–QKt4 and Black brings a Bishop to call Check B–B7 ch. White must move his King. He cannot capture the Bishop with his King because this would put his King in Check from Black's Knight. White's move is K–QR1. Now comes Black's surprise move. He feels that his position is strong enough to risk his Queen and he goes Q–K8! (Figure 34).

Note that White could capture Black Queen now but his position is so desperate that he feels it is more important to get his King out of the blocked position it is in. He must make an escape route and to do so he moves P–R3. Black's next move is another surprise. It is Kt×B! (Figure 35). There is nothing to stop White Rook capturing Black Queen now. This, of course, is what he does. Move

Fig. 33

Fig. 34

Fig. 35

Fig. 36

Fig. 37

Fig. 38

Fig. 39

Fig. 40

Fig. 41

Fig. 42

Fig. 43   Fig. 44

20 is RxQ for White. Black's reply is RxR ch! (Figure 36). White King is still on the run. He cannot capture the Rook so he must move. His foresight in moving out the Rook Pawn enables him to move K–R2. Black continues to press his relentless attack with B–KKt8 ch! (Figure 37). White King forlornly goes to KKt3 but Black hounds him with his Rook. The move for Black is R–K6 ch! (Figure 38). Once more the weary White King moves, this time to KKt4. This time Black does not put White King in Check but he rescues his Knight and brings it into the attack. His move is Kt–K7 (Figure 39).

White should really be concerned to rescue his King but he seems to hope for a distraction by threatening Black's Rook. He moves Kt–KB1. Black ignores this and continues to build up his attack on the King. This time he moves a Knight Pawn and threatens White's Queen, P–KKt3! (Figure 40). White saves his Queen by Q–Q5 and Black calls Check again with P–KR4! (Figure 41). White King goes to KKt5 and Black brings his own King into the fray. White's move is K–KKt5 and Black's K–KKt2 (Figure 42).

Because he is not actually in Check and because he aimed to do it a long time ago, White now captures Black's Rook. Black calls Check again by P–KB3 ch (Figure 43). If you put yourself in the position of the player with the White pieces you will see that White's next move is the only one open to him. He has to move his King and there is only one square available. There are five vacant squares of which four are under fire from Black pieces. So White moves K–KR4 and Black moves up his Bishop, B–KB7 ch! (Figure 44). Now comes White's last despairing move. It is P–KKt3 (Figure

Fig. 45   Fig. 46

Fig. 47

45). He is out of Check for only a matter of seconds. Black now captures this Pawn and calls Checkmate (Figure 46).

Study the position carefully. Black Bishop is Checking White King and it cannot be taken by any White piece. The King cannot capture it without moving into Check from Black Knight. The White Queen is on a wrong diagonal. White King cannot move to the only adjacent vacant square because this would be a move into Check from a Black Pawn!

For ten moves Black has managed without his Queen and in half of those moves he has been able to call Check.

In giving the value of pieces earlier in this article it was mentioned that although a Queen is the strongest piece on the board, a well positioned Pawn can tip the scales at the end of a game. This, indeed was just such a game!

And now to resignations, draws and stalemates. If either player is fairly sure that his opponent will soon effect a Checkmate and if he himself cannot possibly win he may well think it pointless to continue the game. He is therefore well-advised to resign and, of course, this means his opponent has won. On the other hand both players may find themselves without sufficient strength in pieces to effect a mate and it is usual for them to agree a draw.

On the other hand there is one form of draw which players with mating material on the board should strenuously avoid. This is stalemate. If it is your turn to move and the only moves open to you would mean exposing your King to Check when he is not already in Check, then that is a stalemate. You cannot move so you cannot win or lose. The result is therefore a draw. In Figure 47 the player with the White pieces cannot possibly win because he is reduced to a lone King. Black on the other hand has his Queen, a Rook, a Knight, a Bishop and a Pawn on an open file that might have become another Queen. But the result is a stalemate because it is White's move and he cannot move his King without moving into Check. Note that White is not in Check *before* his move. White therefore claims a draw.

Clearly this is a rather exaggerated position and Black has played very badly to allow this position to come about. To avoid a stalemate you must be sure that your opponent *can* move a piece without having to move his King into Check. You may hope for a stalemate if you are losing and your opponent is strong but it can only be a hope. There is no way of forcing your opponent to make the supreme blunder.

A Complete Game Analyzed

Here is a complete game with comments on the moves of both players. If you play this out on your own board you will find it easier to see whether or not you would have made the same moves.

Irregular Defence

White   Black
1) P–K4   P–K4

White makes a standard opening move with a Pawn placed in the centre of the board. Black's reply follows the convention of stopping the opening Pawn from going any further. Black also achieves equality in the game by occupying a centre square.

2) Kt–KB3   Kt–QB3

White brings out his King Knight. The position it now occupies is a threat to Black's King Pawn. Black's reply is bring out his Queen Knight to protect his Pawn. If White captures Black Pawn, Black would capture White Knight. Both players now have opening Pawns in the centre and each has a Knight ready for attack or defence.

3) B–B4   P–Q3

White advances his Bishop to a square from which it could take a Black Pawn (B x BP ch) and put the Black King in Check. This would be throwing the Bishop away if White makes it his next move because Black would reply with K x B. Losing a Bishop to take a Pawn is a poor exchange! On the other hand if White could in move 4 advance his King Knight to Kt5 he could *then* make the Bishop move with safety because the King would be unable to capture except by moving into Check which the rules do not allow. Black's reply is P–Q3. This move serves two purposes. Firstly it frees Black's Knight from its protective role guarding the King Pawn. Black's Queen Pawn now does this. Secondly it opens the diagonal for Black to bring out his Queen Bishop.

4) P–B3   B–Kt5

White's Pawn move is aimed at discouraging Black's Knight from advancing either to the centre (Kt–Q5) or to the Queen's side (Kt–Kt5). White's Pawn is ready to capture Black Knight if he jumps to either of these positions. White has also opened up another diagonal for his Queen.

Black's Bishop has now come out as we anticipated that it might. Black Bishop threatens White Knight but not very seriously because if B x Kt then P x B. But Black has pinned White Knight unless White is prepared to sacrifice his Queen. If White moves his King Knight then Black Bishop captures White Queen!

5) Q–Kt3   Q–Q2

White now takes advantage of the new diagonal for his Queen and goes to Kt3 on the same diagonal as his Bishop. Now if in his next move White Bishop captures Pawn it would be Check and Black King could not capture the Bishop because he would be moving into Check from White Queen.

Black can see this danger and moves his Queen one square so that, if necessary, she can capture Black Bishop if the Pawn is taken.

6) Kt–Kt5   Kt–R3

White is free to move the Knight that was pinned and he brings this up to support the attack he has mounted with his Queen and Bishop. The square under fire is KB7 for White or KB2 for Black. White now has two pieces either of which can capture the Black Pawn on this square. The White Bishop supports the Knight and White Queen supports the Bishop.

Black's reply to White's attack is to bring out his King Knight to a square from which it can capture any piece which dares to take the Pawn which is under threat.

7) BxP ch   KtxB

Now comes White's attack. By taking the Black Bishop Pawn with his Bishop he puts the King in Check. As expected Black captures White Bishop with his Knight. White continues to press the attack.

8) KtxKt   QxKt

In capturing Black's Knight with his own, White knows that Black King cannot be used against him because the King must not move into Check. If Black Queen takes White Knight there could then be an exchange of Queens. This is a risk Black is prepared to take and, though his King is not in Check he decides to capture White Knight with his Queen.

9) QxP   K–Q2

White now switches his attack to the Queen's side of the board. Having failed in his attack on the Black King he elects to gain advantage in material by first of all snatching a Pawn. Black brings his King forward to Q2 to avoid Check if White now captures Black's Queen Rook.

10) QxR   Q–QB5

Throughout the game so far White has done the attacking and Black has defended. In this tenth move the pattern starts to change. As expected White's new attack is aimed at gains in material and

Fig. 48

capturing Black's Rook without loss appears good until you study Black's reply. The move to QB5 is the beginning of Black's winning attack. Study the position carefully. He already has a Bishop covering his K7 square and White has no escape paths open to him. He must start a brisk defence now or lose the game.

11) P–B3   B×P

White's Pawn move is a threat to Black's Bishop and halts the immediate attack but Black keeps the pressure on by capturing the Pawn even though he knows he must surely lose his Bishop. White must capture Black Bishop if he is to stay in the game.

12) P×B   Kt–Q5

White Pawn captures Black Bishop. In terms of material captured White is ahead but the pressure is on and Black's move Kt–Q5 is a further threat and at the same time a possible sacrifice. White should take the Knight with his Bishop Pawn.

13) P–Q3   Q×QP

This is White's fatal mistake. By threatening Black's Queen with his Queen Pawn he had hoped to capture Black's Knight without loss. Black simply captures the threatening Pawn and waits for the kill. It is not far away.

14) P×Kt   B–K2

So White now captures Black Knight. He is still gaining material but to little effect. Black's reply only tempts him to further indiscretion. By moving his Bishop from the back rank Black has exposed his Rook to danger from White's Queen. In fact this does not matter as the next move by both players clearly shows.

15) Q×R   B–R5 mate!

White has fallen for the bait while Black has manoeuvred his Bishop into a winning position. White Queen captures Black Rook but Black Bishop moves to R5 and calls Check – in fact it is Checkmate (Figure 48). White has no piece to effectively intervene. White King is in Check and there is no escape square for him.

A short game this in which there are a number of noticeable features. Neither White nor Black castled in this game which is unusual for players of this stature. White did all the attacking in the earlier part of the game but Black's defence was always adequate. White gained more material but allowed himself to fall into fatal traps. Good aggressive play by White and brilliant cleverly calculated play by unruffled Black. The players were White Rodzynski and Black one of the really great chess players of all time, the legendary A. Alekhine.

Summary

Chess is not a game which is difficult to play nor is it really a difficult game to learn. There are, however, many rules to remember and a beginner should find the following At-a-glance A–Z useful when playing with an opponent who is also a beginner. A glance at the appropriate heading should lead to a quick answer to queries which may crop up in a game. There is also general chess information here.

At a Glance A–Z of Chess

Algebraic notation. This is a system of recording the moves in a game widely used on the continent but not much favoured in English-speaking countries.

The eight files are given the letters a to h from left to right for White and the ranks are numbered 1 to 8. The numbering starts from White's back rank. A move is recorded as the piece (not Pawns) identified by its initial and the combined letter-number of the square of departure and the square of arrival.

Back row. The back row is White's first rank and Black's first rank— that is the first line of squares running from left to right across the board and nearest to each player.

Bishops. Each player has two Bishops one of which is confined to White squares and the other to Black squares. All Bishops are confined to diagonals when they move but, provided the squares are unoccupied, they can move as many squares as they like in one direction. They can, of course change direction in the next move. Bishops capture by occupying the square of a hostile piece. They can put a King in Check if the diagonal from Bishop to King is unoccupied by White or Black pieces. One Bishop starts at the side of the King and the other at the side of the Queen. They are identified respectively as King's Bishop and Queen's Bishop.

Board. There are 64 squares on the board—32 White (or light coloured) and 32 Black (or dark coloured). When the pieces are set up for a game each player must have a White corner on the right of his back rank.

Capture. When any piece makes a capture it occupies the square of the hostile piece which is, in the same move, taken off the board.

This applies to all pieces from Pawns to Kings. A capture is indicated by a cross (x).

Castling. This special move is open to each player once in any game. The conditions governing the move are: The King must not have made a move before castling. The Rook must not have made a move before castling. The squares between King and Rook must be vacant. The King must not pass across a square under attack from a hostile piece. The King must not move into Check. The King must not be in Check. On the King's side the King moves two squares towards the corner of the board and the Rook two squares towards the centre and ends up therefore on the King's other side. To castle on the Queen's side of the board the King moves two squares towards the corner and the Rook three squares towards the centre of the board ending up on the King's other side.

Check. If a hostile King can be captured by a player in his next move then the King is in Check and it is customary for the player to say 'Check'. His opponent is obliged to get the King out of Check by moving the King to a safe square or capturing the attacking piece *or* placing a piece between the attacking piece and the King. The game can then proceed.

Check, discovered. If a player moves a piece which leaves the hostile King in Check from another piece then this is known as a Discovered Check.

Check, double. It is possible for a player to double Check the hostile King. An example is when a Bishop starts in front of a Rook which is in the file occupied by the King. The latter is not in Check but when the Bishop moves to a square of which the diagonal is in direct line to the King then there is a double Check—one from the Rook and the other from the Bishop. The King must escape from both.

Checkmate. If a King is put in Check and cannot escape from the Check, then that is Checkmate and the end of the game.

Chess clock. In tournament chess it is customary to decide before play begins how many moves a player must make within a given time. Special clocks are available with two faces and White's clock is started as soon as play commences. When he has made his move White presses a button to start Black's clock having stopped his own. Players keep a record of their moves and can see from their clocks how well they are keeping within the time limit for the game.

Descriptive notation. Sometimes called the English Notation because it is largely used in the English speaking countries, this is the method of recording games most likely to be of use to the reader. The files are identified by the initials of the pieces which occupy them at the beginning of the game. The ranks are numbered from 1 to 8 for both White and Black starting from the back rank of each. White's King square is K1 and this square, if Black reaches it is K8. In chess literature, White always plays from the bottom of the diagram. The pieces are identified by their initials and Pawns by P unless it is necessary to distinguish between two in which case they are further identified with the initials of the piece they stand in front of at the beginning of the game. A dash means 'moves to', and x means captures. Check is abbreviated to ch. (!) means a good move, (?) a bad move.

Diagonals. Moving across the diagonals of a board simply means moving across the corners. Bishops are confined to diagonals throughout the game. Queens have the option of using the diagonals as do the Kings though the latter, except when castling, are confined to moving only one square at a move.

Development. From the first move in the game each player endeavours to bring out his pieces to positions of advantage on the board. This is known as development. It can be impeded if a player's opponent gains an early advantage and plays an aggressive game. This inevitably means that defence and consolidation are called for and the player may be delayed in developing his pieces satisfactorily.

Draws. If neither player has sufficient strength to Checkmate it is customary for them to agree a draw. A draw can be requested by a player if the same position appears three times as a result of the same move being made by that player.

A draw can be claimed by either player if fifty moves have been made and no piece has been captured and no Pawn has been moved – an unlikely eventuality!

En passant rule. If a Pawn when making its first move advances two squares and avoids capture by drawing alongside a hostile Pawn then it can be captured as if it had moved only one square. The capturing move must be made immediately after the Pawn's two square advance and cannot be postponed until later in the game.

Forced move. This refers to the position a player finds himself in when the move he makes is the only possible move.

Exchange. When a player captures a hostile piece and then loses his own piece it is said to be an exchange. An exchange in which equivalent pieces are lost and won is an even exchange. An exchange in which a Knight or Bishop is captured for the loss of a Pawn is said to have been won – if the Pawn was captured in exchange for the Knight or Bishop the exchange is said to be lost.

Files. The rows of squares which run in line from your back row to your opponent's back row. In chess charts the files are the lines of vertical squares.

Files, open. An open file is one which is unoccupied by Pawns of either colour. Rooks do well in these.

En prise. A piece under attack and which is undefended is said to be *en prise.*

Fork. A fork is a double attack when a piece can, in its next move capture either one of two hostile pieces. To counteract a fork the player should consider a counter attack such as putting the hostile King in Check or capturing the piece responsible for the fork.

Gambit. A gambit usually means to offer a piece for possible positional advantage, and to enable the player making the offer to get early advantageous development. Some named chess openings have the word gambit in them such as Queen's Gambit Accepted or Queen's Gambit Declined.

Interpose. To interpose a piece is to place it between an attacking piece and the King to get the King out of Check. It also applies to relieving other pieces from attack such as placing a Pawn on a diagonal between an attacking Bishop and a Queen. The Bishop would then have to take the Pawn first and, if that square is safe, the Queen might then take the Bishop.

J'adoube. When a player has occasion to touch a piece in order to place it properly on its square and not to move it he should correctly say '*J'adoube*' or, more informally 'I adjust'.

Knights. These are the only pieces in chess which have the power to jump over other pieces (of either colour). The Knight's move is two squares in one direction and then one square in a different direction. He thus makes an L shaped move. The Knight can go two squares up a file and then one across a rank or two across the rank and one into the file. Knights can move forwards or backwards.

Kings. Kings are limited in their moves to one square in any one move except when castling takes place. The two Kings in a game must never be placed on adjacent squares. There must always be one square between them though this need not be vacant. King's can advance or retreat.

King's side. All squares on the right hand side of the board for White and left hand side for Black are referred to as the King's side.

Mate (see Checkmate).

Middle game. After the known moves of an opening and the final moves of the end game comes the major battle which is loosely referred to as the middle game. No precise number of moves constitutes either opening, middle game or end game.

Notation. The two most widely used systems of recording Chess games are Descriptive Notation (also known as English Notation) and Algebraic Notation. Both are described in this book.

Openings. The number of ways of playing the first ten moves of a game are some astronomical figure and the beginner cannot be expected to remember many of them, but he will remember a few as he becomes familiar with them.

Openings have been named after Master players with whom they have become associated, places or tournaments, or in some cases they have been named to indicate the likely course of play.

Pawns. The least powerful of the chess pieces, Pawns do have the chance of promotion if they can be safely taken to the opponent's back rank. The movement of the Pawn is one square forward in its own file except when it is moved for the first time when the player may, if he wishes, advance the Pawn two squares. Pawns capture diagonally and remain in the file on which the capture was made. Pawns never retreat and never hop over other pieces. Pawns can give check to a hostile King.

Pawn, blocked. A Pawn is said to be blocked if it can make no further progress forward because a hostile piece occupies the square immediately in front of it.

Pawns, doubled. When two Pawns of the same colour occupy the same file, as a result of a capture, the player finds he has Doubled Pawns. This impedes satisfactory play and development and should be avoided if possible. Doubled Pawns are weak Pawns.

Pawn, passed. A Pawn which has a clear run in its own file and no hostile Pawns on its adjacent files is known as a Passed Pawn.

Pieces. In this book, and many others, the term pieces refers to any of the chessmen including Pawns. Purists, however, limit the term to Queens, Rooks, Bishops and Knights. The Queens and Rooks are classified as major pieces and the Bishops and Knights as minor pieces.

Pin. A piece is said to be pinned if it cannot or should not move. A Bishop which stands in front of a King to stop a Check from a hostile Rook cannot be moved and is forcibly pinned. A Knight standing in front of a Queen is pinned if he prevents the Queen being captured. The player may have the right to move the Knight but would be well advised not to.

Promotion. When a Pawn reaches the end of its file (the 8th rank) it can be changed to any other stronger piece the player decides on. It is usual to choose a Queen. This is promotion.

Queens. Queens are the most powerful pieces on the board. This is because they can do more than other pieces. They can use ranks, files or diagonals and can move as many squares as the player chooses provided the way is clear, of course. They combine the powers of Rooks and Bishops. They are, like all other pieces, vulnerable and loss of a Queen is more often than not, loss of the game.

Queen's side. All squares on the left hand side of the board for White and right hand side for Black are referred to as the Queen's side.

Ranks. The lines of squares which run from left to right across the board are the ranks. In chess charts the ranks are the lines of horizontal squares.

Rooks. Second only to the Queen in power the Rooks are confined to ranks and files. They never move diagonally nor do they hop over other pieces. Rooks can travel as far as the player decides provided the squares are free and they capture by occupying the square of a hostile piece which is, in the same move, taken off the board.

Sacrifice. A player who allows a piece to be captured is said to make a sacrifice. This is done in the hope of obtaining an advantageous position which is not always obvious to the opponent.

Skewer. A skewer is an apparent attack on one piece whereas it is in fact an attempt by the player to capture a more valuable piece which is in the same line of squares but lying behind the piece attacked.

Stalemate. When a player can move no piece on the board except his King and if the King is not in Check but would move into Check if moved at all, then that is stalemate and the game is declared a draw.

Threat. If a piece can capture a hostile piece that is a threat.

Touched piece. If a player touches a piece the laws of chess decree that he must move it. An exception is when he is adjusting it on its square and this he must announce to his opponent (see *J'adoube*).

White, who plays? The decision as to which player has the White pieces is decided by lottery. It is usual for one or other of the players to conceal in each hand a Pawn of the two colours. His opponent then points to or touches one of the closed fists and plays whichever colour is revealed when the hand is opened.

Checkers

In Great Britain the game is called draughts and is played with Black and White pieces on a Black and White board. In the United States it is called checkers and the pieces are usually red and white and the board dark green and buff. The method of play is the same on both sides of the Atlantic though there are other variations such as Spanish draughts, German draughts, Russian draughts and Polish draughts. Other alternatives to the normal game are losing draughts and diagonal draughts.

The game is played on a board of 64 squares of which 32 are White (or light coloured) and 32 are Black (or dark coloured). Each of the two players has 12 pieces or men and these are round wooden or plastic discs coloured White (or light coloured) and Black (or dark coloured).

The discs are placed on the three rows of Black squares nearest to each player. Before setting out the pieces always ensure that the board is the correct way round by looking to make sure you have a White square in the right hand corner nearest to you (Figure 1). This is exactly the same as for Chess.

All play takes place on the Black squares and movement of the pieces is confined to moving forward on diagonals (across the corners of the squares). The pieces all have the same value and are all confined to the same type of move until they are advanced to the opponent's back row when they are crowned kings. This is done by placing a second disc on top of the successful one so that it is distinguished from the ordinary men. Kings can move in any direction on the diagonals and can retreat as well as advance.

Capturing is achieved by hopping over an opponents piece or pieces and in order to do this the piece to be captured must have a vacant square beyond it (Figure 2). The piece hopped over or captured is taken off the board in the same move. A piece making captures may continue to move for as long as there are hostile pieces to hop over and, in doing so, the piece may change direction (Figure 3). The arrows indicate the move Black makes to capture two White men in one move.

The object of the game is to defeat your opponent by removing from the board as many of his men as possible and to immobilize any pieces he is left with. Each player moves alternately and Black always starts a game. To decide who plays Black in the first game one of the players takes a piece of each colour and conceals these in his clenched fists. He then offers his closed hands to his opponent who chooses (by pointing at or touching) one or the other. Which-

Fig. 1   **Fig. 2**

ever colour is revealed to the player making the choice is the colour he must play. Thereafter players alternate colours in subsequent games played at the same session. Players make their moves alternately and the rules say that if a piece is touched it must be moved. Once a player removes his hand from a piece that has been moved he cannot move it again until his opponent has made his move. In other words you must make sure that you capture all the pieces you can in one move before taking your hand off a piece.

A player who fails to take a piece that could have been taken may be 'huffed' by his opponent. This must be done by the opponent immediately and he can insist that the piece which should have made the capture is removed from the board. A 'huff' is not a move and the player who has claimed the huff then makes his own move. If you have failed to take a piece which could be taken your opponent does have an alternative to 'huffing' you. He can, if he chooses, insist that you take back the move you have just made and he can make you take the piece you have overlooked.

You may find that you have two pieces on the board which can each make a different capture. In this case the choice is yours and if you take a hostile piece you cannot be 'huffed' provided that the piece you moved made all the captures available to it.

Good general advice is that when a game is under way it is usually better to move towards the centre of the board. From here your pieces can attack in two directions instead of being limited to one direction from the side of the board. Always study the position of the pieces very carefully before making a move and do not give your opponent the chance to 'huff' you. Try to follow up the move of a piece with other pieces to stop your opponent capturing lone men. In other words keep your pieces up together especially towards the end of a game. If you are ahead in captures you should go in for equal exchanges, that is be prepared to lose a man to capture one of his.

In competition draughts you should move within five minutes if it is your turn otherwise your opponent may call 'Time' and then you have only one minute to move or lose the game.

The system of recording games is quite simple and the serious draughts player would do well to master it. Figure 4 shows the numbering of the board. The Black squares which are the only ones used for play are numbered from 1 to 32 starting from Black's back row and the sequence in each row is from right to left. The Black pieces are placed on squares 1 to 12 and White on 21 to 32. Figure 1

Fig. 3   **Fig. 4**

shows the pieces set up ready for a game. In Draughts diagrams Black is always shown at the bottom.

The movement of each piece is simply given as the number of the square a piece moves from followed by a dash and then the number of the square the piece finally settles on. Figure 2 shows a Black piece moving to capture a White piece. This is written as 11–18. Captures are not mentioned in the notation. As in chess, opening moves in draughts have acquired names such as the Bristol which is 11–16 or the Edinburgh 9–13. Black, who starts the play has seven moves to choose from. Thereafter his play will depend on White's moves.

Here is a game between players of equal strength which, as you might expect, ends in a draw. If you play this out on your own board you will readily see how good draughts players think ahead. Black opens with 11–15 and White replies with 23–19. Neither player can capture yet. Black's second move is 8–11 to back up the first man moved. White goes 22–17 bringing a second front row piece into play and moving to the side of the board. Black now goes 4–8 continuing to back up his front men. White continues to the side of the board with 17–13. He cannot be 'taken' here. Black ventures into enemy territory with his next move which is 15–18 and White goes 24–20.

The game proceeds as follows: 11–15, 28–24. 8–11, 26–23. 9–14, 31–26. 6–9, 13–6 (first capture). 2–9, 26–22. 1–6, 22–17. 18–22, 25–18. 15–22, 23–18. 14–23, 27–18. 9–13, 17–14. 10–17, 21–14. 6–10, 30–25. 10–17, 25–21. 22–26, 21–14. 26–30 (1st King) 19–15. 30–26, 15–8. 26–22, 32–28. 22–15, 24–19. 15–24, 28–19. 13–17, 8–4. 17–22, 4–8. 22–26, 19–15. 26–30 Drawn.

Players who tire of conventional draughts may care to try some of the variations on the game.

Losing Checkers

This game follows closely the rules and regulations of ordinary draughts except that each player aims to lose his own pieces instead of trying to capture those of his opponent. To 'huff' becomes a little different and even more important in this game and a player who fails to take a piece is made to take back his move and capture the piece or pieces he did not take. In the early moves it is safe enough to go in for equal exchanges allowing your opponent to take one of your men for each of his that you capture. Thereafter try to move

Fig. 5

your men out from your back row and leave spaces between them and the pieces in front of them. The player who first loses his pieces or cannot move those remaining on the board is the winner.

Spanish Checkers

It is usual to turn the board for this game so that each player has a Black square in the right hand corner of his back row. The pieces are set out on the Black squares as for ordinary Draughts and they move in the same way – diagonally forward. Kings, however have greater power in this game. Readers who play chess will be familiar with the Bishops' move, which is through as many squares as the player chooses provided the diagonal is clear. In Spanish draughts a King also has this 'long move' but there must be a vacant square beyond the piece the King wishes to capture so that he can hop over the piece to take it. Kings making the long move need not stay on the vacant square immediately behind the piece taken but may move on along the diagonal to any other vacant square. It is, of course, compulsory to take any pieces available in any one move. Having hopped over all pieces that are available in the one move these are then removed from the board. Once a piece reaches the opponent's back row it is crowned and remains on that square until it is the player's turn to move again. Figure 5 shows the move of a Black King to capture four White pieces in the one move. Other than this the rules for ordinary draughts apply.

German Checkers

In this game the rules of draughts apply and Kings have the same power as they have in Spanish draughts. Kings can move along a diagonal as far as the player likes provided the squares are clear and provided there is a vacant square beyond the piece the King hops over and takes. Movements of the ordinary pieces are, however a little different. They move forward on diagonals but if capturing pieces they can move backwards as well. A piece reaching the opponents back row is crowned in the ordinary way *unless* it can take more men by coming back across the board. In this case the piece continues its move and is not crowned. If there is a choice in the pieces which you can move and which will make captures, you must move the piece which can take the most hostile men in the one move.

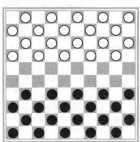

Fig. 6

Russian Checkers

This is similar to German draughts and the same rules apply except the one about pieces becoming Kings. In this game any piece reaching the opponents back row is crowned and then proceeds to complete its move by capturing any other men available to it. The players do not have to make the largest number of captures possible but are free to choose whichever piece they care to move.

Polish Checkers

This differs from the previous games described in that a board with a hundred squares is used (50 White and 50 Black). These are sometimes available in compendiums of games but the reader may find it necessary to make one. Each player has twenty pieces and the decision as to who plays Black is decided as for conventional draughts. The board is placed between the players so that each has a white square in the right hand corner nearest him. The pieces are set up as shown in Figure 6. Black has the first move.

All play is confined to the Black squares and the pieces move diagonally forward. Any piece can capture either forward or backward provided there is a vacant square beyond the piece being taken. A piece is crowned when it reaches the opponents back rank and it then becomes a Queen. As in conventional Draughts crowning is a matter of placing another piece on top of the man who then remains on the square until moved again. If a piece reaches the back rank but can still capture, it must do so and is not crowned. It is compulsory to capture the maximum pieces available. A Queen in Polish Draughts has the same powers as a King in Spanish Draughts. She is entitled to the long move, and can advance or retreat along a diagonal of squares provided they are unoccupied. She captures by hopping over an enemy piece and can either remain on the vacant square immediately beyond that piece or she can continue along other vacant squares.

Maximum capture being compulsory you would have to take an enemy Queen rather than a piece if both were available. When a Queen captures a number of pieces in one move these are left on the board until the move is completed. In this sort of move you cannot hop over the same piece twice. You may, however jump empty squares more than once in the same move. This is a refreshingly different game and one that is well worth trying.

Backgammon

Backgammon is a game in which men are moved round a board according to the throw of dice. Games with this principle have been known for at least 5,000 years, the earliest recorded example being discovered in a royal cemetery of the Sumerian civilisation in Mesopotamia.

Backgammon in most of its modern features has been played at least since the fifteenth century, and there are several backgammon boards in existence that date back to the sixteenth century. The name 'backgammon' itself dates back to 1645, though the games of 'tric-trac' (still the name used in France) and 'tables' were essentially what we know as backgammon.

However there is one very important feature of modern backgammon that was invented as recently as the 1920s, and that is the idea of *doubling*. This is a method by which the stakes can be raised during the course of the game, and it is the biggest single factor in making backgammon the action-packed game it is.

The Rules
Backgammon is a board game played between two players. Figure 1 shows the board set up in the starting position. Each player has fifteen men (variously referred to as pieces, chequers, stones) and the object of the game is to move the pieces round the board and then off the board. The player who first achieves this object is the winner.

Each player has two dice, and he makes his moves according to his dice throws.

The Board
The twenty-four elongated triangles shown in Figure 1 are referred to as 'points'. They correspond to the squares in other board games like chess or snakes and ladders. They are normally painted alternate colours to make it easier to count out the moves. There is no other significance in the different colours.

The board is divided into two halves by a central partition referred to as the 'bar'. In the configuration shown in Figure 1 the points on the right hand side of the bar make up the 'home board' and those on the left of the bar are the 'outer board'. White's home and outer boards are at the bottom of the diagram, while Black's are at the top.

The points have been numbered 1 to 12 starting from the right hand end of the board. This is to facilitate the description of the

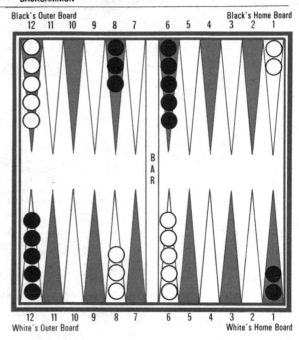

Black's Outer Board 12 11 10 9 8 7 6 5 4 Black's Home Board 3 2 1

BAR

12 11 10 9 8 7 6 5 4 3 2 1
White's Outer Board White's Home Board

moves; actual backgammon boards are not numbered. Points 1 to 6 are the 'home board' points, and 7 to 12 the 'outer board' points.

The Starting Position

At the beginning of a game each player sets up his men as shown in Figure 1. Notice that each player starts with five men inside his home board, on his 'six point' – i.e. on the sixth point counting from the right hand end. Each player has three men in his own outer board, on the eight point; and five men in his opponent's outer board, on the opponent's twelve point. Finally each player starts with two men in his opponent's home board, on his opponent's one point.

The player playing White sits at the bottom of the board, and Black at the top. Notice that White's home board is on his right, while Black's is on his left. The board can be set up in the mirror image position, such that White's home board is on his left. It makes no difference to the play; throughout this article we will use the set-up of Figure 1. Numbers thrown by the dice are printed in red.

The Play

Each player moves his men round the board towards his home

board. White moves anti-clockwise and Black clockwise. Thus the two sides are moving in opposite directions past each other. When a player has brought all his men into his home board (i.e. all his men are distributed somewhere on the points 1 to 6) he can then start to remove them from the board. The first player to remove all his men is the winner.

The players move alternately, and their moves are controlled by dice. Each player has two dice, and preferably a cup for shaking them, and when it is his turn to play he rolls the dice into the half-board on his right. Thus White rolls on the home board side of the bar, and Black on the outer board side. For a throw to be legal dice must come to rest flat on the surface of the board on the side on which they were thrown. If a die finally comes to rest on top of a man, or tilted against the side of the board, it is said to be 'cocked', and *both* dice must be thrown again.

For the first roll of the game, and the first roll only, each player throws one die. The player who rolls the higher number makes the first move, and takes as his roll the numbers shown on the two dice.

Moving the Pieces

When a player has thrown his dice, he must move his men according to the numbers showing on the dice. He considers each number separately: for example, if he rolls a 3–2 he must make a move of 3 and a move of 2, not a move of 5. If a player throws a double (i.e. 1–1, 2–2, 6–6 etc.) he must move the number four times.

There are three types of move: moving round the board, re-entering from the bar, and removing the men at the end of the game.

Moving round the board. Let us assume that the game is about to start. White throws a 5 and Black a 2, so as White has thrown the higher die he has the first move, and takes as his opening roll a 5–2. He must move one of his men five spaces, and one two spaces. He is allowed to move the same man, or he can move two different men. For example, two possible moves that White could play for his five would be to move from Black twelve point five spaces to his own eight point; or he could play a man from White eight to White three. (In future we will refer to Black's twelve point as 'B12' and so on.) For the two White could move any of his men. Figure 2 indicates the possible plays.

There are two restrictions on the movement of men round the board. The first is they cannot be moved past the one point – it is as

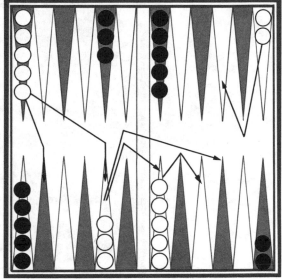

Fig. 2

if the pieces moved on a track which starts at the opponent's one point and ends at the player's own one point. For example, the men on W6 cannot be moved six spaces, as that would entail moving past W1.

The second restriction is that a man cannot be moved to a point occupied by two or more of the opponent's men. So for our example opening roll of 5–2 White could not move from B1 to B6 for the five, as B6 is already held by Black. Similarly if White played from B1 to B3 for the two, he could not then move on from B3 to B8, as B8 is also held by Black in the starting position. So in the starting position White can move from B1 with any number except a five; from B12 with any number except a one (ones being blocked by Black's men on W12); from W8 with any number; and from W6 with any number except a five or a six (fives are blocked by Black's men on W1, and a six would take the man past W1).

Re-entering moves. To introduce the second type of move, let us assume that White played his opening 5–2 by moving one man from B12 to W8, and one from B12 to W11. This leaves the situation shown in Figure 3. The isolated man at W11 is referred as a *blot*.

It is now Black's turn, and we will assume that he rolls a 6–4. One of the ways he can play the roll is to move from W1 to W5, and then onwards to W11. Remember if W11 had been occupied by two or more White men, Black would not have been able to move to that point. However, in this instance there is only one White man at W11, and in this case Black *is* allowed to move there. Furthermore, when the Black man lands on top of him the White blot is said

Fig. 3

to be hit. The White man is removed from the board, and has to be brought back into play at White's next turn. While the White man is in this limbo condition he is put on the bar.

When a player has a man on the bar he must bring it back into play at the first available opportunity. Until he does so he is not allowed to make any other moves. The man must be re-entered on one of the six points in the opponent's home board, as always according to the numbers shown on the dice. For example, if White has a man on the bar and he rolls a 6–2 he must re-enter the man either on B6 or on B2. As for the first type of move, he is not allowed to re-enter the man on a point held by his opponent. So if it happened that Black held B6 (as he does in the starting position) White would be forced to re-enter his man on B2. And if Black held both B6 and B2, White would not be able to re-enter at all with his 6–2, and he would lose his turn.

You will see that the more points a player manages to make in his home board the more difficult it will be for a man on the bar to re-enter. For this reason good players try to make as many home board points as possible (see below).

Bearing off. When a player has brought his men round the board and into his home, such that all fifteen of them are distributed somewhere on his own one to six point, he can start to remove them from the board. This process is called *bearing off*. As with the other types of move it is controlled by the dice, and in some respects it is the reverse process to re-entering. For example, if during the bearing off a player rolls 3–1 he is allowed to remove a man from his three point and a man from his one point, provided he has men on those points. Instead of removing a man from a given point he would also be allowed to move a man from a higher-numbered point.

An additional rule is required to cover the situation in which a player rolls a number corresponding to a vacant point. For example, a player may roll a three when he has no man on his three-point. Then if he has men on higher points he must move one of those; but if he has no men on higher numbered points he must bear off a man from the lower occupied point. This process is described more fully in the example game.

The Doubling Cube

The single feature that makes backgammon such an exciting game is the way in which the stakes can be periodically doubled during the game. The normal and most convenient way of recording the stake is with a *doubling cube*. This cube is usually rather larger than the dice, and on its six faces it has inscribed the numbers 2, 4, 8, 16, 32 and 64. At the beginning of the game the stake is one unit; as there is no 1 on the doubling cube this is signified by placing the cube half-way between the players with the 64 face uppermost.

As the game goes on, the player whose turn it is to roll may offer his opponent a 'double'. This means that the player who is doubled has the option of continuing the game at double the current stake, or of stopping the game and paying out his opponent at the current stake. If the player who is doubled accepts, the cube is turned to show twice the previous stake (e.g. to 2 for the first double of the game) and is placed on the doubled player's side of the table. The next double can only come from the player who accepted the last double.

As an example, after three rolls of a game White may decide to double. If Black accepts, the cube is turned to 2 and placed on his side of the table. The next double can only come from Black. Then if Black redoubles later in the game and White accepts, the cube is turned to 4 and placed on White's side of the table. The double to 8 can only come from White.

Scoring

In a normal game the player who first bears off all his men wins the number of points shown on the doubling cube. So if the stake was £1 a point and the cube was at 8, the winner would get £8.

A second type of win is a *gammon*. If one player removes all his men before his opponent removes any, the winning player is said to have gammoned his opponent, and he collects twice the number of points shown on the doubling cube.

A third degree of win is the *backgammon*. White would win a backgammon if Black had not removed any men and in addition still had Black men in White's home board when the last White man had been removed. In such a case Black would have to pay three times the number of points shown on the cube. In the U.K. it is quite common not to play backgammons–a player can never lose more than twice the doubling cube. Whether backgammons are played is a matter of agreement between the players.

In a normal three or four hour session between good players the margin at the end would be unlikely to be more than thirty points; between bad players it could be higher, as there tends to be more doubling cube activity in a weaker game.

An Example Game

For the opening roll, White throws a 6 and Black a 5, so as his first roll White gets a 6–5. He uses it to move a back man via Black's seven point to Black's twelve point. This will be written in shorthand:

1W. 6–5. B1–B7–B12.

It is now Black's turn, and he rolls a 3–1. He uses it to make his five point by moving a man from Black eight and one from Black six:

1B. 3–1. B8–B5, B6–B5.

The five point is the most important point to make in the early game.

2W. 6–3. B1–B7–B10.

White runs out with his other back man.

2B. 4–3. W12–B9, W12–B10 (hit).

Black hits the White blot at B9, and brings down another man into his outer board. This leaves the position shown in Figure 4.

White now has a man on the bar, and his first duty is to bring it back into play.

3W. 5–2. Bar–B2, B12–W8.

White has to re-enter on B2, and moves down from B12 with the five. Notice that if White had rolled 6–6, 6–5 or 5–5 he would not have been able to re-enter. He would then have lost his whole turn.

3B. 6–2. B10–B4, B6–B4.

Black makes another point in his home board.

4W. 5–5. B2–B7–B12, 2(W8–W3)

White is lucky in that he is able to escape with his back man to B12,

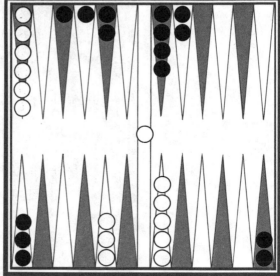

Fig. 4

and to make a point in his own home board. Remember that if you roll a double you move the number *four* times.

4B. 6 – 6 . 2(W1 – W7), W12 – B7, B9 – B3.

Black also gets a double, and uses it to bring his back men out to White's seven point (or *bar point*) and to move two other men towards home.

5W. 5 – 1 . B12 – W8, W6 – W5.

White brings one man down and starts his five point. Now that both sides have rescued their back men they will try to avoid leaving blots where their opponent could hit them. Since the blot on W5 is behind Black's rear-most men it is safe.

5B. 4 – 4 . 2(W7 – W11 – B10)

Black manages to escape from White's bar point.

6W. 6 – 5 . B12 – W7, B12 – W8.

6B. 5 – 4 . W12 – B8, W12 – B9.

7W. 3 – 3 . 2(W8 – W5), 2(B12 – W10).

This leaves the position shown in Figure 5. In the last three moves both players are simply moving round the board and getting their men in as fast as possible. To accelerate this rather boring phase of the game we will give both sides double sixes:

7B. 6 – 6 . 2(B10 – B4), B9 – B3, B8 – B2.

8W. 6 – 6 . 2(W10 – W4), B12 – W7, W8 – W2.

8B. 5 – 5 . 2(B8 – B3), B7 – B2, B5 – off.

Black brings his last three men into his home board. Having done that, he still has one five to play, and he bears off a man from his five point.

9W. 6 – 2 . W7 – W1, W8 – W6.

Fig. 5

Fig. 6

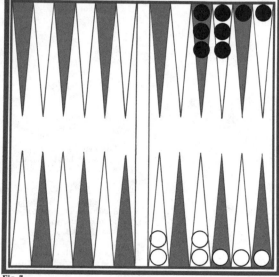

Fig. 7

This leaves the position shown in Figure 6.

Up to this stage neither side has had much of an advantage. But Black's 5–5 makes him a distinct favourite; it is now his turn to roll, but before he does so he *doubles*. White has the option of either conceding one point and getting on with the next game, or of playing on with the stake now at two points. White choses to accept, whereupon he takes the doubling cube over to his side of the table and turns it to 2.

9B. 5–1. B5–off, B6–B5.

Black takes a man off from the five point; since he has no man on the one point he must move a man from a higher point for the one. He chooses to move from the six point.

10W. 2–1. W7–W5, W1–off.

A miserable roll for White. He brings in his remaining man to his five point and takes a man off the one point.

10B. 5–3. B5–off, B3–off.

11W 6–3. W6–off, W3–off.

11B. 5–2. B6–B1, B2–off.

Black has no man on the five, so as he has a man on a higher point (i.e. the six point) he must move from there.

12W. 6–5. W6–off, W5–off.

12B. 6–4. B6–off, B4–off.

13W. 5–5. 3(W5–off), W6–W1.

White takes off his three men on the five point, and then has to move from the six point with the five. This leaves the position shown in Figure 7.

13B. 5–4. 2(B4–off).

Now a new rule comes into operation. Black has no man on his five point, but since he also has no man on a higher point he must bear off a man from the next lower occupied point– in this position, his four point.

14W. 5–5 . 2(W6–W1), 2(W4–off).

For his first pair of 5 s White has to move to his one point; but for the second pair, as he now has no more men on his six point he is allowed to take two men off his four point.

14B. 5–4 . B4–off, B3–off.

15W. 6–2 . W3–off, W2–off.

15B. 2–1 . B2–off, B1–off.

This leaves the following position: White, three men on W1. Black, two men on B3. It is White's turn to roll, but as he is now favourite, before he rolls he doubles. Black accepts, so the doubling cube goes back to Black's side of the table at 4.

16W. 2–1 . 2(W1–off).

White would have won the game outright if he had rolled a double at throw 16. He is still slightly favoured, as Black will not get off if he rolls a one or a two (apart from double 2).

16B. 6–1 . B3–off, B3–B2.

Black fails to get both men off. Since White is bound to get his man off now, White wins and receives four points (the number showing on the doubling cube).

This was rather a tedious game as there was only one hit in the whole game (Black's move 2), and both sides managed to get their back men out easily.

More exciting games occur when there is more blot hitting and when one side or the other manages to block in their opponent's back men.

The Elements of Good Play

The object of the game is for a player to remove all his pieces before his opponent. There are two broad ways in which the player can approach this objective: he can do so directly, by simply running his men round the board at every opportunity while taking little notice of what his opponent is doing; or he can take a more indirect line, and play to slow down his opponent by forming barriers and hitting blots wherever possible. If a player follows either of these techniques exclusively, he will probably lose. In most games a good player will use a combination of these tactics, adapting his game to suit the situation.

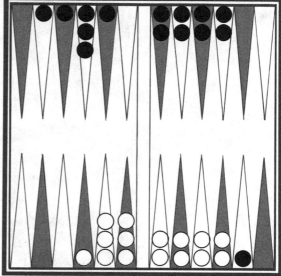

Fig. 8

Blocks and primes. The most powerful blockade against an opponent is six points in a row. Look at Figure 8. The Black man on W2 cannot move as all the points between one and six spaces away from him are held by White. (Remember, if Black throws say a 6–4, he cannot play a ten but must move a separate six and four.) White's succession of points running from W8 down to W3 is called a *prime*.

The lesson to be learnt from this is that it is a good thing to build up groups of consecutive points. In the starting position each player already holds two good points for blocking (his eight and six points), and much early play revolves round building up a block starting with this framework.

Home board points. Look at Figure 9. It is Black's turn and he has a man on the bar. He needs to get specifically a 1 to re-enter his man, odds of about five to two against. But change the position by moving the two men on W2 back to W7 and those on W3 to W8, and now Black only needs a 1, 2 or 3 to re-enter, odds of three to one on. The message here is that the more home board points a player has, the more serious it is for his opponent to be hit. So good players build up their home board whenever they can.

Blots. Clearly when the opponent has a strong home board a player will try to avoid leaving blots where they can be hit. But it is a mistake to play too cautiously, particularly in the early part of the game, and it is often good play in the first few moves to leave blots in order to gain greater flexibility. In a high quality game most of the risks are taken early on.

Fig. 9

Fig. 10

The Opening Moves

This general preamble brings us on to the best way of playing the early rolls. This is quite an instructive topic, as many of the ideas are useful for the later parts of the game.

The opening rolls fall into three principal categories: (i) point-making rolls, which are ones that enable the player to make a useful point immediately; (ii) extrication rolls, which are used to start the back men on the road to freedom; (iii) building rolls, which are used to set up the men to make a useful point at the player's second turn. We will consider them all from White's point of view.

Point-making rolls. 3–1, 6–1, 4–2, 5–3.

With all these rolls it is best to make a point down in the vital area of the board between W8 and W3.

3–1. W8–W5, W6–W5. Figure 10 shows the play of this most desirable opening roll. The five point is the most important point, as it adds to the block already started by W8 and W6, and on top of this is a home board point.

6–1. B12–W7, W8–W7. This roll enables White to make his seven point, or *bar point*. The bar point is the best purely blocking point, as it fills in the gap between the points already held; and as it is six spaces away from Black's back men it blocks 6–6 and 6–5, the best escaping rolls.

4–2. W8–W4, W6–W4. Like the five-point, the four point pulls weight in two ways, as a blocker and as a homeboard point.

5–3. W8–W3, W6–W3. Not such a good point, as it is too far forward to have much blocking effect. However it improves in strength if White subsequently makes his five or four point.

Running rolls. 6–5, 6–4, 6–3.

All are played by running out a back man from B1. With a 6–5 the man gets to safety at B12, with the other two White has to leave a blot either at B11 or B10.

Building rolls. 6–2, 5–1, 4–1, 2–1; 5–4, 5–2, 4–3, 3–2.

None of these rolls does anything appetising immediately; they are used to prepare the ground for making a point at the next turn.

6–2, 5–1, 4–1, 2–1. All these rolls are used to put a blot onto the five point, the idea being that if it is not hit by Black at his first turn White may be able to cover it at his second turn.

6–2: B12–W11–W5.

5 - 1 : B12 - W8, W6 - W5.
4 - 1 : B12 - W9, W6 - W5.
2 - 1 : B12 - W11, W6 - W5.
5 - 4, 5 - 2, 4 - 3, 3 - 2. All these rolls are played by moving two men from B12 down into White's outer board. The idea is that if the blot or blots so exposed survive, White will be well placed to make a good point at his next turn.

The play of doubles. The rules do not allow the first player to get doubles. If the second player gets a double as his first roll, the best way to play them is as follows (again from White's point of view).
6 - 6. 2(B1 - B7), 2(B12 - W7). White makes both bar points. A good roll.
5 - 5. 2(B12 - W8 - W3). White makes his three point from White's twelve point. But if Black had split his back men at his first turn, then it is usually better to play 2(W8 - W3), 2(W6 - W1) if by so doing White can put a Black man onto the bar.
4 - 4. 2(B1 - B5), 2(B12 - W9). White makes Black's five point, a powerful point for defensive operations; and brings down two men into his own blockade.
3 - 3. 2(W8 - W5), 2(W6 - W3). White makes two good home board points.
2 - 2. 2(B12 - W11), 2(W6 - W4). White brings down two builders, makes a home board point.
1 - 1. 2(W8 - W7), 2(W6 - W5). An extremely fine roll, as it enables White to make his bar and five points immediately.

Another consideration in the first few rolls is that it may be possible to hit an opponent's blot. It is usually correct to do so anywhere outside the player's own home board.

Otherwise the players concentrate on the twin themes of extricating their own back men while attempting to trap the opponent's back men.

Other Forms of the Game
Chouette. Though normally backgammon is played between two people, it is possible for more people to play in one game. In such a case one player (the 'man in the box') plays by himself against the others. One of the other players is called the 'captain'. If the captain's side wins a game, the captain becomes the man in the box, the next person in the queue becomes the captain, and the previous man in the box goes to the bottom of the queue. If the man in the box wins, he stays in the box and the captaincy is taken over by the next in line. The players can debate amongst themselves the best way to play a particular roll, or whether or not to double, but the captain has the deciding vote. While the players cannot double the box individually, they may accept or refuse the box's doubles individually.

Tournaments. Backgammon tournaments are becoming increasingly popular. The usual form is to play a knock-out. The winner of each match in the various rounds of the knock-out is the first player to reach a given number of points. The winners of each match are paired against each other in the successive rounds, until finally there is only one unbeaten player.

Hex

Hex is a board game of pure skill for two players. Its rules are very simple, but it is a game of considerable interest, and deserving of more attention than it has yet received.

Hex is played on a diamond shaped board ruled into equilateral triangles, the standard size board having ten triangles along each edge (see Figure 1). Play takes place on the points of intersection of the lines as in Go, and not within the triangles.

Algebraic notation is used to define points, and for this purpose vertical lines are ignored. Thus the central point is referred to as F6, and not F11 or L6.

Moves are also made as in Go—starting with the board empty players alternately place men on any vacant point, Black moving first. Once played men are not moved, and there is no capturing.

Each player's object is to build a continuous chain of adjacent men linking any point on one of the sides marked with his colour

Fig. 1

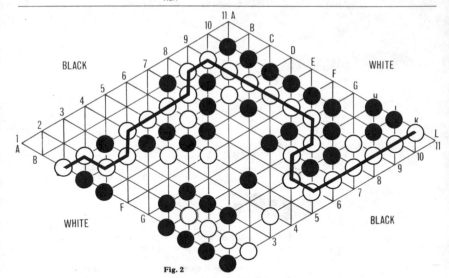

Fig. 2

to any point on the opposite side. Corner points may be used by either player to reach his side.

Figure 2 shows the end of a game of hex which White has won. The heavy black line picks out the continuous chain of men with which he has linked his two sides. Note that a winning chain can turn and double back as much as it likes as long as it has no gaps. Notice also that a game of hex cannot be drawn. There is no way Black could now connect his two sides without the chain crossing the white one somewhere.

We will now examine the game which ended as in Figure 2. You are advised to play the moves through on a board.

Moves 1–20 (see Figure 3)

Black 1: The strongest opening move is on the centre point–however, as this gives Black a considerable advantage it is customary to bar opening there, or sometimes on the entire short diagonal. The latter rule was in force in this game.

White 2: A typical reply.

Black 3: This makes a 'double connection'–the two black men cannot be disconnected because as soon as White plays F7 or F8 Black plays the other.

White 4: Tries to block Black 3 from the lower right side.

Black 5–White 9: More double connections by Black, and more blocks by White. Black has a rather inflexible position, but White has a weak point at K5.

Black 9–Black 15: Black cuts White off from the lower left side, and the following plays look rather submissive on Black's part. However, he is being chased in the direction he wants to go (towards A1), so

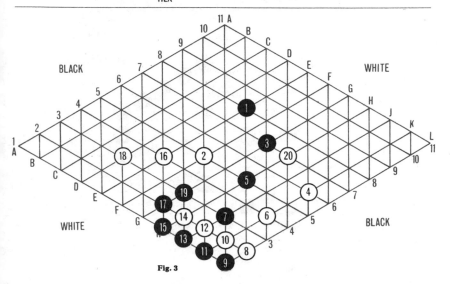

Fig. 3

Black is happy knowing that White cannot keep this up too long.

White 16: This man threatens to connect both to the lower left side and to White 14.

Black 17: Threatens to break both these connections, so;

White 18: Preserves the possibility of connecting to the lower left side, and hints at a possible winning chain via the C9 area.

Black 19: Carrying out the threat to disconnect 14 from 16.

White 20: A subtle move, threatening to link the white men (and therefore disconnect the black ones) with a play at H4. Without White 20 Black could parry this threat by disconnecting White at his weak point of K5 e.g. White H4, Black K5, White H6, Black G6, White J5, Black H7, White J6, Black J8, etc. However, White 20 protects this weakness at K5.

Moves 21–40 (see Figure 4)

Black 21: A very solid reply.

White 22: He has to play somewhere in this area as Black 1 is now potentially connected, via double connections and directly, to L1 on the lower right side, and he must therefore disconnect it from the upper left side.

Black 23: Trying to block White 22 from the upper right side; but;

White 24–White 34: In a forced sequence White connects his 22 to the upper right side using his 20 and 4 on the way. Of course the chain still has some gaps, but these are all of the 'double connection' variety, so Black has no way to break through.

Black 35–White 36: Black's only hope is to push through between White 2 and 22, and White's defensive block at a distance is usually the right way to handle such a frontal assault.

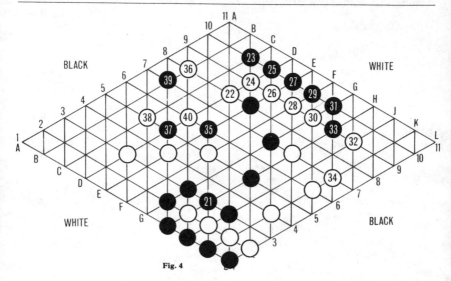

Fig. 4

Black 37 – White 38: White is prepared to abandon his 2 and 16. He doesn't mind which way his winning chain runs!
Black 39: An attempt to confuse the situation.
White 40: Probably best, but . . .

Moves 41–68 (see Figure 5)

Black missed a chance to win with 41 D4. After missing this chance, the game goes downhill for him – he plays his remaining moves only in the hope of a mistake by White.

After White 44 he threatens a double connection with the upper right side with B10 or A11. Black 45 prevents this, but White just plays 46 and uses the connection he established with moves 24–34. White 50 and 52 are standard replies to an attempt to break a double connection to a side point. The remaining moves are trivial as they consist of threats to break double connections and their replies.

As in most games of strategy, it pays in hex to keep your options open as long as possible. Black lost this game because of a too solid style of play, especially in over-reliance on the double connection in the opening stages.

Hex was invented in Denmark in the 1940s and enjoyed a brief vogue there and subsequent pockets of interest in the U.S.A. However, there is almost no literature on the game, and at the time of writing the game is not manufactured. It is however quite easy to make a board and to use Go stones or counters for the men, or you can play with a pencil on isometric drawing paper.

Some players prefer a board drawn as a tesselation of hexagons, playing inside the hexagons instead of on the intersections as in the version shown here. The game comes to the same thing, but

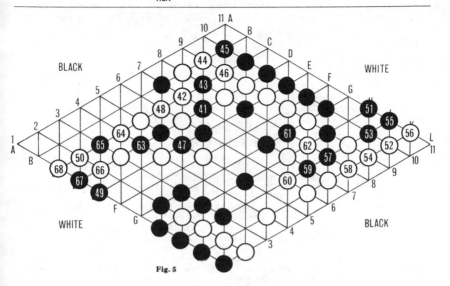

Fig. 5

the board is far harder to draw!

Other size boards than the one shown may be used. I think that as the game comes to be studied more larger boards may well be used.

The lack of hex literature is an advantage for the player who likes a game that depends mainly on over-the-board ability rather than prior book study. It is of course an irony of this and all such games that as general interest in it grows, so also will the amount of book work required to become a stronger player.

Reversi

Reversi is a board game for two using an ordinary draughtsboard (chequerboard) and 64 identical men similar to draughtsmen with the two sides of each man in contrasting colours usually, as here, black and red.

The game was invented in England in the late nineteenth century when it became briefly popular. It continues to enjoy a modest following but should be better known as it is skilful and fast-moving with dramatic changes of fortune and is also a good family game.

Many variations of Reversi have been tried (for example, on different size boards) but the version given here is the standard one. Cheap sets are readily obtainable but the men may easily be improvised.

81	82	83	84	85	86	87	88
71	72	73	74	75	76	77	78
61	62	63	64	65	66	67	68
51	52	53	54	55	56	57	58
41	42	43	44	45	46	47	48
31	32	33	34	35	36	37	38
21	22	23	24	25	26	27	28
11	12	13	14	15	16	17	18

Fig. 1

63	64	65	66
53	54	55	56
43	44	45	46
33	34	35	36

Fig. 2

63	64	65	66
53	54	55	56
43	44	45	46
33	34	35	36

Fig. 3

Preparation for Play

Players toss for colour then each takes 32 men and arranges them in front of him, own colour uppermost.

The board is placed between the players without regard to orientation as the colours of the squares have no significance in the game.

Before we go further it is necessary to annotate the board for reference. An adequate notation is shown in Figure 1 with the colours of the squares omitted for clarity. It will be seen that each row (rank) is numbered progressively up the board in tens, and each column (file) progressively from left to right in units.

The board is now dressed by the players alternately placing two men, one at a time, on the four central squares. Clearly only two arrangements are possible, with like men either side-by-side (Figure 2, preferred by experts) or diagonally opposite (Figure 3).

Play

Red plays first and places a man on any vacant square orthogonally or diagonally adjacent to a square already occupied by a black man such that the black man is flanked by two red men. It can be readily seen that Red has four, and only four legal plays in either of the two initial arrangements. When a man has been trapped in this manner it is reversed to show the colour of its captor. For example, if the board were dressed diagonally (black men on 45 and 54), and Red played first on 35, the black man on 45 would be turned over, when there would be four red men on the board and only one black man (on 54).

Now it is Black to play and he can occupy 34, 36 or 56, reversing one red man in each case.

Object of the Game

The object of the game is to have a majority of your colour on the board at the end. Play ceases when all the squares have been filled or when neither player has a legal move (i.e., cannot make a capture). If at any time one player is unable to move, he misses his turn.

Strategy

As the board fills up from the centre, opportunities will occur to capture several men in a single play. Men captured are determined solely by the last piece played, when every enemy man in an unbroken line between it and the next friendly man *in any and every*

Fig. 4

direction are captured and reversed. Theoretically, as many as 19 men can change sides in one play though about half this number is the usual maximum.

Figure 4 shows a game in progress with Red to move. In this position, Red has five plays:

25 – reversing the two men on 35 and 45
33 – reversing the two men on 34 and 35 and the man on 44
42 – reversing the three men on 43, 44 and 45
53 – reversing the man on 54
64 – reversing the men on 34, 44 and 54

Remember that the man played alone dictates the men captured. Thus if Red here plays 33, then after reversal of 34, 35 and 44 the black man on 45, although surrounded, is not reversed.

All captured men must be reversed at once but there is no requirement to make the numerically largest capture.

Notice that if there is a gap anywhere in a line of men flanked by two men of the opposite colour, either between the men in the line or between one of the end men and a flanking man, then none of the men is reversed. Similarly, a line of men cannot be trapped if one of them is on the board edge as then it is impossible to satisfy the conditions of capture. However, if the line runs along the board edge, then the men can be captured unless a corner square is occupied by one of the group when capture again becomes impossible.

It will be seen from this that certain squares can be more valuable than others. Figure 5 identifies best squares to occupy (white) and worse (red) with shading showing relative values of the others.

Fig. 5

It will be seen that the four squares diagonally in from the corners are especially to be avoided because their occupancy is likely to allow the opponent into the strong corners securing all adjacent men in three directions.

This is only a relative guide however, useful as all such guides are useful, but not to be followed slavishly as positions can often arise where square values may vary from those shown.

The concept of key squares nevertheless remains at the root of Reversi strategy and it is usually better to forgo the capture of, say, five men, if an important square can be gained for, say, the capture of only two or three men.

Generally speaking, one should aim at filling in the centre before expanding outwards to the sides (notice in Figure 5 that the 12 squares that surround the four dressed squares in the centre are all classed as valuable).

It is not easy to see ahead accurately more than a move or two in Reversi except in the closing stages of a game, but with practice one can develop a feel for good and bad formations—and unlike so many games, Reversi, because of its fluctuating fortunes, can never be dull.

Wari

There is a whole family of games, commonly referred to generically as Mancala, whose common features are that they are games of skill, usually for two players, in which a number of stones or beans, initially distributed among two, three or four rows of cups, are redistributed or 'sown' according to certain rules; contents of cups are captured from time to time by one or other of the players, the winner being the player who acquires more than half of the available stones.

Mancala has been described as the national game of Africa and has a good claim to being the oldest board game extant as it is believed to have been popular during the Empire Age of Ancient Egypt well over 3,000 years ago. There are at least two hundred recorded regional variants of Mancala, each with its own local name. One of the most widely played is Wari, originating in West Africa where the 'boards' are often simply holes scooped out of the ground (though boards are also carved from wood, often elaborately) with the 'stones' usually beans, pebbles or shells.

A Wari board consists of 12 cups arranged in two parallel rows of six with a large cup at each end, one for each player, to keep prisoners (Figure 1).

Fig. 1

Play

The two players face each other across the board which is placed lengthways between them, each player assuming control of the row of six cups nearest to him.

The board is dressed by placing four stones in each of the 12 cups, there being no differentiation between the stones of the two sides.

The players decide who shall start, and the first player lifts *all*

Fig. 2

the stones from any cup of his choice *on his side of the board* and sows the stones one at a time into successive cups in an anti-clockwise direction starting with the cup immediately to the right of the emptied cup and continuing round his opponents cups if necessary. The second player then takes all the stones from one of the cups on *his* side of the board (4 or 5 as the case may be) and sows them similarly, still in an anti-clockwise direction.

Play continues in this way until one player puts the *last* stone from one of his cups into an opponent's cup that contains *one* or *two* stones (i.e., two or three stones after distribution has been completed). The player is entitled to all the stones in this cup as prisoners. He scoops them out and puts them in his large hole at the end of the rows. If there are also precisely two or three stones in the *preceding* cup, and this cup is also on the opponent's side, then these stones too are taken prisoner. Similarly with the next cup. If any cup has less than two or more than three stones in it, however, then these stones are immune from capture as are the stones of any cups which preceded it in the distribution, regardless of their contents. Some simple examples will serve to explain these points.

Let us call the players White and Black, and annotate the cups on White's side A–F and those on Black's side a–f, from left to right looked at from White's side in each case. The starting position is then as shown in Figure 2. The arrows indicate direction of play.

Supposing White starts and elects to pick up the stones in cup E. He must pick up *all* the stones. He then sows them anti-clockwise, dropping the first stone in F, the second in f, the third in e and the fourth in d. As d does not now contain either two or three stones, no captures are made and the turn ends. We can record this simply as E(4), the letter indicating the cup emptied and the number of stones in it. There is no need to indicate the player, as each can only empty a cup on his own side of the board and can only capture stones on his opponent's side. Let us continue a move or two: f(5); B(4); a(5)

The position is now as shown in Figure 3. Black's last play was into cup E which now has two stones in it. Accordingly, these stones are removed and are now Black's prisoners. If D had had 2 or 3 stones in it, Black would have captured these as well. If each of the cups A–E had had either 2 or 3 stones in them after the distribution from a, then Black would have taken the contents of all these cups.

There are only a few other rules. If a cup contains more than 11 stones and hence at least one circuit of the board is completed, the

Fig. 3

cup from which the stones were lifted must remain empty. Thus if 12 stones were distributed, the last stone would be dropped into the cup immediately beyond the starting cup.

A player may not empty or leave empty *all* the cups on his opponent's side. He must play so as to leave at least one stone for his opponent to sow (it is hard to find a parallel of this compassionate rule in European games). If he is unable to do so, he (the player) takes all the stones remaining (which must perforce be on his side of the board) and adds them to his prisoners and the game is over.

Sometimes in the late stages of a game a position arises where no further meaningful plays are possible (for example, if White has only one stone left at C and Black only one stone left at c, these two stones will simply follow each other round). In this case, the players take up the stones on their respective sides of the board and the game is over.

Hints on Play

There is no chance in Wari, so theoretically a 'best play' can be calculated in any position. In practice, of course, the possibilities to be considered are astronomical except in the late stages of a game, so precise computation is out of the question.

Simple tactics become evident after a game or two. For example, a cup containing two stones is obviously vulnerable to an enemy cup that contains the correct number of stones to reach it. The weakness can be defended by (a) emptying a cup that will allow a stone to be added to the two thus making that cup impregnable; or (b) playing so as to add a stone to the enemy cup so that it will overshoot its target; or (c) emptying the cup and distributing the two stones. This last is not usually satisfactory as the second player has only to feed one stone into the empty cup to make it vulnerable again.

An aggressive game calls for a build-up in your right-hand cups. If the number of stones in any cup is such that the last stone sown in that cup will be sown in home territory, then clearly that cup is inoffensive and the stones in it poorly deployed. Aim to get several of the opponent's cups simultaneously under attack.

Mah Jong

Mah Jong is a game for four players (two- and three-player versions exist but are unsatisfactory). Mah Jong has affinities to the card game, Rummy, and like that game, the element of luck is considerable while still leaving scope for skilful play.

Mah Jong in its present form is probably about a hundred years old, a development of early Chinese card and domino games, themselves derived from ancient Chinese paper money. Mah Jong cards (narrow strips of pasteboard) are still used, but the game is commonly played with tiles, once made of ivory or bone and often backed with wood, particularly bamboo, but now almost invariably manufactured of plastic.

The game is widely played today throughout the Far East and among Chinese communities everywhere. One of the distinctive sounds in the back streets of Singapore and Hong Kong is the audible shuffling of the tiles – 'the twittering of the sparrows'.

Mah Jong was first introduced to the West as a card game before the turn of the century but it was not until after the First World War, when it reappeared in its present form, that it acquired any popularity. The Mah Jong craze of the 1920s, particularly evident in America, soon passed, a victim of proliferating rules and the rising appeal of Contract Bridge.

Rules

There are two basic games; the uncomplicated Mah Jong of the East, essentially a gambling game, and the Western version which has many 'special hands', more elaborate scoring and sometimes extra tiles. Although a number of attempts have been made to codify Mah Jong, there are no universally acknowledged rules, certainly for the Western game, though the version offered here, a compromise between the two extremes, has achieved wide acceptance. Nevertheless, rules should always be agreed before play to avoid misunderstandings.

Equipment

Tiles. A modern set comprises 136 tiles of which 108 are 'suit' tiles and 28 are 'honour' tiles.

There are three suits in Mah Jong; Bamboos (commonly called 'sticks'), Characters (sometimes called 'numbers') and Circles ('dots'). There are 36 tiles in each suit, four of each number from one to nine.

The honour tiles consist of four each of Winds (East, South,

Fig. 1

West and North) and Dragons (Red, Green and White). The reverse side of all tiles is uniform, invariably plain. The 34 different values are shown in Figure 1. Notice that the ones and nines of each suit are known as terminals.

A few sets also have decorative tiles known as Flowers and Seasons, each tile different and numbered. These earn bonus points but otherwise have no part in the play and these days they are little used.

Bones. These are really counters or chips, but are long and thin with the value of each stamped on it. Common denominations are 10, 100 and 500.

Dice. Two conventional dice are used in the preliminaries.

Wind Disc. This is simply a marker to show 'prevailing wind' (i.e., the dealer).

Racks. Sets often include racks to hold the hands of each player. Tiles can also be stood on end, blank side facing the other players, or held in the palm of the hand.

Fig. 2

Preliminaries

Few games can have such elaborate preliminaries as Mah Jong. Some enthusiasts consider these add flavour to the game.

1) One player takes one each of the wind tiles and shuffles them face down. Each player then picks up a tile, the shuffler taking the last one. East is first dealer, who chooses his seat. South sits on his right, North on his left and West opposite him. Note that this does not correspond to our arrangement of the compass points.

2) The 136 tiles are now mixed face down with all players taking part in the shuffling. Each player then builds a wall 17 tiles long and 2 high, all tiles face down. When the walls are complete they are moved together to form a hollow square. This is the Great Wall of China, secured against demons (Figure 2).

3) The dealer (East Wind) now throws the dice, adds the two numbers together and counts round the walls *anti-clockwise*, beginning with his own. Thus if East threw a 2 and a 5, totalling seven, he would count 'East 1, South 2, West 3, North 4, East 5, South 6, West 7'. To determine the point at which the wall will be broken, West (or whichever player at whom the count ended) then throws the dice and adds the total to that of East's throw. If West threw two 3's, for example, making 13 in all, West would then start counting along the tiles of his wall *from right to left*, breaking the wall between the 13th and 14th tiles. (If West had thrown a double 6, making a total of 19, he would have continued counting round the corner onto South's side.)

4) The players now draw their hands from the wall in the following manner. East, as dealer, first takes the four tiles (two stacks of two)

231

immediately beyond the break. Each of the other players do like-wise in turn (South, West, North), the wall thus being dismantled clockwise. This procedure is repeated three times when each player has twelve tiles. East then takes the next two tiles and the other players in turn take one more each from the wall, always the tile nearest the break and top before bottom. The hands, which are concealed from the other players, are now complete and play can start.

Object of the Game

The aim of each player is to make the highest score which is usually synonomous with being the first to go Mah Jong (go out), similar to Rummy. A player may go out when he has arranged his hand into four sets and a pair, or completes a special hand (see below).

There are three kinds of sets:
1) A sequence (CHOW); any three consecutive tiles of the same suit
2) A triplet (PUNG); any three identical suit or honour tiles
3) A four (KONG); any four identical suit or honour tiles.

A pair is any two identical tiles.

In the hand shown in Figure 3, the player is waiting for a North Wind or an 8 of Characters to go out.

Play

1) Dealer starts by discarding a tile of his choice face up inside the wall. All players now hold 13 tiles. Dealer's subsequent discards are laid face up in a continuous row so that the other players can see what he has discarded and in what order. The other players follow the same procedure. An alternative system is for discards to be placed face up at random within the wall.

2) After the dealer has discarded, and assuming no other player wants his discard (see below), play will continue anti-clockwise. South will take the next tile from the wall (at the point where North removed the last tile for his hand), discarding at will, and so on until a player goes Mah Jong, or Wu as it is sometimes called.

3) A set can be made in two ways:
a) It can be picked up in the initial hand, or drawn from the wall, or a combination of these. This is known as a *concealed* Chow, Pung or Kong.
b) It can be completed by picking up the third tile (or fourth in the case of a Kong) discarded by another player. This is known as an

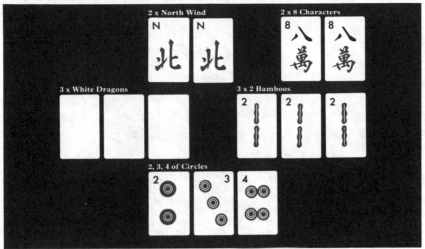

Fig. 3

exposed or open Chow, Pung or Kong. (An exposed Kong can also be obtained by adding a tile drawn from the wall to an exposed Pung but not by claiming a discard to add to an exposed Pung.)

4) Concealed sets (except Kongs, see below) are not disclosed until the end of play. They are worth double exposed sets (except Chows). Exposed sets are placed face up in front of the owner, between the rack and the wall.

5) Only the discard of the last player can be claimed, and that before the next player has picked up a tile. Only the next player in sequence can claim a discard to complete a Chow, but any player can claim a discard to complete a Pung or a Kong or to go Mah Jong (completing a set *or* the necessary pair to go out). The player or players requiring the discard shout 'Chow', 'Pung', 'Kong' or 'Wu', as appropriate. Precedence is in ascending order of value, with a player claiming a Chow having lowest priority and a player calling Wu, highest. Where more than one player is claiming Wu, the player first in rotation of play has prior right.

6) A player who wins a discard takes the tile into his hand and *at once* completes a set, which is then exposed, or goes out. If he does not go out, he must himself discard before completing his turn. A discard may not be claimed to keep in hand nor to add to an exposed Pung. The turn of play then passes to the player immediately to the right of the player claiming the discard. Thus if East throws away and North legally claims the discard, then play will again pass to East; South and West having effectively lost their turns.

7) A special procedure occurs when a player completes a Kong. If this is picked up in the initial hand, then the player must wait until his turn when he declares it, placing it on the table, the two central tiles face up and the outside tiles face down to show that it is a concealed set. He then draws a tile from the wall *but does not*

discard. If a player completes a concealed Kong during play and claims it, or claims a discard to make an exposed Kong, or draws the fourth tile to add to an exposed Pung, he must draw a further tile from the wall and discard in the usual way when his turn ends. This procedure is designed to ensure that the right number of tiles are always in hand to go Mah Jong (four sets and a pair). A player with an exposed Pung may hold the fourth tile in his hand but elect not to complete the Kong (because, for instance, he wants the fourth tile for a Chow). In this case he cannot claim points for a Kong if another player goes Wu, nor can he draw another tile. He may subsequently, however, decide to convert his Pung into a Kong when he follows the procedure set out above.

8) If nobody has gone Mah Jong when the wall has been reduced to 14 tiles (the 'dead wall', often separated slightly from the main wall at start of play), the game is abandoned without scoring.

Scoring

Scoring, like the preliminaries, can be complicated. First, the winner (the player to go out) adds up his points as below.

Scoring Table

Points awarded for	Amount scored
– going Mah Jong	20
– going Mah Jong and drawing last tile from wall (i.e., not a discard)	2
– going Mah Jong with the last tile from the wall (excluding the 14 dead tiles)	2
– an exposed Pung of	
simple tiles (2–8)	2
terminal tiles (1, 9)	4
honour tiles	4
– an exposed Kong of	
simple tiles	8
terminal tiles	16
honour tiles	16

Concealed Pungs and Kongs count DOUBLE.
Chows score NOTHING, whether concealed or exposed.
Pairs score as follows:

Dragons	2
Dealer's (prevailing) wind	2
One's own wind	2

Notice in particular that Chows earn nothing while Pungs and Kongs of terminals earn the same as honour tiles, and concealed sets are worth double exposed sets. Certain pairs can also earn points, as shown. They score the same whether the pair was concealed or completed from a discard to go out. Some schools allow a number of additional bonuses but these are omitted in this description for simplicity.

When the points are added, they are *doubled* for *every time* that the following conditions can be satisfied:

1) Holding a Pung or Kong of:
a) Dragons
b) Dealer's (prevailing) Wind
c) Own Wind
2) The tile to go out is drawn from the wall
3) The tile to go out is the last tile of the wall (excluding the 14 dead tiles)
4) The hand is all of one suit with Winds or Dragons
5) The hand is all Pungs

They are *doubled twice* whenever the hand contains a triplet or four of the player's wind *when he is dealer* and *doubled four times* when the player's hand is all of the same suit or all terminals or all honours tiles.

Payment

Only the player who goes Mah Jong scores his hand. The other players each pay him the total score, rounded up to the nearest ten. The dealer (prevailing wind) pays *double*, but if he is the player who goes Mah Jong all the other players pay him double.

Some players score every hand, each player settling the difference between his score and those of the other players, but this is very confusing and is not recommended.

It is usual to agree a limit score for a hand. This is usually 500.

Example of Scoring

East is dealer and goes Mah Jong, drawing his last tile from the wall, with the following hand:

Concealed Kong of East Wind
Exposed Pung of Red Dragons
Concealed Pung of 1 Circles
Concealed Chow (3, 4, 5 of Bamboos)
Pair of Green Dragons

He scores:

Going Mah Jong	20
Drawing last tile from wall	2
Concealed Kong of East Wind	32
Exposed Pung of Red Dragons	4
Concealed Pung of 1 Circles	8
Concealed Chow	0
Pair of Green Dragons	2
	68

He doubles his hand once for:
   Pung of Dragons
   Going out with tile from the wall
He doubles his hand *twice* for:
   Kong of dealer's wind when dealer
   The hand thus earns four doubles, making a total well in excess
of the limit hand, hence the total score for payment is 500. But East
is dealer, so each of the other players must pay him 1,000 points.
There are no other payments.

Special Hands
Many consider that Mah Jong was suffocated by the proliferation
of 'special hands' introduced from time to time 'to make the game
more interesting'. However, certain of these hands, including one
or two admitted in the Chinese game, have achieved general
acceptance and are given below. They are all 'limit' hands.
1) *Concealed Triplets* Four Pungs and a pair, ALL tiles drawn
from the wall. Sometimes Kongs, if concealed, are also allowed in
this hand.
2) *Four Big Winds* Four sets of Winds plus a pair.
3) *The Snake* 1–9 of a suit plus one of each of the Winds with any
tile paired. All tiles except the last must be drawn from the wall.
4) *Heavenly Hand* (Dealer only) Go Mah Jong with the 14 tiles
dealt; i.e., without any play taking place.
5) *The Gates of Heaven* A Pung of 1's, a Pung of 9's, and one each
of the tiles 2–8, one of them doubled and all tiles of the same suit.
6) *All Pair Honour Hand* 7 pairs of honour and/or terminal tiles.

Hints on Play
It is necessary to strike a balance between building a high-score
hand and going Mah Jong as soon as possible. The dealer (whose

awards and penalties are doubled) should always strive to go out.

As with Rummy, discards can be important indicators of opponents' hands – watch them.

It is always advisable to monitor the pool of dead tiles – it is not much use waiting for a second Green Dragon to complete your pair if three have been discarded!

An open-ended consecutive suit pair – say, 4 and 5 of Circles – obviously offers better chances of a Chow than a pair with only one end open (say, 1 and 2) or a split pair (6 and 8).

Defer the discard of a tile you think may be wanted – particularly the dealer's wind.

Be alert for the tiles you want – a good player plays quickly to prevent the other players claiming discards.

If a game has been going on for some time, strive to go out rather than trying to improve your hand – other players are likely to be near Mah Jong. Most winning hands, unlike the example given above, are low-scoring.

Dominoes

Dominoes, like playing cards, are not a game but a whole family of games of varying complexity and suitable for almost any number of players.

The history of dominoes is obscure but they likely came from China where they have been in use for many hundreds of years. It is interesting that Chinese dominoes and playing cards are virtually indistinguishable. The origin of the name is also clouded and there are several theories, but none of them is particularly convincing.

Domino games are generally simpler than other games in this book because their scope is more limited but it is nevertheless possible to develop considerable skill in play.

Most games of dominoes are played with a double-six pack which consists of 28 tiles (see Figure 1). The tiles themselves are black or white with the spots—known as 'pips'—in a contrasting colour, usually white or black respectively. Each tile is divided into two, each half representing a number between 0 (blank) and 6. Notice that if the blanks are excluded the other tiles correspond to every possible combination of the throws of two dice. One can consider the single blank tiles as the throws of a single die with the double-blank to complete the set. (There are no blanks in the Chinese pack.)

Double-nine and double-twelve packs are used in some multi-player games but are not discussed here as these packs are not seen very often.

Certain procedures are common to all or most domino games:
1) The pack is first shuffled face down, all the players taking part.
2) Players each draw a domino from the pack to determine first lead. Highest double takes precedence, or if there are no doubles, highest domino (total pips). Tiles are again shuffled before play, which is clockwise.
3) A number of dominoes are now drawn by each player, the manner of dealing and the numbers taken depending on the game. Tiles in hand are concealed from the other players.
4) In almost all games, players take it in turns to put a domino face up on the table; second and subsequent dominoes are joined to form one continuous chain or 'leg' with pips matching on adjacent dominoes and with doubles placed at right angles to the leg. Thus there are two open ends to a domino chain which can be conveniently made to turn corners to keep the playing area manageable.

Fig. 1

5) When a player cannot match from hand either of the dominoes at the ends of the chain, he is blocked and signifies this by knocking on the table. In some games he may draw a tile from the stock, or 'boneyard' as it is usually called, or receive one from another player, but otherwise misses his turn.

6) The object of most games is to be the first to go out – i.e., get rid of all one's tiles – but in some games this is secondary to making scoring plays.

7) Partnerships are usual in four-player games. Partners sit opposite each other as in Bridge.

8) The score may be kept on paper but a cribbage board is often used for this purpose, particularly in pub games and it has the advantage of allowing all players to see easily the state of the score.

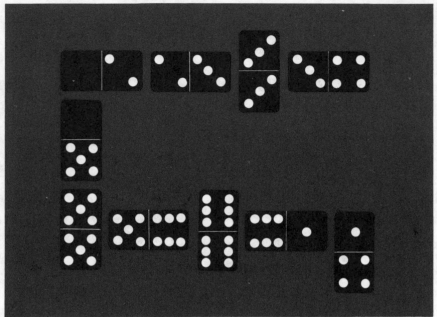

Fig. 2

The Block Game

The Block Game can be played by two, three or four players (in partnership), and is probably the most widely played of all domino games.

Preparation for the two-player variant is as above. Each player takes seven dominoes from the boneyard into hand. The holder of the highest double plays first by placing it in the centre of the table. If neither player holds a double the tiles are reshuffled.

The second player places a domino, one end of which must match the 'starter', with this end against the double but at right angles to it. The first player on his second turn has a choice between placing a matching domino against the starter or against the end of the second player's domino. Play continues in this fashion, doubles always being placed at right angles to the leg. A player who is unable to play must pass his turn. If both players are unable to add to the leg, the hand ends; the player with the smaller total number of pips on the tiles remaining in his hand is the winner and he scores the difference between this total and the total of his opponent's pips. If one player goes out (or 'domino') he scores the total of his opponent's remaining tiles. Thus if A goes out and B has the 6–3 and 4–1 left, A scores 14. A game is played to an agreed total – 50 or 100 is common.

Each player also draws seven tiles in the three- and four-player variants. In the latter, all the dominoes are in play so the hand must be started with a double 6. The hand ends when *one* player goes out; the partnership scoring the total pips of the opponents' dominoes *less* the pips of the remaining partner.

Figure 2 shows a two-handed Block game in progress. Play was started with a double-6. Both ends of the leg are 4-spots so only a domino with a 4-spot can be played. Half the dominoes are, of course, out of play in the boneyard.

The Draw Game

This is very similar to the Block Game except that the starter may be any domino and a player may, on his turn, *whether he can add to the leg or not* draw one or more dominoes from the boneyard *except that the last two may not be touched*. Thus if player A in a two-player Draw Game puts down the 5–4, B may elect to draw a tile from the boneyard. He can then put down a domino or draw another tile from the boneyard, and so on. Only when a player has drawn *all* the remaining tiles in the boneyard (except the last two) can he pass. Thus if B cannot play to the leg and there are three tiles in the boneyard he must draw one tile and must play this tile if he can do so, otherwise he may pass. In the four-player version, players draw only six dominoes each at the start, leaving four in the boneyard. Scoring is the same as for the Block Game.

Fives-and-Threes

This game is also for two, three or four players (in partnership). Each player draws seven tiles, as for the Block Game. Lowest double takes first drop (starts). Every time the combined total of both ends of the leg is a multiple of three or five, the player completing the total, scores according to the following table:

Total at *both* ends	Score
3	1
5	1
6	2
9	3
10	2
12	4
15	8
18	6
20	4

Each 3 or 5 in the total scores one point; hence 15 is the top-scoring total (five 3's plus three 5's). When a player is blocked he

Fig. 3

must pass. The player (or partnership) who goes out scores an additional point.

Figure 3 shows a two-player game of Fives-and-Threes in progress. The plays, with points scored, were as follows:

Player A – double 1 (no score)
       B – 1 – 6 (no score)
       A – 1 – 3 (3 points)
       B – 6 – 2 (1 point)
       A – 2 – blank (1 point)
       B – double 3 (2 points)
       A – 3 – 5 (1 point)
       B – 5 – 6 (2 points)
       A – blank – 3 (3 points)
       B – double 6 (8 points)

Thus with ten tiles down, B leads by 13 points to 8.

The Star

The Star, or Cross, also known under several other names, is best as a four-player, non-partnership game.

Each player draws seven tiles and whoever holds the double-6 places it in the centre of the table. The next player must play a 6-spot but may place it *either* at right-angles to the starter *or* in line with it. The next three plays must add 6-spots to the starter so that a cross is formed. Once the cross has been formed players continue and score as in the Block Game. Any player holding the two remaining 6-spots has an advantage as he can secure one arm of the cross for at least one round.

Bergen

A good game for two, three or four players. In the two- and three-player versions, each draws six dominoes; four players draw five.

Lowest double is played and holder scores 2 points. If all doubles are in the boneyard, lowest tile is played but the owner does not score for it. Play rotates as usual except that if a player cannot match, he draws one tile which he must play if he is able. If he still cannot play, he passes.

The object of the game is to match both ends of the leg. When this is done, the player scores two points for a 'double-header'. If the domino at one end is a double, then the player matching it, or playing the double, gets 3 points for a 'triple-header'. (Hence the 2-point score for the double starter.)

The first player to get rid of all his tiles scores an additional point.

It pays to hold back doubles in this game in order to cap a double-header with a triple-header. As in most domino games, one cannot opt to pass.

There are a whole fund of other domino games, many drawn from oral tradition and with regional differences that are a social study in themselves. There are a few solitaire games. A very simple one calls for the player to draw five tiles from the pack. Starting with any domino, he plays from his hand as long as he can. When he is blocked, he again makes his hand up to five by drawing from the boneyard. He wins if he succeeds in playing out the whole pack.

Hints on Play

1) In most games it pays to go out first, so this is a primary aim.

2) With choice of plays, select from the longest suit. This enhances the chance of being able to add to the leg in the next round, particularly in a two-player game. As an extreme case, if every 5-spot were held, three tiles could be put down in succession without interference (a 5-spot at the end of the leg followed by the double-5 and another 5-spot). Naturally, if both legs can be controlled in this way there is considerable advantage.

3) Always conceal whether a play is made from choice or necessity.

4) With a little practice it is often possible to form some idea of opponents' hands. In a two-player game, if one player passes the second player may be able to identify certain tiles in the boneyard.

5) Mental arithmetic and a quick sight of exposed tiles are particularly useful in the harder games (e.g., Fives-and-Threes).

Halma

Halma was invented as a proprietary game in the late 19th century, and was very popular. It is still played, even though the patent has long since lapsed. It has not received such detailed analysis as games like Chess and Go, but is a game with considerable scope for skill. Since the 1930s a game based on Halma, Chinese Checkers, has taken some of its popularity. Chinese Checkers is usually played on a board in the shape of a six-pointed star, and is suitable for from three to six players.

The Board and Pieces
The board is a square of 256 small squares. At each corner heavy lines mark off enclosures, called camps, as shown in Figure 1. The camps mark off 13 squares, but in two diagonally opposite corners the camps are enlarged to mark off an additional six squares. The pieces are counters of a different colour for each player.

The Players
The game is for two or four players. With two players, each has 19 pieces, which are set up in the larger camps as shown in Figure 2. With four players, each has 13 pieces set up in the smaller camps as shown in Figure 3. With four players, each may play for himself, or they may play in pairs, partners sitting diagonally opposite each other, and assisting each other in the manner described later.

The Object of the Game
The object of the game is to move all of one's pieces from their starting camp to that diagonally opposite. The first player to do so wins. In partnership play, the first pair to transfer all their pieces wins.

The Play
Players move one piece at a time, in turn clockwise. There are two ways to move. The *step* is a move to an adjacent square in any direction, along a file or column, or diagonally. The *hop* is like a taking move in draughts, whereby a piece may hop or jump over an adjacent piece, again in any direction, to a vacant square beyond. A hopping move may continue, and a piece may hop over as many other pieces as possible. The pieces hopped over may be one's own, or one's partner's or opponent's. There is no taking, and pieces hopped over remain where they are on the board. No move may combine a step and a hop. Hopping is not compulsory. Stepping and hopping moves are shown in Figure 4, A showing how a piece may step in any

one of eight directions, and B showing a piece in a continuous hop over friendly and opposing pieces.

Strategy

Halma is a race game, so strategy must consist in devising ways of moving pieces across the board as quickly as possible. Clearly hopping is the quicker way, and as Figure 4 indicates, the formation of 'ladders' suitable for hopping will enable pieces to advance several squares at a turn. Of course ladders can equally be used by opponents moving in the opposite direction. Players should attempt to form ladders more suitable for themselves than opponents, and to block opponent's ladders. A new dimension is added to partnership play in that partners can form ladders of use to each other.

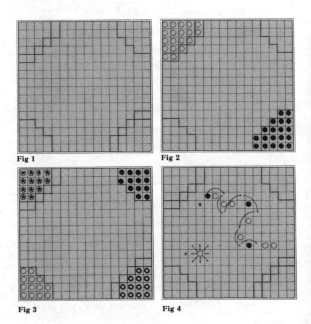

Fig 1   Fig 2

Fig 3   Fig 4

Nine Men's Morris

Nine Men's Morris is a game with its origins in ancient history. Layouts have been found on articles, in manuscripts and in tombs dating from various times, including one cut into roofing slabs at Kurna dating from around 1400 BC. It is called the Mill in the United States and Germany (*Muhle*) and is also known as *Morelles* or *Merels*. It has similarities to the children's game Noughts and Crosses, or Tit Tat Toe. It was at its most popular in the 14th century and acquired the name Morris in England possibly due to the board resembling the patterns made by Morris dancers. Three Men's Morris and Six Men's Morris are also played. Each game is for two players.

Fig 1

The Board and Pieces
The layout of the board is shown in Figure 1. It will be seen that there are three concentric squares, with four joining lines, which make 24 intersecting points arranged in 16 lines of three points each. Each player has nine counters, with contrasting colours for each player. No counters are on the board at the start of the game.

The Object of the Game
Play takes place on the 24 intersecting points on the board. Each player attempts to arrange three of his pieces in a line on the board. Such a line is known as a *mill*. This entitles him to remove any one of his opponent's pieces from the board, except any that are themselves forming a mill. A player who can reduce his opponent to two pieces only or blocks him from making a legitimate move wins the game.

The Play
The play is in two distinct phases. In the first phase, players alternately lay each piece onto one of the 24 points. A player making a mill is entitled to capture any enemy piece, which becomes dead. A possible end to the first phase, with all pieces in position and none so far captured, is shown in Figure 2. In the second phase players alternately move one piece along a line to an adjoining vacant point, still attempting to make a mill. A mill can be made any number of times by moving one of the pieces on one turn (called opening the mill) and moving it back on the following turn, thus closing the mill again and removing another opposing piece. A player with only three pieces left, forming a mill, must open the mill on his turn, even if it means losing a piece and thus the game.

246

Fig 2

Fig 3

Fig 4

Strategy

To discuss strategy, it is necessary to number the points on the board, and this is done in Figure 3. As an example of the way the game progresses, consider the position in Figure 2, with all pieces played. Black can form a mill in three moves, by moving 12-7, 11-12 and 17-16. White cannot prevent this mill, if Black moves first. On the other hand, White can form a mill in two moves, by moving 5-8 and 6-5. However, Black can prevent this mill by moving 4-5 as soon as point 5 becomes vacant. So if both players attempt these mills, the game might proceed: B 12-7, W 5-8, B 4-5 (to prevent the mill), W 15-3, B 11-12, W 10-11, B 17-16 (forming a mill). Black then removes W 11. White must now attempt to block 11 and 17 to prevent Black opening and closing this mill, so W 20-17, B 12-11, W 22-10, B 11-12 (forming a mill). Black removes W 8, again has two points (11 and 8) on which to open and close the mill, and is on the way to victory.

Let us imagine what might happen should it be White's turn to move first from Figure 2. Suppose White attempts to complete a mill on 2,5,8 with the piece on 18. The game proceeds W 18-13, B 12-7, W 13-9, B 7-8. Black must form a mill first, as White still cannot prevent the mill on 16,12,7. Therefore White's best procedure is W 5-8, B 4-5, W 8-7. White has prevented the threatened mill, and the game should develop into a long battle.

It is believed that, like Noughts and Crosses, with correct play by each player Nine Men's Morris will be a draw. Probably the best points to occupy in the first phase of the game are 5,11,14,20. From each of these a piece may move in four directions. The eight points allowing three moves are probably more valuable than the 12 allowing only two.

If the first player begins on one of the four favoured points (say 5) and the second player fails to respond with a piece on an adjacent point (in this case 2,4,6 or 8), then the first player can force a mill. This, too, has similarities to Noughts and Crosses. However, in this case, the first mill does not guarantee a win. Play out the following: W 5, B 11, W 8, B 2, W 9, B 7, W 13, B 18, W 14, B 15, W 6, B 4, W 21. White now has a mill on 6,14,21. Whatever piece he removes, Black replaces. Let us say White removes B 11. The game proceeds B 11, W 19, B 20. White now has one piece left. He cannot place it on 12 or 17, or Black will play B 16 and he will be unable to move next turn, and so lose the game. If he places it on 16, Black will put his last piece on 12 or 17, and White has only one more move. If White places his

Fig 5

Fig 6

Fig 7

last piece on any vacant point on the outside square, Black will place his last piece on an adjacent square, and follow White's piece round the board until White can move no further. So Black wins without having made a mill. It must not be assumed, however, that a mill made in the first phase of the game will lead to defeat.

A player who forms two mills will almost certainly win, and a double mill is particularly deadly. Positions to try to achieve are shown in Figure 4. Black's triangle of pieces allows two opportunities for mills to be made on 16 and 23, a valuable position in the first phase. White's position allows mills to be made on every turn in the second phase, by moving the piece on 5 to 8 and back.

Variation
It is sometimes allowed that a player reduced to only three pieces may on his turn move any piece to any vacant point, not being restricted to a point adjacent to the piece to be moved. Since this convention only enables a well-beaten player occasionally to win, it is not recommended.

Three Men's Morris
Three Men's Morris is played on a smaller board, as shown in Figure 5. Each player has four pieces, which are alternately placed on the intersections, each player trying to form a mill, which wins the game. Once the pieces are played, they are not moved, and like Noughts and Crosses, correct play by both sides means every game is drawn.

A refined version uses the board shown in Figure 6. Each player has three pieces, and once they are played to the board, pieces are moved along the lines to adjoining points, in an effort to form a mill. A player forming a mill wins. Correct play ensures a win for the player going first.

Six Men's Morris
Six Men's Morris is played on the board shown in Figure 7. Each player has six pieces, and the game proceeds in two phases, as for Nine Men's Morris. The lines connecting the two squares are for the purposes of moving pieces, and a piece at each end of any of these lines is not a mill, which has to be of three pieces in a line.

Dice Games

Craps

Craps is a gambling game played with two dice, perhaps the oldest of all gambling implements. Early dice players used astragals, the ankle bones of cloven-footed animals (usually sheep), which have distinct faces. The modern game of craps developed during the twentieth century from an old English game called Hazard, which was popular all over Europe (but was not the game Chuck-a-Luck, which is sometimes called Hazard). Craps is now the most popular dice game, and in Las Vegas, the gambling capital of the world, the craps tables usually are the busiest. It is also the gambling game with the fastest 'action'.

Craps can be played either in casinos or privately. In casinos there will be a staking table (of about 10 feet by five feet) and the game will be operated by employees. All bets will be made against the bank. In private games, the only equipment necessary is the dice, and bets will be made amongst the players. In private games, therefore, the range of bets allowed will normally be smaller than that in casinos, and the odds paid for each bet will also differ, since there is no need to build in a percentage profit for the casino. The casino game will be described first, as it is the more complicated. In this article all numbers which represent a total thrown by the dice are printed in red.

Casino Craps

Craps in a casino will be played on a table like that in Figure 1. There are many different styles of layout, but that in the illustration is typical, and will serve to describe the bets. Seated at the centre

Fig 1

TOTAL	POSSIBLE COMBINATIONS	NUMBER OF WAYS	ODDS AGAINST
2		1	35–1
3		2	17–1
4		3	11–1
5		4	8–1
6		5	31–5
7		6	5–1
8		5	31–5
9		4	8–1
10		3	11–1
11		2	17–1
12		1	35–1

Fig. 2

of the table (at the top. in the diagram) will be the boxman, who controls the game and keeps watch on all transactions. Opposite him will be the stickman who handles the dice and looks after the betting on the centre section of the table. On each side of the boxman will be a dealer, who looks after all bets at his end of the table. The gamblers stand round the table to left and right of the stickman, and use the casino's chips, which will usually vary in colour with the denomination.

The player who throws the dice is the shooter. He rolls the dice across the table so that they hit a backboard (which surrounds the table) before coming to rest. The first roll is known as his 'come-out' roll. The totals 7 and 11 are 'naturals', and should either be thrown the shooter wins immediately. The totals 2, 3 and 12 are 'craps', and mean the shooter loses. Should any other total appear it becomes the shooter's 'point', and the dealers at each end of the table place a marker in the box containing that number. The shooter then continues to roll the dice in an attempt to throw his point before he throws a 7. If he throws his point, he wins; if he throws a 7 he loses. Other totals do not count. A 7 therefore is a natural and a winner on the come-out roll, but a loser thereafter. Should the shooter win, the dice are said to 'pass' and a bet on this is called a 'right' bet. It is possible to bet that the dice 'don't pass' or 'miss-out', and this is a 'wrong' bet.

On this simple base is built a complex betting structure. However, the game remains one of chance only, and its main attraction to games players lies in examining the probabilities concerning the outcome of throwing two dice and comparing them with the various odds offered against the bets allowed. Figure 2 shows the 36 ways a pair of dice may fall, and lists the true odds against any total appearing. There are eight ways in which a shooter may come out with a natural 7 or 11, so that in the long run twice in every nine rolls the shooter will win immediately. There are a total of four ways in which the come-out roll may be a crap 2, 3 or 12, a loser for the shooter on one roll in nine. On the remaining six rolls in every nine, the shooter will make a point, and his chance of winning will vary with his point. To discover the shooter's overall chance of winning, a total of 1980 rolls must be considered to avoid fractions. Table 1 summarizes these rolls.

Table 1: Shooter's Probability of Passing

Come-out roll	Number of times thrown	Number of winning coups	Number of losing coups
2 crap	55	—	55
3 crap	110	—	110
4 point	165	55	110
5 point	220	88	132
6 point	275	125	150
7 natural	330	330	—
8 point	275	125	150
9 point	220	88	132
10 point	165	55	110
11 natural	110	110	—
12 crap	55	—	55
Totals	1980	976	1004

Thus, in the long run, of every 1980 come out rolls, the shooter will win 976 and lose 1004, and since the bank offers even money for a pass bet, it will enjoy an advantage over the shooter of 1·414 per cent.

Using the table above, it is possible to calculate the bank's percentage advantage in all the craps bets it will allow.

The bets and advantages are as follows:

Win, Do, Pass or Front Line. This is a bet that the shooter will pass, and the stake is placed on the space marked 'line' on the table. This line might on other tables be marked 'pass line' or 'win'. The odds offered are even money. As calculated above, the bank's advantage is 1·414 per cent.

Lose, Don't, Don't Pass or Back Line. This is a bet that the shooter will lose, and the stakes are placed on the 'Don't Pass' space. The odds are again even money. As there are more ways in which the shooter can lose than win, the bank must adjust the bet to retain its advantage. The 'Don't Pass' line in Figure 1 states the adjustment: 'Bar 6, 6'. This means that if the shooter comes out with a double-6, don't pass bets are void, and await a further throw. A double-6 will occur 55 times in the total of 1980 rolls listed in Table 1, and if these are barred, the shooter can lose only 949 times, while still winning 976 times, so the don't pass bettor finds that the casino keeps its advantage, although it is slightly less, 1·403 per cent. Some casinos bar double-1 rather than double-6, and their advantage remains the same. Others bar 1, 2, which occurs twice as often as double-1 or double-6, and their advantage rises to 4·385 per cent.

Come. This is a bet made when the shooter has already established his point. It is the same as a pass bet, except that the shooter's next roll will be considered as his come-out roll. The stake is placed in the box marked 'come'. If the shooter's next roll is a natural, the come bettor wins immediately. Similarly he loses if the next roll is a crap. Alternatively, the next roll might establish a point for the come bettor, in which case the dealer will move the stake to the appropriate point box. The bet is then the same as a pass bet, except that the shooter and the come bettor will have different points and will win or lose at different times in the sequence of rolls. The odds offered are even money. The bank's advantage is, as for pass bets, 1·414 per cent.

Don't Come. This bet is the opposite of a come bet, made when the shooter has established his point. As with a don't pass bet, the double-6 is barred (or the double-1 or 1, 2 as explained earlier). The don't come stake is placed in the box marked 'don't come', and moved by the dealer to the blank square below the appropriate point square when the shooter has made a new point for the don't come bettor. The odds offered are evens. The casino's advantage is 1·403 per cent (or 4·385 per cent if the 1, 2 is barred).

Big Six and Big Eight. These are bets that a 6 or an 8 will appear before a 7, and the stakes are placed in the appropriate box. Reference to Figure 2 shows that a 7 will be thrown six times to every five for a 6 or an 8. The odds offered are even money, so the bank enjoys an advantage of 9.091 per cent.

Field. This is a bet that any of a group of numbers will appear on the next roll. The stake is placed on the space marked 'Field' on the table. The group of numbers on the table in Figure 1 is 2, 3, 4, 9, 10, 11, 12. Figure 2 shows that one of this group will appear 16 times in 36. The odds offered are even money, but to give the bettor a fairer bet, the double-6 and double-1 are paid double, i.e. at odds of 2 – 1. This means that the bettor on the field can expect a return of 34 chips for every 36 staked, an advantage to the bank of 5·556 per cent. The field varies, and some casinos will offer the 5 instead of the 4 in the field, but will not pay double on the double-1 and double-6 The bank's advantage remains the same.

Hardway. This is a bet that 4, 6, 8 or 10 will be made the hard way, i.e. by means of a double, before it is made any other way or before a 7 is thrown. The bets are placed in the appropriate place in the centre of the table, where it will be seen that the bank offers 8 *for* 1 (7 *to* 1) on hardway 4s and 10s, and 10 *for* 1 on hardway 6s and 8s. Since there are eleven ways in which a 6 or 7 can be thrown, and only one is a double-3, the correct odds for a hardway 6 are 10 – 1. In offering 10 *for* 1, the bank thereby takes an advantage of 9·091 per cent, and takes the same for hardway 8s. The bank's percentage on hardway 4s and 10s is 11·111 per cent.

Place or Box Numbers. These are bets that a chosen number will be thrown before a 7. Stakes are placed on the line above or below the respective point number. On 4 and 10 the bank pays odds of 9 – 5. Reference to Figure 2 shows the correct odds to be 2 – 1, so the bank's advantage is 6·667 per cent. On 5 and 9 the bank pays 7 – 5, its advantage being 4·000 per cent. On 6 and 8 the bank pays either 7 – 6, in which case its advantage is 1·515 per cent, or even money in which case its advantage is 9·091 per cent. Note that if the casino offers odds of 7–6 on place 6 and 8 bets, it is pointless backing Big Six and Big Eight at even money, where the bank enjoys nearly six times the advantage.

Buy or Lay Bets. A buy bet is similar to a place bet in that the player bets that a point number will appear before 7. The difference is that on the buy bet the casino will pay winners at the correct odds: for points 4 and 10 at 2–1, for 5 and 9 at 3–2, and for 6 and 8 at 6–5. However, it will exact a commission of 5 per cent of the stake. Since the minimum commission will be the minimum stake, the gambler must stake 20 times the minimum or pay a higher percentage commission. The casino's advantage on these bets is 4·762 per cent. Reference to the percentages for place bets shows that the player does better to buy bets on 4 and 10 and to place them on 5, 6, 8 and 9. Lay bets are the opposite of buy bets, i.e. the player bets that 7 appears before the point. The true odds are paid: for points 4 and 10 at 1–2, for 5 and 9 at 2–3, and for 6 and 8 at 5–6. The 5 per cent commission is this time exacted on the winnings rather than the stake, i.e. 1 chip commission will be levied on a stake of 40 on points 4 and 10, 30 on points 5 and 9, and 24 on points 6 and 8, since each of the bets will win 20 chips. The casino's advantage is respectively 2·439 per cent, 3·226 per cent and 4·000 per cent. The bets are made by the player placing his stake on the table and calling the point he wants. The dealer removes the house commission (called 'vigorish') from the stake and places the stake in the correct box.

Other Bets. There are various other bets or combinations of bets possible at craps. A few are shown on the table in Figure 1. Most are 'one-roll action' bets, and are settled on the result of one roll. For instance, a gambler can back 7 to appear on the next throw. The odds are 5 *for* 1, and the bank's advantage 16·667 per cent. Odds of 30 *for* 1 are offered for double-1 and double-6, with the same advantage to the bank. Odds of 15 *for* 1 are offered for 3 and 11, the advantage still being 16·667 per cent. All craps are offered at 8 *for* 1, an advantage to the bank of 11·111 per cent.

Free or Odds Bets. When the shooter has a point, casinos allow players who have bet on pass, don't pass, come or don't come to double their bets, and the second half of the bet is paid at the correct odds. Thus pass or come bettors will get 2-1 on points 4 and 10, don't pass or don't come bettors will get 1-2. The odds offered on 5 and 9 will be 3-2 and 2-3 respectively, and on 6 and 8, 6-5 and 5-6. For example, a come bettor with a point of 6 and a stake of five chips will be allowed a free or odds bet of five chips on 6, to be paid at odds of 6-5. As the casino will not deal in fractions of a chip, the stake on this particular free bet must always be in multiples of five, and the player will be allowed to round up or down his stake to the nearest multiple of five. If his stake is only one or two chips he will not be allowed a free bet at all. The casino allows the free bet to speed up the action, and takes no commission on it. Thus the player should always accept it for the maximum stake allowed, and correspondingly reduce the bank's advantage on the total bet. Free bet stakes are not placed flat on the table, but overlap the edge of the original stake.

The bank's overall advantage on the bet can be calculated by reference to Table 1. Of the 1980 rolls summarized, the bank returns to the pass line bettor 976×2 chips (assuming one chip per bet), or 1952 chips. The table shows that 1320 of the 1980 rolls will result in a point and if the pass bettor takes the free bet each time he will stake a further 1320 chips, and, since the bets are paid at the correct odds, can expect 1320 chips back in return. Thus, if he always accepts the free bets, his total stakes on the 1980 rolls will be $1980 + 1320$, or 3300 chips, from which in the long run he will expect $1952 + 1320$ back, or 3272. So he will expect to lose only 28 chips in 3300, a casino advantage of only 0·848 per cent. Don't pass bettors will do even better, with an advantage to the bank of only 0·832 per cent. This is the lowest advantage the casino takes in crap games, except for some casinos in Reno, where free bets are allowed of double the original stake. A player making full use of these bets will reduce the casino's advantage to 0·606 per cent on pass or come bets and 0·595 per cent on don't pass or don't come bets.

Private Craps

Craps played privately is a much simpler game than casino craps. The only essential equipment is a pair of dice, although a blanket or carpet might be used to roll them on, and a backboard for the dice to rebound from is advisable. Because of the lack of a staking table, the bets are fewer and simpler.

The first shooter places a sum of money before him as his 'centre' bet, and the other players are invited to 'fade' it. The shooter is betting he will win; the other players put up an amount equal to his stake to bet he will lose. It is an even money bet. As in the casino game, the shooter wins if he throws a natural 7 or 11, loses if he throws a crap 2, 3 or 12, and continues to roll if he establishes a point.

Meanwhile, the other players bet among themselves on whether the shooter passes or not. Come and don't come bets are also made. Once a shooter has thrown his point, he and other players may bet that he will or will not make it. The correct odds are paid, i.e. 6−5 that he will make 6 or 8, 3−2 that he will make 5 or 9, and 2−1 that he will make 4 or 10. Sometimes even money is bet on the shooter making a point of 6 or 8, but this is incorrect, and gives the wrong bettor a tremendous advantage. Hardway bets are common. If the shooter's point is 4 or 10, 8−1 are the odds against making it the hard way. It is 10−1 against making a hardway 6 or 8. The players may make other bets among themselves, but those already mentioned are the commonest.

The shooter keeps the dice while winning; as soon as he misses out he passes the dice to the next player in rotation.

Strategy
Craps is a game of chance, and skilful play consists only of knowing the proper odds and probabilities for each bet, and making bets which are arithmetically sound. In private crap games the wrong bettor generally has an advantage of 1·414 per cent, a significant advantage over a long period. In casino games, a sound bet is merely one with a small advantage to the casino. The player will therefore avoid, for example, Big Six, Big Eight and hardway bets. Wrong bettors face a slightly smaller disadvantage than right bettors. If the free or odds bets are made whenever possible, the casino's advantage can be kept below 1 per cent.

Dice Games

In this section are described a selection of games which require only dice and sometimes a sheet of paper on which to keep a score. Most dice games are very simple, many are games of chance only, and even those games which allow skill to be exercised depend considerably more on chance. This leads to many of them needing a gambling element for their attraction, and some are indeed pure gambling games. Nevertheless the simplicity of dice games can be an asset when an awkward number of players of varying standards require games needing only intermittent concentration.

The games are arranged in order according to the number of dice required, beginning with two games requiring only one die.

It is advisable to play all dice games with a dice cup, which should be shaken before the dice are thrown. When players throw from their hands, sooner or later one player will develop secret or outspoken suspicions about another player's lucky throw.

Twenty-one

Any number may play, and only one die is required. It is not necessary to keep a score sheet. Players each roll a die to determine who takes first throw, lowest first. Play then proceeds clockwise.

Each player on his turn throws the die as often as he wishes, adding his scores together, in an attempt to score 21, or as near to 21 as possible, without exceeding it. A player may stop when he likes, when the turn passes to the next player clockwise. A player who exceeds 21 is out of the game. The player nearest to 21 at the end of the round wins. Should two or more players be equal, they play off a deciding game between them.

Strategy A player with a score of 18 has an even chance of improving his score by taking another throw. It would therefore be unwise for an early player to stop with a score lower than 18. Once a target has been set, later players will continue to throw until they have at least equalled or bettered it. The later his turn in the round, the better a player's chance of winning.

Variation To speed the game up, two dice might be used until a player reaches a score of 14, when he discards one and continues his turn with one die. Of course, he might exceed 21 before changing to one die.

Gambling When played as a gambling game, all players begin by contributing one chip to a pool. Additionally, each player who exceeds 21 must add another chip to the pool. This alters the strategy only a little, as a player playing last and facing a total of 21 would be advised to risk an extra chip attempting to improve even from a score of 20, provided there were ten or more chips in the pool. The extra chip has the effect of reducing the early player's disadvantage, as a good score could force the later players to exceed 21. It might be decided that in the gambling game players who tie should share the pool rather than play off. After the first round, the first player should be the player to the left of the first player in the previous round, and play should continue until all players have played first an equal number of times.

Pig

Any number may play Pig and one die is used. Players throw for turn, the lowest throwing first, and the turn passing clockwise. A player may throw the die as often as he wishes, adding together his scores. When he decides to stop, his score is entered against his name on a score sheet. However should he throw a 1, his turn ends and he scores nothing for the turn. The first player to reach 100 wins.

Variation The game can be played with two dice. A player throwing a 1 with either die loses his score for the turn. A throw of a double carries a bonus. A throw of double 1 scores 25 for the turn, irrespective of how many had already been accumulated by previous throws on that turn, and the dice pass to the next player. However, any other double thrown doubles the score shown for the throw (i.e. double-4 counts 16), and the player may continue throwing if he so desires.

Strategy A player must decide when to be satisfied with his score. The state of the game will influence the decision. A player well behind will find it necessary to take a risk in attempting a big score. Generally, anything above 15 is a reasonable score, but runs of 50 or so are not rare. It would be a brave player who continued beyond 50.

Gambling Pig is not usually played as a gambling game, but if desired players can either contribute to a pool, to be taken by the winner, or losers can pay off the winner at an agreed amount per ten points.

Barbudi

Sometimes known as Barbooth, Barbudi is a gambling game played in Mexico and Eastern Europe, which requires two dice. Any number may play and bet, but only two players at a time are involved in the action. Traditionally, miniature dice are used, but any dice are suitable.

The players throw a die, and the highest thrower becomes the *shooter*. The player to his right becomes the *fader*. (In Barbudi, the 'action' passes anti-clockwise). The fader puts up a stake of whatever amount he wishes (unless maximum and minimum amounts are agreed beforehand) and places it in the centre of the table. The shooter covers as much of the stake as he wants. If all is not covered, the player to the fader's right has the option of covering all or some of the remainder, and so on round the table until the stake is covered. If any remains uncovered, the fader withdraws it. The shooter may give up his opportunity to be shooter and pass the dice to the player on his right, who becomes shooter. Similarly, the fader may decline to put up a bet, in which case the player on his right becomes fader. In placing his bet, the fader stipulates a one-shot or two-shot decision, the meaning of which will become clear later.

When the fader's bet has been covered, the shooter and the fader throw alternately, shooter first, to decide the fate of the bets.

In a one-shot decision game, either player wins if he throws double-6, double-5, double-3 or 6-5 (see Figure 1). Either player loses if he throws double-1, double-2, double-4 or 1-2 (see Figure 2). Bets are immediately settled. If the shooter wins, he remains shooter for the next round, and the fader remains fader. If the fader wins, he becomes shooter for the next round, and the player on his right is the new fader.

In a two-shot decision game, a throw of 6-5 wins only half the bet, and a throw of 1-2 loses only half. Either player can then decide to end the round there, with winners taking only half the opposing stake as winnings, and losers retaining the other half. If the shooter won, he remains shooter, otherwise the fader becomes shooter for the new round.

On the other hand, both players can agree to continue to shoot for the second half of the stake. In this case all stakes are left on the table. If the shooter won the first half, he remains shooter for the second half. If the fader won the first half, the players reverse roles for the second half of the bet, and the old fader has the privilege of shooting first as the new shooter. When the decisive throw is cast, if the same

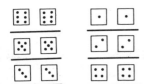

Fig 1   Fig 2

side won both halves of the bet they collect their winnings. If each side won one half of the bet, then each bettor withdraws his own stake. When the second half of a two-decision game is contested, both the shooter and the fader lose their roles, whoever wins, and the shooter for the next round is the player to the original fader's right.

Variation Some players find the one-shot or two-shot decision needlessly complicates the game, and ignore it, treating all games as one-shot games, where all bets are immediately settled on a winning or losing throw. However, the 6-5 and 2-1 throws retain some significance, as a shooter who loses by throwing 2-1 or by the fader throwing 6-5 can retain his position as shooter for the next round.

Gambling The game can only operate as a gambling game. Played privately, it is an even game, with no advantage to either shooter or fader. However, it is a popular game in clubs and casinos in some parts of the world, and in these games the gambling house usually takes 5 per cent of the losing bets before paying out the winnings, in effect taking $2\frac{1}{2}$ per cent commission on all money staked. This is a heavy commission to attempt to overcome over a long period.

Four-Five-Six

Four-Five-Six is cometimes called See-Low, and is derived from a Chinese game called Strung Flowers, which is described as a variation later. It is a banking game suitable for any number of players and requires three dice. All players throw the three dice, the highest thrower becoming first banker.

The banker puts up a stake, or bank, and players in turn to his left may cover all or part of it, until it is all covered, or until no more players want to bet. If any part remains uncovered, the banker withdraws it. The banker then throws the dice, and continues to throw until he achieves one of the following significant throws:

1. A throw which wins all bets immediately. These are (a) any triplet; (b) 4-5-6; (c) any pair with a 6.
2. A throw which loses all bets immediately. These are (a) 1-2-3; (b) any pair with a 1.
3. A throw which establishes a point for the banker. These are any pair with 2, 3, 4 or 5.

In the last case, the odd die represents the banker's point, and the play on the round continues.

The first bettor to the banker's left throws the dice, and continues to throw until he throws a significant throw. If he throws a combination listed in (1) above, he wins. If he throws a combination listed in (2) above, he loses. If he throws a point for himself, as listed in (3) above, he wins if his point is higher than the banker's, loses if it is lower, and ties, and recovers his stake, if his point is the same. The next bettor to his left then settles his bet in the same way, and so on until all bets are settled.

The banker retains his bank for the next round, unless (a) he loses the whole bank in the course of the play, in which case the bank passes to the player on his left or (b) a player throwing against the banker's point throws a triplet or a 4-5-6 combination, in which case the bank passes to him on the next round, the banker withdrawing any of the bank which is remaining after the round has been completed.

Strategy Four-Five-Six is a game of chance, and no strategy applies but it should be recognised that the banker holds an advantage of about 2.47 per cent, due to the fact that in his initial roll there are 27 outright winning throws against 21 outright losing throws, and of 60 point-making throws he will win 25, lose 28.33 and tie 6.67. Half of all possible throws of three dice produce a significant throw.

Variation The Chinese game Strung Flowers has the following variations:

1. All players throw the dice for choice of first banker, and the player who throws most 4s becomes banker. Players who tie throw again until a decision is reached.

2. Players place their stakes in front of them, and the banker covers each in turn. This assures that all players who wish to do so can play on each round. It is advisable to agree on a maximum stake beforehand.

3. All stakes are made in multiples of three, for reasons which will become clear immediately.

4. When both the banker and player throw a point, the bet is settled according to the difference in the two points. Thus if the difference is one point, only one third of the stake is won and lost; if two points, two thirds; if three points, all the stake. This has the effect of very slightly increasing the banker's advantage.

5. The banker loses his bank only when he makes a point which is beaten by a player's point. The bank then passes to the banker's left at the end of the round.

This last variation ensures that by agreement a game can continue until all the players have enjoyed the bank an equal number of times.

In the Chinese version, a throw of 4-5-6 is known as *Strung Flowers*, 1,2,3 as the *Dancing Dragon*, and a pair with an ace as *Ace Negative*. Many will think it a more pleasing version of the game than Four-Five-Six.

Buck Dice

Buck Dice is a game which finds a loser rather than a winner. Any number can play, and three dice are used. Players throw the dice to decide (a) who takes first throw and (b) who establishes a *point number*. The lowest player throws one die, and whichever number he throws becomes the point number for the game. The highest player then takes the first throw. Play proceeds clockwise.

The first player throws all three dice, and scores one point for each point number that he throws. He continues to throw the three dice, keeping count of his points, until he fails to score on any throw, when his score for the turn is entered on a score sheet and the dice pass to the player on his left. A player who throws a triplet, other than the point number, scores a *Little Buck*, which is worth five points. A triplet of the point number is *Big Buck*, and all the thrower's previous scores are wiped out and he is given a total of 15.

As players reach 15 points, they retire from the game, so Big Buck earns immediate retirement. The last player left is the loser. Each player must end exactly on 15, and if during a turn a player scores points which take him beyond 15 (for example by throwing two points or Little Buck when his score is already 14) he loses his score for that round and passes the dice to the next player.

Variation This variation is played as a gambling game. All players contribute one unit to a pool, and the game produces a winner, who takes the pool, rather than a loser, as above.

The first thrower also establishes the point. He throws a single die, and a throw of 4, 5 or 6 establishes the point number. Should he throw 1, 2 or 3 (on this throw called a *Mulligan*), he must throw again, and must continue to throw until he establishes a point of 4, 5 or 6. However, after the Mulligan, which is 'free', each time he fails to establish a point he must add another unit to the pool. This counters the big advantage a player has in going first.

Once the point is established, the first player throws the three dice and rethrows them each time he scores, until a throw fails to produce a score, when his score for the turn is entered on the score sheet and the dice pass to the next player, clockwise. Scoring is more varied than in the parent game. Each point number scores one, but a player who scores two point numbers in one throw is credited with Little Buck, worth five points. Any triplet other than the point number is also Little Buck, and scores five points. A triplet of the point number is Big Buck, and wins the game immediately irrespective of the current score.

Also any combination of smaller numbers thrown which add up to the point number score a point. Thus if the point number is 6, a throw of 1,2,3 earns a point; 2,4,6 earns two points; 3,3,1 earns a point.

A player must score 15 exactly to win (but need not complete his turn once a throw has taken his score to 15). Should a throw take his total past 15, he loses the score for that throw only, and his turn ends.

Unless the game is won with Big Buck, a player failing to score at the end of the game must add one unit to the pool. Some will think it a weakness of the game that occasionally a player will win on his first turn, leaving other players to contribute an extra unit to the pool without having had a turn – but at least before the first player is decided, all players have an equal chance.

Chuck-a-Luck
Chuck-a-luck is a banking game, using three dice. It is basically the same game as Crown and Anchor, once popular with the Royal Navy, and now occasionally to be found operated illegally on street corners and racetracks.

The game cannot be played without gambling, and a layout should be made on which stakes can be placed. This is shown in Figure 3. Players place their bets on whichever number they fancy will appear at least once in a throw of the dice.

The banker then throws three dice, and pays out as follows: on all single numbers thrown, he pays out bettors at even money; on all pairs, he pays out bettors at 2-1; on a triple he pays bettors at 3-1. He collects losing bets, and another round begins.

Fig 3

Fig 4

This game is popular in casinos, where instead of throwing the dice the banker may tumble a birdcage (see Figure 4). An advantage is held by the casino (or the banker in a private game) arising from the fact that doubles should be paid at 14-1 and triples at 215-1. This amounts to an advantage to the banker of 7.87 per cent. It is advisable therefore in private games for the bank to circulate.

Sometimes casinos and carnivals, particularly in America, will operate a wheel called a Chuck-a-Luck wheel or Big Six Wheel, in which combinations of three dice are shown on a giant upright wheel, which is spun to decide the winning combination. These wheels do not show all 216 possible results of a throw of three dice. They might show, for instance, just the 56 different combinations (ignoring the fact that with three dice, 4,3,2, for instance, can be thrown six ways), in which case the operators enjoy an advantage of 12.50 per cent. Other wheels have a casino advantage of 22.22 per cent. All these wheels are to be avoided.

Yacht

Yacht is one of the most interesting dice games, calling for judgment. It is one of many 'category' games, some others of which are described later. Any number may play. Five dice are required. A special score sheet must be ruled up (Figure 5) showing the players and the various categories in which they may score.

Players throw to determine who goes first – lowest starts. Each player has up to three throws at each turn. After the first throw of the dice, he may set aside any that he wishes to keep, and rethrow the remainder. He may do the same after the second throw, but after the third throw the five dice represent his score. He may, if he wishes, stop after the first or second throw. He must then decide into which category on the score sheet to enter his score. The categories and scores are:

Yacht (five of a kind): scores 50.
Big Straight (2,3,4,5,6): scores 30.
Little Straight (1,2,3,4,5): scores 30.
Four of a Kind ⎫ scores the total
Full House (three of one kind, two ⎬ number of pips
  of another ⎪ showing on the
Choice (any five dice) ⎭ five dice.
Sixes : scores six points for every 6 thrown. Similarly *Fives* scores
  five points for every 5, and so on.

The play ends after 12 rounds with each player having entered a

	CHRIS	MARY	KAREL	JOHN
YACHT				
BIG STRAIGHT				
LITTLE STRAIGHT				
FOUR OF A KIND				
FULL HOUSE				
CHOICE				
SIXES				
FIVES				
FOURS				
THREES				
TWOS				
ACES				
TOTAL				

Fig 5

score in each category. A player must select a category, even if he scores nothing for it, and once a category is filled, the score for that category cannot be superseded by a later, higher score. For instance, if a player throws 5,5,5,5,3 and already has his categories for *Four of a Kind* and *Fives* filled, he must decide whether to score 23 for *Choice*, three for *Threes*, or zero in any other category. Players often dispense with awkward throws by entering zero in the *Aces* category, as maximum score for this category is only five.

After 12 rounds, the scores are added for each player, the highest being the winner.

Strategy Players should attempt to score the big scores at the top of the list of categories. A player with 2,3,4,5 has two chances of completing a straight with one throw to come, the odds against achieving either *Big* or *Little Straight* being 2-1. However an 'open' straight (e.g. 2,3,5,6) presents only a 5-1 chance of completion. Players with a triplet on the first or second throw will probably throw the other two dice, attempting *Yacht*, *Four of a Kind* or *Full House*. A player ending with, say, 4,4,4,4,2, will usually do better to score it in *Four of a Kind* rather than *Fours*, since a later throw of 4,4,4,6,3 could then score 12 in *Fours* where it would be useless elsewhere, unless *Choice* were still open, in which case 21 would be scored. As mentioned above, players often dump a poor throw in *Aces* or *Twos*, since these categories cannot score highly. Occasionally, near the end of a game, a player might register a poor throw as zero for *Yacht*, since most players in a game will not score for *Yacht*. Naturally, a

	LEIGH	SUE	GLYN	IAN	
SMALL ENERAL	60				
FOUR OF A KIND		40			
FULL HOUSE		30		30	
STRAIGHT	20		20		
SIXES		18	18	24	
FIVES	15		15		
FOURS	12				
THREES					
TWOS					
ACES		0	0	3	
TOTAL					

Fig 6

player will bear in mind which categories are still open to him when re-throwing his dice. For instance, if the only two categories left are *Fives* and *Big Straight*, it would be pointless retaining a pair of 6s.

Gambling If gambling is required, players usually pay the winner according to the points difference, at an agreed sum per 10 points.

General

This is another 'category' game, played on the same lines as *Yacht* but with different categories and a different scoring system. The system of play is the same.

The categories are shown in the score sheet (Figure 6). Some scores have been entered as if a game were in progress. The scoring for the first four categories varies according to the throw on which the score was made.

Big General is five of a kind made on the first throw of any turn. It is not entered on the score sheet, as a throw of Big General wins the game immediately.

Small General is five of a kind made on the second or third throw, and scores 60.

Four of a Kind scores 45 on the first throw, 40 on the second or third.

Full House scores 35 on the first throw, 30 on the second or third.

Straight (either 1,2,3,4,5 or 2,3,4,5,6) scores 25 on the first throw, 20 on the second or third.

Sixes, Fives, Fours, Threes, Twos and *Aces* are scored as in Yacht.

An ace in one category only is 'half-wild'. In *Straight*, an Ace may be counted as a 2 or 6, but not 3,4, or 5. Thus 1,3,4,5,6 or 1,1,3,4,5 can both count as a *Straight*.

General is an extremely popular game among Puerto Ricans. The strategy is similar to that of Yacht.

	PETER	CAMILLA	KIM	IAN	
CRAG					
THIRTEEN					
HIGH STRAIGHT					
LOW STRAIGHT					
EVEN STRAIGHT					
ODD STRAIGHT					
THREE OF A KIND					
SIXES					
FIVES					
FOURS					
THREES					
TWOS					
ACES					
TOTAL					

Fig 7

Crag

Crag is a 'category' game included here because the principles are similar to Yacht and General, but it is interesting because it is played with only three dice and is a quicker game than the others. Any number may play.

In Crag, a player may make only two throws per turn. The categories are shown in the score sheet (Figure 7).

Crag is any pair plus a third die in which the three dice total 13, e.g. 4,4,5 or 6,6,1, and scores 50.

Thirteen is any three dice totalling 13, and scores 26.

If a *Crag* is thrown, and the *Crag* category is already filled, the throw may score as *Thirteen*.

High Straight (4,5,6), *Low Straight* (1,2,3), *Even Straight* (2,4,6) and *Odd Straight* (1,3,5) all score 20.

Three of a Kind scores 25.

Sixes, Fives, Fours, Threes, Twos and *Aces* score as in Yacht.

Drop Dead

Drop Dead is a fast, simple game using five dice, especially suitable for games involving children. Players throw a single die to decide the order of play, lowest going first. Ties are rethrown.

The first player throws the five dice, and if no 5s or 2s appear, he scores the total of the numbers thrown, and rethrows the five dice. However if any dice show a 5 or 2, he scores nothing for that throw,

Throw		Score	Running score
1		0	0
2		0	0
3		11	11
4		0	11
5		4	15
6		6	21
7		0	21

Fig 8

puts aside the dice showing 5 or 2 and rethrows the remainder. Each throw he makes without a 5 or 2 scores the total showing, and he continues to throw until all dice are eliminated. His score is then noted on the score sheet and the dice pass to the left for the next player to throw. A specimen turn is shown in Figure 8. When all players have thrown, the player with the highest score is the winner.

The game provides lower scores than might be imagined, and anything over 20 is a good score. It is interesting to note that the odds against scoring with five dice are 211-32 (about 13-2), against scoring with four dice are 65-16 (about 4-1), against scoring with three dice are 19-8 (nearly 5-2) and against scoring with two dice 5-4. With one die remaining, there is a 2-1 on chance of scoring. Therefore players tend to discard dice quickly, but occasionally run up a score with only one die remaining. A player who scores with five dice is in a strong position.

Variation For a longer game play might continue until each player has had five turns.

Qualify

Qualify is a banking game, using five dice. When played socially each player should hold the bank in turn. First banker is decided by each player rolling one die, highest becoming banker.

Each player puts up a stake, which is covered by the banker. It is advisable to agree a maximum stake. The banker takes no part in the play. Each bet is settled in turn, beginning with the player to the banker's left.

The object of the game is to score 25 points or more.

The first player throws the five dice, and sets aside the highest die as a contribution to his score. He then rethrows the four remaining dice, again setting aside the highest, and so on until he throws the last die singly, and totals his score.

If his score is 25 or more, he wins his bet; 24 or lower and the banker collects his stake.

Although 25 seems a high number for five dice, the thrower should be in with a chance on his last die (i.e. have a score of 19 or more) in about three-quarters of his turns, and should have an even or better chance (21 or more) in about half his turns. No less an authority than Ely Culbertson thought the banker had no advantage, but experience suggests that it might approach as much as 20 per cent.

Number of times point number appears	Odds paid
26	4-1
27	5-1
28	6-1
29	8-1
30 or more	10-1
13	5-1
10 or fewer	10-1

Fig 9

Twenty-six

Twenty-six is a game for any number, which uses ten dice. It is a banking game. Players throw a single die to decide first banker: highest wins.

The player on the left of the banker puts up a stake (it is advisable to agree on a maximum beforehand) and chooses a point number, from 1 to 6, which he announces. He then throws all ten dice from a cup 13 times, keeping a running count of how many times the point number appears. It is best if the banker writes down the running total after each throw, so that no argument arises as to how many throws have been taken. Should the thrower score 26 or more, he wins; less than 26 he loses his stake to the banker, unless he scores 13 or fewer than 11, in which case he wins. The banker pays winners according to the table in Figure 9.

The odds quoted are thought to be fairest. Wherever Twenty-six is played, the odds vary from game to game, and a game operated by a gambling house will offer considerably shorter odds.

In effect, the number of times a point would be 'expected' to be thrown is 21.67, so a score of 26 or more is difficult to achieve, and the bank should show a profit in the long run. At the end of each round the bank passes to the next player clockwise.

Variation Fourteens is a similar game to Twenty-Six, also using ten dice. However, in Fourteens, a player nominates his point number *after* his first throw. Should his first throw produce a triplet or better, the number of the triplet or better becomes his point number, and he is credited with the number of times it appears. Should his first throw not produce a triplet or better, then he can choose and announce any point number, and is credited with a score of three for his first throw.

He has four further throws, totalling the number of times he throws his point number, and wins if he scores 14 or more, when he is paid at odds of 8-1. If his last four throws fail to produce a point number, he also wins and is paid at 8-1. Again, the bank should show a profit.

Poker Dice

Poker Dice is played with a special set of five dice, whose six faces are shown in Figure 10. It can be played with standard dice. The first player is chosen by lot, and thereafter for each round, the player on his left throws first. Later players have an advantage over earlier players. Players contribute to a pool, to be taken by the winner.

Fig 10

On his turn, a player throws the five dice, and can set aside any he wishes to keep, and throw the remainder a second time. The object is to get the highest ranking poker hand. The rank of the hands are shown in Figure 11. Hands without a pair are of no value.

The first player's throw is noted, and subsequent players must attempt to beat it. When the throw is beaten, the new highest hand is noted. The player to have the highest hand at the end of the round wins.

With all hands except the two straights it is necessary to note the value of the hand within the rank to distinguish between hands of equal rank. For example, Four Queens will beat Four Jacks. With a Full House, the value of the triplet decides the winner, and the value of the pair decides only if another throw produces the same triplet. For example, Three Tens and Two Queens beats Three Nines and Two Aces, but loses to Three Tens and Two Kings. Similarly if two hands produce Two Pairs, the value of the higher pair has first importance. With Four of a Kind, Three of a Kind, Two Pairs and One Pair, the value of the odd dice are not significant. It should be decided beforehand whether, in the event of a tie, the winners play off or divide the pool.

Rank of hands in Poker Dice	
1	Five of a kind
2	Four of a kind
3	Full house
	(three of a kind plus a pair)
4	High straight
	(A.K.Q.J.10)
5	Low straight
	(K.Q.J.10.9)
6	Three of a kind
7	Two pairs
8	One pair

Fig 11

Liar Dice

Liar Dice is a game for two players, using two sets of Poker Dice whose faces are illustrated in Figure 10. It is an awkward game to play, because each player throws separately, and neither player must see his opponent's hand until the showdown, so a screen must be erected between the two players. It is also a game of bluffing, and of all dice games most resembles the card game Poker. Standard sets of dice may be used. Each player throws a single die, higher becoming first *caller*.

Each player then throws his five dice, so that his opponent cannot see them. The caller then announces whether or not he is satisfied with his hand. If he is, play continues. If he announces he is dissatisfied, his opponent has the right to decide to play or not. The caller may announce 'either way' leaving the option to his opponent.

If play is to continue, the caller announces his hand. Here the element of bluff enters, because the caller (and either player on subsequent announcements) may announce any hand he pleases, higher or lower than the actual hand held. Announcements must be in full, and specify each die, for example 'Three Kings, Ace, Jack' or 'Two Tens, Two Nines, Queen'.

If his opponent thinks the caller is bluffing, he may remove the screen immediately, and wins if the caller's hand is lower than announced. If the caller's hand is as announced or better, the caller wins. However if the caller's announcement is accepted, then the opponent must announce a higher hand. Now the caller has the choice of accepting or removing the screen. Removing the screen clearly is tantamount to calling one's opponent a liar, hence the name of the game.

Should the caller now accept his opponent's call, he may set aside any of his dice he wishes to keep, and rethrow the remainder. He must then announce a higher hand than his opponent, whose options are once again as on the first round. Play continues thus until each player has had two re-throws (i.e. three throws including the initial throw). After his opponent's third throw, the caller must remove the screen.

The game is usually played best of three or best of five hands, the loser paying the winner an agreed stake.

Strategy The object of announcing a lower hand than that held is to keep a little in hand as the hands improve through the play. The object of announcing a higher hand than held is to hope that the opponent accepts it and fails to beat it in his turn. A bluff should not be so high as to invite the opponent to remove the screen, as he wins if he does. The most difficult choice arises when either player announces three of a kind on his first roll, as this is a better hand than can be expected, but not high enough to be a fairly sure bluff. Always announce a Straight correctly, and remove the screen on your first option, as this hand is extremely difficult to improve with a re-throw. It is usually best to announce high hands, such as Full House or better, correctly and remove the screen on your turn. If the caller has a good hand on his first throw, an announcement of 'either way' risks his opponent not playing, but if the call is accepted, the caller knows he has a better hand than his opponent expects.

Roulette

Roulette

Roulette is a gambling game of chance, in which the winning and losing is decided by a ball falling into a numbered pocket on a wheel which spins in one direction while the ball rolls in the other. Although no skill is required to play it, it has a fascination for games players with a liking for arithmetic because of the ingenuity of the systems which gamblers have invented for years in an effort to make their fortunes. The search for an infallible system continues despite periodic and mistaken claims that it has been found. Roulette is primarily a casino game, but home sets are marketed widely, and it is possible to hire full-size wheels and tables.

The use of a pocketed wheel and a ball for gaming dates back to about the year 1700 when a game called hoca became popular in casinos on the continent of Europe. In England a game called E.O. was played in which, instead of numbered compartments, all the pockets were lettered E or O (for even or odd). A game more similar to modern roulette was developed in Europe in the eighteenth century. Called boule, and still played today, it consists of a stationary wheel set in a bowl around which a ball is rolled. There are eighteen pockets numbered 1 to 9, two pockets for each number. Gamblers can back any number to win (and be paid 7 to 1 if successful), or back various groups of four numbers at even money. The number 5 is always a loser on these even-money bets. The bank thus can expect to retain over 11 per cent of all money staked, a much worse proposition for the gambler than playing roulette.

Roulette itself has also been played since the eighteenth century, and became very fashionable towards the end of the nineteenth, when the casino at Monte Carlo began to flourish and receive patronage from the royal families of Europe.

The Equipment

The basic equipment for roulette consists of the wheel and ball, and the table on which the bets are made. The wheel used in the Monte Carlo casino (Figure 1) has 37 pockets, numbered 1–36 and 0 (zero). The pockets are alternately red and black, except the zero pocket which is green. The numbers are arranged so that the high and low numbers, and the odd and even numbers also alternate as far as possible. In American casinos, the wheel is different (Figure 2). It has an additional zero pocket, numbered 00. As will be seen later, the effect of this extra pocket is to make betting on roulette much less attractive in American casinos than elsewhere, where a single zero is used. The arrangement of the numbers is

Fig. 1

Fig. 2

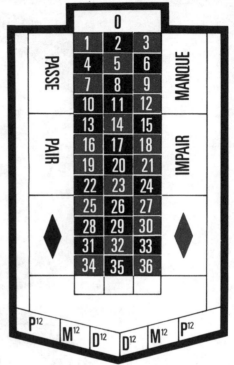

Fig. 3

different on the American wheel, although the eighteen red numbers on the Monte Carlo wheel are also red on the American wheel.

The table is of green baize cloth, marked in red, black and gold, although again the conventional layout differs in Monte Carlo and America. The layout of the table has no effect on the game, and indeed in Britain, where the Monte Carlo wheel is used, the table found in many casinos will be of the American pattern (but without the 00 space). The Monte Carlo table is illustrated in Figure 3 and the American table in Figure 4. The table in casinos might be double-ended, i.e. there will be a staking layout each side of the wheel, the zero being closest to the wheel at each end. The double-ended table allows more players to make bets in comfort.

The Casino Game
In a casino, roulette will be operated by croupiers, who will spin the wheel, rake in losing bets and pay out the winners. Bets will be made with the casino chips, which will usually be of a different colour for each player. When a game is in full swing, the wheel will be spun approximately every two minutes. Soon after setting the

Fig. 4

wheel and ball in motion the croupier will call 'Rien ne va plus' and no more bets may be made on that spin. The French language is traditionally used in describing roulette, although in English-speaking countries and particularly America this custom might not be observed, and 'Rien ne va plus' becomes 'No more bets'.

The bets allowed fall into two categories, the even-money bets and those offering other odds.

The even-money bets are as follows:
Rouge, which is a bet that a red number will win
Noir, which is a bet that a black number will win
Pair, which is a bet that an even number will win
Impair, which is a bet that an odd number will win
Manque, which is a bet that a low number, 1–18, will win
Passe, which is a bet that a high number, 19–36 will win.

The stake is placed on the appropriate place on the table layout.
A player making a successful bet on one of these combinations will win an amount equal to his stake. An important difference

between European and American casinos arises regarding these bets. In most European casinos, should zero turn up, the stake is not automatically lost. It is put 'in prison' and remains on the table for another spin. Should the bet win on the second spin, the player is allowed to retain his stake, but does not collect any winnings. This is equivalent to the player losing half his stake should zero turn up, and in some casinos he may be allowed to withdraw half his stake and forfeit half. In American casinos, the bet will automatically be lost should zero or double-zero win. This convention puts the American gambler at a considerable disadvantage compared to the European gambler.

The other bets are as follows:

En plein (straight). This is a bet on a single number, and the stake is placed on the number on the table. It is allowable to bet on zero, and, on the American wheel, the double-zero. The odds paid are 35−1. The American gambler is still at a disadvantage since whereas the true odds are 36−1 on the European wheel, they are 37−1 on the American wheel, there being an extra pocket. The same disadvantage applies to the remaining bets.

A cheval (split). This is a bet on two adjacent numbers on the table layout (not adjacent numbers on the wheel), and the stake is placed on the line between the two numbers. Zero or double-zero can be combined with a number adjacent to it. The odds paid are 17−1.

Transversale pleine (street). This is a bet on any three numbers in a horizontal line on the table, such as 22, 23, 24. The stake is placed on the outer line of the row. Zero or double-zero may be combined with any two adjacent numbers by placing the stake on the corner common to the three numbers. The odds paid are 11−1.

En carré (square). This is a bet on a block of four numbers forming a square on the table, such as 13, 14, 16, 17. The stake is placed on the corner common to all four numbers. Zero in Europe can be backed in conjunction with 1, 2, 3 by placing the stake on the outside corner common to the zero and the row 1, 2, 3. The odds paid are 8−1.

Transfersale simple or *sixaine* (line). This is a bet on six numbers comprising two horizontal rows, such as 31, 32, 33, 34, 35, 36.

The stake is placed on the outer corner common to the two rows. It is impossible to include the zero or double-zero in a *transversale simple*. The odds paid are 5−1.

Colonne (column). This is a bet on one of the three vertical columns of twelve numbers on the table. The stake is placed in the blank box at the foot of the column on the Monte Carlo table. On the American table (Figure 4) the three columns are marked '2−1', and these are the odds paid.

Colonne à cheval (split column). This is a bet on two adjacent columns, the stake being placed on the line between the two boxes at the foot of each. The odds paid are 2−1 on, or 1−2.

Douzaine (dozen). This is also a bet on twelve numbers. The alternatives are the low numbers, 1−12, the middle numbers, 13−24 or the high numbers, 25−36. The stake is placed on the Monte Carlo table on P (première) for 1−12, on M (moyenne) for 13−24, or D (dérnière) for 25−36. On the American table, the stake is placed on 1st Dozen, 2nd Dozen or 3rd Dozen respectively. The odds paid are 2−1.

Douzaine à cheval (split dozen). This is a bet on any two adjacent dozens, the stake being placed on the line between the appropriate two boxes on the table. The odds paid are 2−1 on, or 1−2.

In the casino game, the odds offered for each bet ensure an advantage to the casino. Where a wheel with one zero is used, and bets on even-money chances are placed in prison when zero wins, as in Europe, the casino will expect, in the long run, to win 1·35 per cent of all money staked on even money bets, and 2·7 per cent on all other bets. In American casinos, with a wheel with two zeros, and no in prison rule, the casino will expect to win 5·26 per cent of all stakes. The casino will impose a minimum and maximum stake for all bets.

The Private Game
When roulette is played privately, the bets and odds are exactly the same as in the casino game. This means that in most cases, the bank will show a profit at the end of the session. It may be that the host, or the supplier of the equipment, will take on the role of the bank,

in which case he will expect to win. However, it is possible for all players to share the bank, thus giving each an equal chance of winning or losing.

The way to do this is for each player to contribute an equal amount before play begins to the bank. The total sum contributed forms the bank's capital. At the end of the game the money remaining in the bank is divided equally among the players. Since the bank expects to win, this will usually be more than the amount contributed.

It may be, of course, that not every player will wish to share in the bank. In this case, players may have unequal shares in the bank. For ease of calculation let us say there are ten players. Fix the bank's capital as 1,000 units (which might be £10 or £100, or $1,000), and offer each player 100 units. Say only six players wish to have a share in the bank, and all take 100 shares. This leaves 400 shares over. If all six players would like further shares in the bank, then lots may be drawn to decide which four may purchase a second hundred shares. The total of 1,000 shares, and the lots of 100 per player, are suggested so that the ultimate sharing-out of the bank's capital becomes easier. For example, if the capital in the bank at the end of the game is 4,200 units, each holder of 100 shares receives 420 units in the share-out. Another system is to allow each player to buy as many shares as he likes, up to a maximum. The only disadvantage is that if the total shares taken are, say, 730, the final sharing-out will involve awkward fractions.

If during the course of the game the bank runs out of capital, then the players holding shares must replenish it by the same amount as their original shares.

As in the casino game, minimum and maximum stakes should be set. The following table suggests minimums and maximums in units.

	Minimum	Maximum	Odds
En plein (single number)	1	2	35−1
A cheval (two numbers)	1	4	17−1
Transversale plein (three numbers)	1	6	11−1
En carré (four numbers)	1	8	8−1
Transversale simple (six numbers)	1	12	5−1
Colonne and Douzaine (twelve numbers)	2	25	2−1
Even-money and other bets	4	100	

The game would operate more conveniently if counters were

Roll	Winning Number	Colour	Odd or Even	High or Low	Column	Dozen
1	3	R	O	L	3	1
2	17	B	O	L	2	2
3	8	B	E	L	2	1
4	14	R	E	L	2	2
5	36	R	E	H	3	3
6	0	–	–	–	–	–
7	9	R	O	L	3	1
8	17	B	O	L	2	2

Fig. 5

used as stakes rather than currency. Four colours might be used, to represent one, two, five and ten units. There should be a good supply of counters, so that players running out during the game may purchase more. All money collected for counters, including those forming the bank should be kept to one side. At the end of the game, when the counters in the bank have been distributed among the shareholders, all players cash in their counters.

It is an advantage if one member of the party, instead of playing, acts as banker and croupier. If the party plays regularly, the banker might be decided by rotation. Should nobody be willing to perform this task, then one of the players may look after the bank, but he must be careful to keep his own capital and the bank's separate. If the banker plays, the game will be slowed down.

A fixed period of play should be agreed beforehand. This prevents embarrassment should some players wish to stop when others wish to continue. If about four hours is agreed for the session, then it might be divided into two halves of 50 spins each, with an interval for refreshment. The host should prepare a ruled sheet of paper with 100 lines numbered 1–50 and 51–100, with three columns for each line. After each spin he should enter in the columns the winning number, the colour, and whether it is odd or even. This will ensure that the agreed number of spins are made, and it will enable system players to check the sequences. If the players wish it, three additional columns might be added to indicate whether the winning number is high or low or in which column or dozen it is contained. Figure 5 shows the beginning of such a full chart. It is because the croupier has to spin the wheel, settle the bets, keep the chart and generally see that the game proceeds properly, that it is advised that he should not play himself.

Systems

For games players who prefer their fortunes to depend on skill, or skill allied to chance, rather than on chance alone, the pleasure of roulette comes from an appreciation of staking systems, and the invention or choice of a plan and putting it into operation.

It is impossible, of course, to devise a system which will guarantee to win. On every bet made at roulette, the bank enjoys an advantage of at least 1·35 per cent, and no clever manipulation of numbers is going to alter that.

The best known and simplest of all staking systems is the martingale, or 'doubling-up' system. It is used on the even-money bets, as listed above. The player stakes one chip on, say, red. If it loses he doubles his stake and his next bet is two chips. Another loss and he stakes four chips. Eventually, he will win, and when he does his win will equal all his previous losses plus one chip. Since ultimately a win is a certainty, the system cannot lose. However, the 1, 2, 4, 8, 16 progression very rapidly reaches large numbers. After ten successive losses, the player has already lost 1023 chips and must stake 1024 on the next spin. Red once came up 28 times running at Monte Carlo, so even a Rockefeller, had he been backing black, would have needed to send for more funds. In practice, of course, a run of losers soon necessitates a stake above the maximum allowed, so the martingale is unworkable.

The system is more fun played in reverse. Instead of doubling losing stakes, winnings can be left on the table to double, and will mount as quickly as the stake does in the martingale system. If it is decided to collect the winnings only after eight successive wins, the number of chips taken will be 256. And as the stake is never more than one chip, it will take a long time to pay back 256 chips.

Another popular system is to increase the stake by a chip after a loss, and to decrease it by one after a win. The idea, as with the martingale, is to have the larger stakes on the winners, and if winners and losers alternate there will be one chip more on each winner than each loser. Unfortunately sequences are never as neat as that, but the system has the merit of keeping stakes within reasonable limits.

There are fewer systems for backing single numbers, and they usually rely on the fallacious 'law of averages'. The most popular is backing 'sleepers', which are numbers which have not won for some time and are consequently considered 'due'. A number can be expected to win, on a 37 number wheel, once in 37 spins on average. The *systémier* waits until a number has not appeared for 111 spins (3 × 37) and then backs it 37 times with a single stake, then increases the stake to two chips, and after a further 37 spins to three chips. The theory is that numbers rarely sleep for as many as 222 spins, but it will be noticed that the system does not necessarily show a profit when the expected win comes. In any case, the system is based on the premise that past results will affect future ones, which on a fair wheel is clearly erroneous.

A more valid system, perhaps the most interesting of all, is another based on the even chances, the 'cancelling-out' system. The player begins by writing down a short series of numbers, say

1, 2, 3, 4 or 2, 2, 2 or 1, 1, 2, 2. He backs one of the even money chances, and his first stake is the sum of the two outside numbers of his series. Were the series 1, 1, 2, 2, his first stake would be $1 + 2 = 3$. Should he win, he cancels the two outside numbers, leaving his series as 1, 2. His stake is therefore again 3, and should he win again his whole series is cancelled, and he is six units to the good. Should his second bet lose, he adds the losing stake, 3, to his series, which becomes 1, 2, 3 and his next stake is again the sum of the outside terms, in this case $1 + 3 = 4$. The beauty of the system is that every time the player wins, he cancels two numbers in his series, and every time he loses he adds only one, so that his series will always ultimately be cancelled out. And every time it is, he will win the sum of the numbers in his series – in the example followed, six units. The system's only drawback is that when a long adverse sequence occurs the stake can mount quickly.

The variety of roulette bets allows the player to invent systems as simple or complicated as he pleases. It will be noticed, for instance, that the third column on the roulette table contains eight red numbers and only four black. Suppose the player backs this column at odds of $2 - 1$. He can expect to lose roughly twice for every win, but he can hedge his bet by also backing black. If his column bet wins, he must win at least one chip overall, perhaps three. When his column bet loses, his bet on black stands a better than even chance of saving his total stake, because there are 14 possible black winners in the first two columns to only ten reds. The backer has 26 of the 37 numbers on his side. It sounds an attractive plan, but it is a snare. The column bet will lose one chip in 37 to the bank, the bet on black one chip in 74, and there is no way of adding the two losses together to make a win.

Although the advantage in roulette must always be with the bank, the game is an enjoyable way to lose money, and serious students get their pleasure from the never-ending search for a plan which offers the promise of a good win with minimal losses.